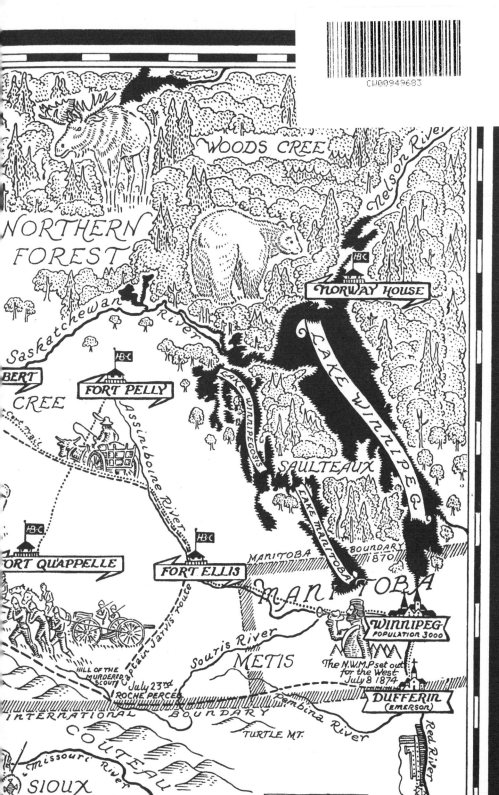

THE
LAW MARCHES WEST

BY

SIR CECIL E. DENNY, Bart.

Late Inspector North-West Mounted Police

EDITED AND ARRANGED BY

W. B. CAMERON

Author of 'When Fur Was King,' etc.

WITH A FOREWORD BY

HON. A. C. RUTHERFORD, K.C., LL.D.

Chancellor of the University of Alberta and First Premier of the Province

DENNY PUBLISHING

Published by Denny Publishing Limited
6 Cotswold Business Village
Moreton-in-Marsh
Gloucestershire
GL56 0JQ
United Kingdom

First published March 1939.
This edition published September 2000.

Set in 12/15 Garamond.

A catalogue record for this book is available from the British Library.

Printed by St Edmundsbury Press, Bury St Edmunds, Suffolk

Prepared for the publishers by The Write Idea, Cambridge.

ISBN: 1-903680-00-X

Contents

Foreword

Before reading a book it is desirable and quickens interest to know something with regard to the author.

Cecil Edward Denny was born in Hampshire, England, on the 14th of December 1850. He was the second son of the Rev. Robert Day Denny, and half-brother of Sir Arthur Denny, Baronet, and succeeded to the title upon the death of Sir Arthur in February 1922. After his preliminary education he attended Cheltenham College and colleges in France and Germany.

At the age of nineteen he emigrated to the United States of America, and engaged in farming on land purchased for him by his father. This farm is now a suburb of the City of Chicago, Illinois. He was a guest at the Sherman House when Chicago was swept by a great fire in 1871.

Mr. Denny loved adventures and was to become a romantic and picturesque figure in the life of the North-West of Canada.

In February 1874 he crossed over to Toronto, Ontario, and obtained a commission as Captain in the North-West Mounted Police, then being organised, and in due course proceeded to the North-West Territories of Canada, one of the first three hundred officers, non-commissioned officers, and men which comprised that force.

In the winter of 1874–5 he assisted in constructing Fort Macleod, and in August 1875 he was in charge of the detachment of police that built Fort Calgary.

Captain Denny resigned from the Mounted Police in 1882, and accepted the office of Indian Agent for the Cree and Assiniboine Indians. He was located at Fort Walsh in the North-West Territories. He was one of the signers of the notable treaty of 1877 made by the Government of Canada with the Indians. For several years he was in charge of the Indian tribes under this treaty. He was made an honorary chief by the Indians, and was known as Chief 'Beaver Coat' owing to his wearing a beaver overcoat.

In 1885 Captain Denny operated a ranch near Fort Macleod. In this year the Riel Rebellion broke out, and he was specially requested by Sir John A. Macdonald, Prime Minister of Canada, to take charge of the western plains Indians. At the close of the rebellion he received the thanks of the Canadian Government for his efforts in preventing them going on the war-path. After the rebellion Captain Denny returned to his ranch, and also did some special scout work for the police.

He visited England, and upon his return went to British Columbia, where he remained for two years as Police Magistrate at Fort Steele, during the construction of the Crow's Nest Pass railway line.

Captain Denny occupied many other positions in the service of the Government. He was in charge of the N.W.M.P. pack-train on the Peace River exploration expedition from 1904 to 1906. For several years he was Fire Ranger in the Athabasca and Lac la Biche districts in Alberta, and afterwards acted in the same capacity during the construction of the northern railways in Alberta.

From 1992 to 1927 Sir Cecil Denny was Archivist for the province of Alberta, and assisted in the Provincial Library in Edmonton. He was superannuated in 1927. Following a long illness he died in the University Hospital, Edmonton, on 24th August

1928, at the age of seventy-eight. He was accorded a public funeral in Calgary from the Church of England cathedral, and was buried in the Mounted Police plot in Union Cemetery in the city which he had assisted to establish over fifty years previously.

Sir Cecil Denny was never married. He was extremely fond of children, and they delighted to have him tell stories of his adventures. He was the author of numerous magazine and newspaper articles relating to western Canada and western life, and also the author of a notable book, *The Riders of the Plains*, long out of print.

Sir Cecil Denny led a colourful and useful life in western Canada. He first came when there were scarcely any white inhabitants. The Indians and buffalo roamed over the prairies where are now located many prosperous farmers and numerous cities, towns, and villages have grown up. He was well equipped to write a history of his time.

I have read the manuscript of this book, *The Law Marches West*, by Sir Cecil Denny. It is a most interesting work. It is a worthwhile authentic addition to the historical works relating to the history of the great North-West of Canada, and in particular of the province of Alberta.

A.C. Rutherford
Edmonton, Alberta, 1938

Introduction

In the long history of law enforcement, the reputation of the Mounties has always been of the highest calibre, their name and uniform recognised the world over.

One of the founder members of the Mounties was Sir Cecil Edward Denny, a great pioneer and adventurer in his own right. He was one of the group of men who in 1874 embarked on a 1,000-mile march across the great plains of Canada, from Winnipeg to the foothills of the Rocky Mountains, befriending the Indian tribes and establishing law and order in this hitherto wild place.

The Law Marches West is Sir Cecil's fascinating first-hand account of that pioneering journey. First published in 1939, it has stood the test of time both as a highly enteraining read and a valuable contribution to the history of the Canadian Mounted Police. This 2000 edition, with additional archive photographs to complement the original text, is published on behalf of the Denny Family Archive Trust.

Richard Denny, Publisher
September 2000

A group of bloods at Fort Calgary, Alberta, 1878. Sir Cecil Denny seated on chair in background.

I

A Challenge and the Answer

Violence was in the saddle over Canada's West – battle, murder, and sudden death, a composite of evils which, from the Red River to the Rocky Mountains, year by year, exacted a grisly toll. Red man warred upon red man, tribe upon tribe, and the white man warred and preyed upon them all. When in any land homicide, unless privately avenged, goes unpunished, thieving and plundering are accounted virtues, and a life snuffed out is only a life less, conditions admittedly are bad.

This does not mean that the law was flouted. There was no law. True, at one of the few tiny isolated settlements centred about his trading post on some northern lake or river, a Hudson's Bay Company officer might occasionally hold the semblance of a court. He represented such authority as the country knew. But since there existed no legal machinery for their enforcement, decrees issuing from such a tribunal seldom effected anything. In the great treeless region drained by the Bow, Belly and South Saskatchewan rivers were neither trading posts nor settlements; the contacts of the Indians there with their pale-skinned brethren had been of such a character as not to inspire the tribesmen with any love for the white man, and the trader venturing on territory looked upon as their own risked not only the loss of his goods but of his scalp. So the reputable dealer in furs stayed away.

The white men whose activities were in the main responsible for the frequent atrocities in this region operated chiefly along the international boundary. Some at least were outlaws, fugitives from justice and Montana courts, with records of crimes behind them. At their headquarters on the Belly River not far from the site of the present city of Lethbridge, they had built a fort, and labelled it, most appropriately, 'Whoop-up'. Whoop-up was a dot of riot in the wilderness, a depot whence was dispensed to the various tribes a vile concoction euphemistically called liquor, but for which the Indian had a fitter name – 'fire water'. For fire water in very truth it was. Buffalo in uncounted thousands still roamed the plains and the business of these enterprising gentry was highly profitable. Its effect upon the red men was anything but that. Crazed by the poisonous stuff they virtually threw away their robes; quarrels and fighting inevitably broke out, and terror and devastation ran through the camps. Nor did the traders themselves balk at using their rifles upon the natives, either wantonly or in drunken abandon. They shamefully abused the men and debauched the women. The situation was serious, and constantly growing worse. It called for immediate and drastic measures of repression.

The authorities at Ottawa were fully informed regarding conditions in their recently-acquired territory in the North-West. In 1870 Lieutenant W. F. Butler (subsequently knighted and a major-general in the Imperial Army) had been commissioned to investigate the situation on the ground, and made a voluminous report. The Government had also the reports of Captain Palliser, Colonel Robertson Ross, Sanford Fleming, Hudson's Bay Company officials, missionaries and others resident or visiting in the West. But action could not be taken at once. Time was required to decide upon a policy and to put it into effect.

However, plans were at length completed, and in May 1873 the Prime Minister, Sir John A. Macdonald, gave notice of his intention to introduce a Bill respecting the administration of justice and the establishment of a police force for the North-West Territories. Questions had been asked on the floor of the House by the Hon. Alexander Mackenzie (afterwards Premier), Donald A. Smith (afterwards Lord Strathcona), and others. Sir John, minister in charge of western affairs, and the Hon. Joseph Howe stated that the Government was alive to its responsibilities in that direction.

Sir John, who in later years took a deep interest in the North-West Mounted Police, had been making a study of different organisations, more particularly the Royal Irish Constabulary, and had determined on having a force of the hardiest and best-trained men procurable, men who had either seen service in other corps, or in the lumber woods, men of courage and good physique, good riders and good shots, capable of meeting the difficulties facing any force penetrating that wild and virginal land.

Finally, on 20th May 1873, the Bill passed. It provided for a civil force in uniform, drilled in simple movements taken from the British Cavalry Regulations, and to be conducted much upon the system of a cavalry regiment. Discipline was to be enforced by the power conferred on officers by a section in the statute which provided for a maximum punishment of six months' imprisonment with hard labour and the deprivation of one month's pay.

And thus was taken the first step in the mustering of a corps the daring and resourcefulness of which have carried its fame around the world, and brought lustre to the name of Canada – the North-West Mounted Police.

'Ordinarily speaking, no more wildly impossible undertaking was ever staged than the establishment of Canadian authority and Canadian law throughout the western prairies by a handful of mounted police.' So wrote the Hon. Frank Oliver, pioneer newspaper-man and member of the Federal Cabinet, many years later. In large measure world opinion took for granted that lawlessness must accompany pioneer conditions. Canada's Mounted Police was a challenge to that idea.

The pay of the police as first organised was on the following scale: The Commissioner, a salary not to exceed $2,600 a year, and not less than $2,000; superintendents, not exceeding $1,400, and not less than $1,000; paymasters, not exceeding $900; quartermasters, not exceeding $500; surgeons, not exceeding $1,400, and not less than $1,000; veterinary surgeons, not exceeding $1,600; ordinary constables at the rate of $1.00 per day; and sub-constables, 75 cents a day. Looking back at the rate of pay granted the original force of Mounted Police, and the work they performed, it seems but poor remuneration, but the lure of the unknown, and the prospect of great adventure, brought thousands to apply for enlistment when only hundreds were required.

Although the Bill had passed the Dominion Parliament in May 1873, it was not until September of that year that recruiting officers were sent out. By October three troops of fifty men each had been organised, making a total of one hundred and fifty men, with an inspector and two sub-inspectors to each troop, 'A', 'B' and 'C'. Lieutenant-Colonel George A. French, who had been what was termed loaned to Canada by the British Government, and had been inspector of artillery, and in command of 'A' Battery, R.C.A., at Kingston, Ontario, was appointed Commissioner of the force.

The first contingent was sent in the fall of 1873, via the 'Dawson Route', to Winnipeg, Manitoba, and stationed at Lower Fort Garry, to remain until the following spring, when the remainder of the force, which would be recruited during the winter in Toronto, would join them and bring up all transport, supplies, etc., required for the arduous journey to be taken into the unknown West. They would also bring up enough horses to provide each man with his trooper, and teams enough to move the transport.

It may be of interest to many who are acquainted with Major-General Griesbach, of Edmonton, to know that the first man to enlist in the first one hundred and fifty men of the original North-

West Mounted Police in 1873 was A. H. Griesbach, his father, who had served previously in the 15th Hussars and Cape Mounted Rifles. He was the first regimental sergeant-major of the force, and retired as superintendent in 1903 on pension. The late Major-General Sir Samuel B. Steele, and the late Lieutenant-Colonel Robert Belcher, enlisted at the same time.

In November 1873 Sir John A. Macdonald was defeated in Parliament, and was succeeded as Premier by the Hon. Alexander Mackenzie. In Sir John A. Macdonald's Government the North-West Mounted Police had been under the direction of the Minister of Justice, an office held by the Premier. In the new Cabinet, this portfolio was held by the Hon. A. A. Dorion, who then assumed control of the force. The troops 'A', 'B' and 'C' were sent west by the Great Lakes and the 'Dawson Route' to the Red River country. This was a most difficult route in summer, the portages through the mud and clouds of mosquitoes being enough to try the endurance of the hardiest, but as this party travelled in the fall they escaped most of the plagues of the hot season.

The troops arrived at Lower Fort Garry, 'the Stone Fort', an old Hudson's Bay Company post twenty miles north of Winnipeg, at the end of September. This force of one-hundred and fifty men was what the Government at Ottawa at first considered sufficient to patrol three hundred thousand square miles of country in the lawless state I have endeavoured to picture. On the arrival of Lieutenant-Colonel French at Fort Garry in November he was able to see from such information as he could gain there of the conditions of the West how inadequate for the work before them such a small force was, and on his return to Ottawa, he urged upon the Government the necessity of a much larger force, and on his recommendation it was increased to three hundred men.

Pending the arrival of the Commissioner, Lieutenant-Colonel Osborne Smith, commanding the Western Military District, had temporary command of the force, and as soon as they were located in the Stone Fort he arrived from Winnipeg and swore them in, each man being given a warrant with his name and rank, the first and only one issued in the force. On the return of Lieutenant-Colonel Smith to Winnipeg, Superintendent Jarvis remained in command until the arrival of the Commissioner, Inspector Walsh doing duty as adjutant. Sergeant-Major Griesbach took charge of the discipline, and instructed the men in foot drill, while Sergeant-Major Steele took over the breaking-in of the horses, and instructed the non-commissioned officers and men in riding.

The foot and mounted drill was continued in fair weather and foul, and from early morning until late at night. Much weeding out of bad characters among the men was needed. The three troops were reduced in number, and were not brought up to full strength until the following spring, when the remainder of the force arrived.

This united force was the first to give assistance to settlers entering the country, a party of men, women and children, with a couple of teams of horses on their way to Winnipeg from Prince Arthur's Landing, now Port Arthur. These were the first of many thousands who in after years men of the Mounted Police helped to settle on the land either as stockmen, farmers, or in business, and over whom at all seasons a watchful care was exercised to enable them to earn their livelihood in peace and security.

Much discomfort was caused the men at Fort Garry by the lack of adequate winter clothing, that forwarded from the East having been delayed until spring by the impassability of the 'Dawson Route'. During the stay of the Commissioner at Fort Garry he came into communication with officers of the Boundary Survey, which had been carried to a point four hundred miles west of the Red River. He was fortunate in being able to obtain much reliable information concerning a portion of country of which little was known and for this he was principally indebted to Captain Cameron, R.A., Commissioner, and to Captain Andrews, R.E., the Chief Astronomer.

It was understood that the expedition westward would start in the spring, and the question of supplies and transport was thoroughly gone into while Commissioner French remained. On his return to Ottawa in February 1874 he found the Government alive to the necessity of increasing the force to three hundred men as advised. He also recommended that stores and provisions should be transported westward by the force itself; also that cattle for slaughter should be driven along on foot, and the need for carrying pork or pemmican in quantities be thus avoided.

Colonel French reports:

> *In the spring of 1874 arrangements had to be made for the supply of arms, ammunition, and stores of every description. Uniforms had to be designed and supplied, men enlisted, requisitions made to the Imperial Government for field guns and stores, horses to be purchased, and a tremendous amount of work done in a very short time.*

In April 1874 most of the men required were assembled at the New Fort, Toronto, and every endeavour was made by all ranks to pick up as much instruction as possible in the limited time available for drill, riding, target practice, etc. The regimental sergeant-major was an old officer of the 13th Hussars, Captain Miles, who, with the assistance of Sergeant Francis, a Crimean veteran, did splendid work in drilling the recruits, both in the riding school and on foot. Practice with the nine-pound guns was also carried out under the instruction of Inspector Jackson, an ex-officer from the battery at Kingston, and a gun team formed. There was much rifle practice, and as the majority had been used to arms, more or less, the instruction proceeded satisfactorily.

In the riding school things did not go so well, as the recruits, for the most part, were unused to horses, and many accidents occurred. As the Commissioner stated, the practice the men would have on the long march west would make of them good horsemen before its conclusion. The horses, purchased in Toronto, were exceptionally good, the price averaging $150 per head. They were all over fifteen and a half hands, and were admitted to be the best ever shipped from that city.

The first uniform consisted of a red tunic, black breeches with two white stripes, forage cap and helmet, high black leather boots, heavy dark blue overcoat with cape, belt with revolver and cartridge pouch, and Snider carbine. The trouser stripes were afterwards changed to red, and later again to yellow, as at present. The saddles were of the 'McClellan' make. They were a poor type of saddle, with high uncomfortable cantle, and the carbine in a bucket at the side was most awkward, the butt projecting over the top of the saddle, making it very difficult to mount.

II

En route and a wild night with the elements

During the preparation at Toronto, Lieutenant-Colonel French paraded the men on several occasions, and told of the hardships to be encountered on the journey westward. He also advised any who might be of faint heart to apply for discharge, which he promised to grant, but few availed themselves of the opportunity. The force collected at Toronto was therefore an unusually efficient one, made up of the hardiest men that could have been got together in any country, as the Commissioner said. Tied down by no stringent rules or articles of war, but only by the silken cord of a civil contract, those men by their conduct gave but little cause for complaint, and on the 8th July started on an expedition at which veteran soldiers might well have faltered. Day after day on the march, night after night on picket or guard, and working at high pressure daily for months from daylight until dark, and too frequently after dark, with little rest even on the day sacred to rest, the force ever pushed forward, delighted when a pure spring was met with, and still uncomplaining when salt water or the refuse of a mud hole was the only liquid available. At times the whole force was obliged to drink liquid which, when passed through a filter, was still the colour of ink. The fact of horses and oxen dying for want of food never disheartened or stopped them, but pushing on, on foot, with dogged determination, they carried through the service required of them under difficulties which can only be appreciated by those who witnessed them.

The force which left Toronto in June 1874 comprised sixteen officers, two hundred and one men, and two hundred and forty-four horses. Nine carloads of wagons and agricultural implements were attached to the trains at Sarnia, and another containing thirty-four horses was taken on at Detroit. The route from Toronto to Dufferin, a point in Manitoba near Pembina, North Dakota, where the three troops from Winnipeg had instructions to proceed and meet those from Toronto, was through the United States by permission granted by that Government, via Chicago and St. Paul, thence to Fargo, North Dakota, about one hundred and fifty miles from Dufferin, and the terminus at that time of the Northern Pacific railroad.

It was understood that very little personal baggage could be taken, as the transport was limited and most of it needed to convey provisions and forage. It is curious today to remember what a vague idea we really had of the journey before us, and the country westward along the mountains, and I doubt if any expedition of such importance ever before undertook a seven-hundred-mile march across vast plains without competent guides, believing that at the end of it they would have to subdue lawless bands of desperadoes, with such complete faith in themselves and such ignorance of what they were to encounter.

On leaving Toronto we had a fairly well organised force; people all over Canada took the greatest interest in the organisation and its success. The journey throughout was watched not only in Canada, but in England with lively interest, and the greatest anxiety was manifested as to the fate of the little band when many months passed after its departure and no word whatever had been received of the expedition.

Lieutenant-Colonel Richardson, afterwards Judge Richardson, of the Department of Justice, under which the police force then was, although guided in military matters by the Queen's Regulations, arrived from Ottawa, and held a last conference with the Commissioner. He also brought the final instructions from the Government. We were ready on Friday, 5th June 1874, to load the transport horses and baggage in two special trains that should take us without change to Fargo. The loading was accomplished after the hardest kind of work by the morning of 6th June, and the trains pulled out, amid adieus and good wishes, and with many presents forced upon the men, about midday, to the accompaniment of martial bands, exploding torpedoes, and encouraging cheers.

Quarters on the trains, particularly at night, were rather cramped. The horses were unloaded three times a day for feed and water, occasioning considerable delay, and also hard work at the stops. We took meals at the different stations, arrangements having been made beforehand so that everything was ready on our arrival, and sometimes our numbers taxed the accommodation of the smaller stations. However we fared well, no pains being spared to give us the best they had. We arrived at Chicago on 7th June, and put up at the stockyards, unloading the horses and feeding them in the pens during the night. A strong picket of two officers and thirty men kept guard over them. A heavy thunderstorm made it unpleasant for those on duty, and the men were thoroughly soaked and tired by morning. There were few hotels near the stockyards, it was difficult to get meals, and the men who slept in the cars were glad enough to get away on 8th June.

In St. Paul, reached on the 10th, it rained continually during our stay. Few of us had waterproofs, the uniforms being packed and the men travelling in plain clothes. The horses had to be marched from the train into town, a considerable distance, to find stable room. St. Paul at that time was only a moderately-sized town, and our stock required most of its stables. We remained a night, putting up at the Metropolitan and the Merchants' Hotels. The dealers in clothing had a windfall in the sale of waterproofs and overcoats to the contingent. We left on the 11th for Fargo, our next and last station. It rained steadily until we arrived next day, when it cleared and we had beautiful weather.

Fargo at that date was a small place, consisting of a station, one or two small stores, and one hotel. We unloaded everything, and after picketing and feeding the horses, got out and began assembling the wagons. This proved a tedious business, as they came in detached parts. Eventually all cars were emptied and the contents placed on the ground, so that the parts could be picked out as required. The saddlery from England was also in pieces, each box complete in itself, but it was soon sorted and put together by the saddlers. When one looked round and saw acres covered by sections of wagons and stores of all kinds, it appeared as if we should not get away for a week, but by the evening of the 14th not only were the wagons loaded, but all had pulled out and made camp some six miles from Fargo. A guard consisting of twenty men, with myself as officer in charge, did duty that night, this being the first real duty on the plains. We finished adjusting the loads at midnight of the 15th. The horses also were branded on the hoof with their respective numbers. Four horses which escaped from the picket at this camp were never recovered.

On 16th June the force moved out for Fort Dufferin, one hundred and eighty miles distant, with horses in prime condition, and the men in good spirits. We travelled by troops, 'D' supplying the advance guard, and 'F' that in the rear. We made thirty-six miles on the first day, and camped on the bank of the Red River.

On 16th and 17th June we again made marches of thirty-four and thirty miles.

The long marches during these first days were a mistake, and with our heavily loaded wagons had much to do with animals giving out and dying subsequently on the longer and more arduous journey across the plains. The days were hot and the flies bad, but we were beginning to get hardened to the work. Our rations were scant, consisting only of biscuits and tea. On the 18th we made another thirty-five miles, and a horse died on the trail. On this day we saw the first Indian camp of Sioux, and to us who had never seen Indians, they were quite a novelty. On the 19th we camped near an American military post at Pembina, on the frontier between North Dakota and Manitoba. The American officers were most hospitable, and the men did a good deal of fraternising with the American soldiers.

We crossed over at this point into Manitoba, and reached Dufferin on the 19th June. Here we met the three troops, 'A,' 'B' and 'C', from Fort Garry. They had been joined a few weeks before leaving by Lieutenant-Colonel James F. Macleod, C.M.G., who had been appointed Assistant Commissioner of the force. He had previously held the rank of Assistant Brigade-Major in General Wolseley's Red River expedition, and for his services had received the rank of Lieutenant-Colonel and the C.M.G. On meeting these three troops, several days were spent in making mutual acquaintances, rearranging the loads for our journey across the plains, distributing horses and wagons among the six troops, transferring men, branding the animals and getting ready generally for the long march.

On the night of 21st June a terrible thunderstorm struck our camp, accompanied by wind and hail. Nearly all the tents went down. The horses had been picketed to long, heavy lines stretched over posts. Over two hundred broke loose and stampeded through the camp, overturning wagons, flattening the tents and knocking down and severely injuring several of the men. Confusion reigned. Ebon darkness split by vivid lightning, stinging hail, and the charge of maddened horses created a pandemonium not easily forgotten. The thunder was deafening, making it almost impossible to give orders. Officers and men alike were only partly dressed, but there was no panic, and two constables, Wilde and Francis, with three sub-constables, Oliver, Barton and Sinclair, managed to secure horses, and mounting bareback, followed after the racing herd. The darkness was so dense, however, that they could see nothing, and soon returned. We passed a miserable night in the open, but when morning dawned warm and bright we dried our clothes, repitched the camp, and were soon once more our cheerful selves.

Sixty men were detailed to follow the horses, and after some days the majority were recovered, but twenty-five were never seen again. A few were found dead, and those brought back were much the worse for their wild race. Some had travelled nearly fifty miles before being picked up. Colonel French purchased horses in Winnipeg to replace those lost. We had other storms while at Dufferin, but the horses were hobbled and well guarded, and there were no more stampedes.

The troops numbered from 'A' to 'F', and were composed of an inspector, two sub-inspectors, and fifty non-commissioned officers and men each. The horses and transport wagons were also divided equally among the troops. The two nine-pound guns were attached to 'D' troop, with Sub-Inspector Jackson in charge. The horses required shoeing, which with our small portable forge, took time. Parades were held, and there was much drilling. Bad whisky was easily obtainable, and several undesirable characters were discharged for drunkenness and other offences. The weather remained unsettled during our stay, making it hard for the men to get through the work. They grumbled considerably, and six or seven men deserted at Dufferin, but we were doubtless better off without them. At Dufferin came the first pay-day since leaving Toronto. It was also the last many of us saw for a year, since direct communication with Ottawa was opened only long after our march across the plains ended.

The baggage allowance over and above the kit was fifty pounds to each officer, and ten pounds per man, not enough to allow transport of any luxuries. One hundred and twenty oxen and carts were purchased, and thirty half-breeds engaged to drive them. Each carried five hundred pounds of forage ration and other supplies.

We were all in readiness for the start by 6th July, when word came from across the Line that a large band of Sioux had attacked and murdered a number of settlers at St. Joe, a small town in Dakota, and the officer commanding the United States troops in that vicinity got in touch with Colonel French, asking his co-operation in cutting off these Indians should they cross into Canada. Three troops, armed and mounted, started for the point where it was supposed the Indians might enter. They returned next day, having seen no Indians. This entailed a delay of two days, and on our last night at Dufferin another tremendous thunderstorm swept our camp, but no damage was done.

July 8th at last saw our start westward, with three hundred men, three hundred and ten horses, one hundred and forty-two work-oxen, one hundred and fourteen carts, seventy-three wagons, thirty-three head of beef cattle, two nine-pound guns and two mortars. We carried a six-months' supply of tea, sugar, flour, biscuit and bacon, besides baggage, ammunition and forage; also supplies of tobacco, matches and other small articles. Much baggage was of necessity left behind and most we never saw again. Some twenty men deserted from Dufferin, and thirty horses were lost or died, but the force generally was in good shape and spirits. We camped the first night, after a twenty-mile march, on the Murray River. Thus began the real journey to which we had all been looking forward since the organisation of the force, our destination being, according to information from different sources, a strong fort called Whoop-up at the junction of the Bow and Belly rivers, some seven hundred miles to the westward.

In the *Mounted Police Blue Book* for 1874, an interesting account is given in Lieutenant-Colonel French's report of the appearance of the force as it left camp for the westward march. As it may be of interest, I give it in full:

> *On our first starting we had, of course, the usual difficulties of balky horses and unruly oxen to contend with, but after a few days we had but little trouble in this respect. Our train was, I*

suppose, the largest ever seen in these parts; closed to a proper interval it was a mile and a half long, but from advance to rear-guard it was more nearly from four to five miles, owing to the uneven rate of travel of horses and oxen, and the breaking of wheels and axles of that imposition of the country, the Red River cart. The column of route presented a very fine appearance. First came 'A' Division with their splendid dark bays and wagons. Then 'B' with their dark browns. Next 'C' with bright chestnuts drawing the guns and small-arm ammunition. Next 'D' with their greys, 'E' with their black horses, the rear being brought up by 'F' with their light bays. Then a motley string of ox-carts, ox-wagons, cattle for slaughter, cows, calves, mowing machine, etc., etc. To a stranger it would have appeared an astonishing cavalcade – armed men and guns looked as if fighting was to be done. What could ploughs, harrows, mowing machines, cows, calves, etc., be for?

But that little force had a double duty to perform – to fight if necessary, but in any case to establish posts in the West. However, we were off at last, the only man in Winnipeg who knew anything about the portion of the country to which we were going, encouraging me with the remark: 'Well, if you have luck you may be back by Christmas, with forty per cent of your horses.' By the time the force left Dufferin the comparatively large number of thirty-one men were absent without leave, the Sioux murders of St. Joe, thirty miles west, having the effect of quickening the movements of several in this respect. I anticipated the backing out of a certain number, and fortunately brought twenty spare men, so that the force was not so short-handed as some supposed.

III

1874: The famous march of the North-West Mounted Police

ON 9th July we resumed our march, starting late in the afternoon. Overnight in a heavy storm twenty head of horses stampeded, but were recovered next morning. We waited half a day for the carts to catch up, the half-breeds being in the sulks over some fancied grievance. At this camp, to save our horses, three loads of luxuries the Commissioner thought could be spared were sent back. Reports reaching us of depredations committed by Sioux Indians across the Line, for several days mounted sentries watched over the horses at night. After leaving the Pembina River both men and horses suffered through lack of good water. Frequent thunderstorms made guard detail unpleasant.

We travelled for a considerable way along the Boundary Survey road, which made marching comparatively easy. We remained a short time at Pembina Mountain, a beautiful spot. Here we met the first locusts, the air being literally alive with them, and the ground thickly covered. Vegetation this year was devastated in Manitoba by the clouds of these insects passing toward the west. We crossed Pembina Mountain on the 13th of July, and encountered another heavy storm that night. With hailstones the size of marbles, and lack of grass owing to the locusts, the horses fared badly and suffered in consequence. So far we had travelled at the rate of some twenty miles daily. The only game seen was a few antelope, none of which could be approached. West of Pembina Mountain we saw the first buffalo skulls, but many hundred miles had yet to be traversed before we met the living animals.

At Pembina Mountain we were joined by a party of half-breeds selected by the Governor of Manitoba. They brought presents for Indian chiefs, and were supposed to assist the force as guides and interpreters, but we found later they knew nothing of the country west of the Cypress Hills, and the only Indian language they understood was Cree. Of Blackfoot they knew nothing.

On 17th July we met a returning party of the Boundary Survey. They reported having fired on a party of Indians caught in the act of an attempted raid upon their horse herd. Our rations from this point were cut down, as it was evident the journey would take much longer than anticipated at the slow rate of progress, and it was doubtful if we had sufficient for the long stretch ahead.

The horses now began to give out, and the train stretched over many miles. On the 19th the rear guard under me was so far behind that we were forced to camp alone, with no water for horses or cattle or any rations for the men. To make matters worse, it rained all night. We caught up with the main body at the Souris River, where we rested for several days. There was no settlement here at this time, although it has since become thickly populated and one of the best wheat-growing sections west of Winnipeg. A number of men were left at Souris River in charge of sick horses, with some transport we were unable to move. At the second crossing of the Souris we met more of the Boundary Survey returning, their work being completed. Feed was very scarce, the grasshoppers being still numerous, and more horses giving out, we had to leave them. The eastern horses, unaccustomed to grazing or looking out for themselves, could not stand up under the hardships.

On 28th July we arrived at Roche Perce. It was a full day before the stragglers came in, Colonel Macleod having remained behind to see that all arrived. The horses were in bad shape from scarcity of feed and water, hundreds of miles remained to be covered, and the prospects for a successful termination to the journey began to look none too rosy. Rations for the men were again cut down, and they fared none too well. At Roche Perce, two hundred and seventy miles from Dufferin, we made a long halt, and 'A' troop, in command of Inspector Jarvis, with Sub-Inspector Gagnon as subaltern, was detailed to proceed via Fort Ellice, Fort Pitt, and Carlton to Edmonton. S. B. Steele was sergeant-major with this troop, which took with it fifty-five of the weakest horses, twenty-four wagons, fifty-five carts, sixty-two oxen and fifty cows and calves. Sub-Inspector Shurtliff and twelve half-breeds also accompanied the party. Their instructions were to wait at Edmonton for further direction. They arrived on 27th October after a most difficult journey between Carlton and Edmonton, eighty-eight days including stoppages from Roche Perce. Much of the country was timbered, and it was necessary to clear miles of road for the wagons.

It was expected that Colonel Macleod, with a considerable portion of the force, would join Colonel Jarvis at Edmonton, but owing to unforeseen circumstances this arrangement was changed. Colonel Jarvis therefore remained at Edmonton during that winter, and no word from Colonel Macleod was received until the following spring, though he was in communication with the east via Winnipeg through the Hudson's Bay Company's packet to that place. There was also continuous movement of freight and travellers by dog- and horse-sleigh along this northern route; thus his division was not so isolated during that winter as was that of Colonel Macleod, who wintered in the southern part of Alberta.

On Inspector Jarvis's detachment leaving for the north, we overhauled and reloaded our wagons. Most of the sick horses and men who were for the time incapacitated having gone with him, the main body was relieved of much encumbrance and, feed and water at Roche Perce being good, our horses picked up wonderfully. Coal found at this point was used in the forge. A week's rations were cooked in advance, and wood for fuel was loaded, as it was expected no more would be found for a long distance. By the 30th of July our diminished force was ready for another start.

We made twenty-six miles on the 31st, still finding good feed and water. The weather remaining fine, the horses did fairly well and covered more ground. Up at daylight, camp was struck and we were on the move by 5 o'clock. Guard duty was heavy. An officer, a picket and fifteen men were detailed every night, and the officer next day had to take either the advance or rear guard. We therefore found enough to do, especially as, when on rear guard, we had to bring up the stragglers and exhausted teams, often arriving many hours after camp had been pitched and settled for the night. Too much praise could not be accorded the men, who worked well and cheerfully under most trying and unfamiliar conditions.

The country through which we passed was full of lakes teeming with ducks and geese. We shot as many as we cared to and they made a welcome addition to the different messes. On several occasions men became lost while hunting, and remained out all night, although rockets were fired to guide them into camp.

On 3rd August a tornado struck the camp, and all the tents were levelled. We stood by the horses until morning to prevent a stampede. The following day I was on rear guard and sighting some antelope in the distance went toward them to try to get a shot. Utterly without experience of prairie peculiarities, I rode straight into what looked to me like a perfectly solid patch of ground. It was alkali, and my horse went down until his head only appeared above the surface. I managed to scramble to firm footing as he sank, and was deeply chagrined. Marking the place, I set out afoot for help. I walked miles before meeting Colonel Macleod, who had a spare horse with what was called lasso harness. He had been using this horse to help teams stalled on the trail. Informed of my predicament, he was good enough to return with me. We doubted that even if we found the place, we should find the horse still

Fort Edmonton, 1874

above ground, but after searching for a long time we located him, with his head still showing above the surface. With much difficulty we got a rope around his neck and managed to haul him out. He was exhausted, and it was not until nightfall that I manoeuvred him into camp. For weeks he was unfit for work, but at length recovered, and I subsequently used him on many a hard expedition.

On 4th August Colonel Macleod went south with a train of empty carts to Wood Mountain and a Boundary Survey camp, from which Colonel French thought supplies of forage and possibly pemmican might be obtained. At this point we left the Boundary Survey trail, which here crossed into the United States, and thereafter we had to depend on the compass for direction. Our guides had proved most unreliable.

Colonel French states in his report of 1874:

> *After leaving the B. S. road, I surveyed our route as well as (under the circumstances) I could. It entailed on me a very large amount of extra work. I had to be on the alert to take the altitude of the sun and find our latitude. I plotted out the work*

and marked it on Palliser's map. At night I had frequently to wait up until 1 or 2 a.m. to obtain the magnetic variation of the pole-star. But I was well rewarded for my trouble a month later when, without guides, I was enabled with a certain amount of confidence to strike out for the forks of the Bow and Belly rivers by compass and find the place within a short distance of that calculated on.

On the 6th we crossed a coteau, the altitude being three thousand feet above sea-level. We rested here a day or two. Great prairie fires flamed to the south, but they did not reach us. The pull up this coteau was a hard one on the horses, particularly with the heavy nine-pound guns. These guns gave us more trouble and crippled horses than all the rest of the transport. We had lost since leaving Dufferin ten horses, and the carts and wagons on our line of march sometimes stretched out for miles.

We had met no Indians thus far, although we were nearing the country in which they might be expected. We were also fast approaching the buffalo country, and were constantly on the look-out for these animals. Here the first death occurred, a man of 'E' troop succumbing from fever brought on by wet and exposure. This event cast a gloom over the force.

On 8th August we sighted the first buffalo, but could not get near enough for a kill. I was on rear guard, and can well remember the view from the top of the plateau, our party moving along in the distance, with the Old Wives' Lakes visible several miles to the west. A few buffalo grazed near the lakes. As far as the eye could reach stretched a boundless prairie, partly burned. It was indeed a wonderful sight to us who had never seen the western prairies in their wild beauty, a sight never to be forgotten by those who witnessed it.

We here sent forward from the rear guard for rations, as we were two days behind the party owing to our many exhausted horses. The main force was camped at the Old Wives' Lakes before we overtook it. We remained here several days, waiting for Colonel

Macleod, who arrived the day after we joined the camp. He brought a supply of dried buffalo meat and pemmican, and several cartloads of oats, which were much needed for horses dying daily for want of them. He was accompanied by Lieutenant-Colonel L. W. Herchmer, who was in charge of the Boundary Commission stores at Wood Mountain. Colonel Herchmer joined the force some years afterwards as Superintendent, and eventually became its fourth Commissioner. Colonel Macleod again left for Wood Mountain for a further supply of forage, and we proceeded on our way westward.

Old Wives' Lakes lay some five hundred miles from Dufferin. They were slightly salt, and the water was bad for the horses. Ducks, geese and pelicans abounded, and there was plenty of shooting.

On 12th August we met the first camp of Indians. They were Assiniboines, and not an imposing lot or a good type of the plains aborigine. At this point we established what was called Cripple Camp, and as grass and water were good, fourteen wagons, twenty-eight of the poorest horses, and seven men were left, with a half-breed and some footsore cattle and stores that were not urgently needed. Colonel Macleod was also to leave oats on his return from Wood Mountain. This party was to remain until picked up by that part of the force which would return later on. A sergeant was placed in charge.

Our rations were cut down to half a pound of bread per man a day. Sugar we had been without for some time. Colonel Macleod arrived from Wood Mountain on 15th August with a further supply of oats, which did much to save the horses. The Boundary Survey camp lay only forty miles to the south of us, but we were soon too far away to send there for more supplies. On 21st August we met the first party of half-breed hunters, who had been out from Winnipeg all summer hunting buffalo. Their carts were loaded with pemmican and buffalo robes. A Catholic priest, Father Lestance, accompanied them and their families. They had left

Winnipeg in the early spring, and been as far west as the Cypress
Hills. Their transport was ponies and carts. They reported no feed
between us and the Cypress Hills, buffalo in great numbers having
eaten off all the grass.

These hunting parties were annual affairs. They slaughtered thousands of buffalo, as several carcasses were required to make a sack of
pemmican weighing about one hundred and fifty pounds. Much of
the meat was left rotting on the prairie. A hundred or more animals
might be killed in a single hunt and the waste was enormous. The
buffalo hunters lived a happy life, camping all summer and returning in the fall with carts groaning with their loads of pemmican and
robes, from the sale of which they were provided for the winter and
enabled to start again in the spring. Their guns were chiefly flintlock muskets purchased from the Hudson's Bay Company, repeat-
ing and breech-loading guns being rarely seen among them. They
often came into collision with the Blackfeet and other Indians in
the vicinity of the Cypress Hills, and many were killed on both
sides. They also took every opportunity to steal horses from Indian
camps, the Indians in retaliation frequently setting them afoot,
when they found themselves in a bad way, but were generally rescued by other camps of half-breeds in the vicinity or the friendly
Crees, who sometimes hunted near the Cypress Hills. After meeting this party, bands of buffalo were often seen in the distance but
too far off to be reached by us. For fuel we used buffalo-chips (dried
buffalo dung). It made a capital though not lasting fire. It served us
during the remainder of our journey and, except when in the vicinity of wood, in many subsequent trips, even in winter, when we dug
it from under the snow.

We found the half-breeds' report of bad water fully justified, most
of it being unfit to drink, salty, or in the small ponds polluted by
the buffalo. On 25th August we sighted the Cypress Hills, and
camped near a creek of clear cold water, with good feed around it.
Here we cut some hay and carried it with us. A camp here of several days refreshed both men and horses. Several antelope and deer

were killed in the hills, the first fresh meat we had enjoyed for a long time. The horses, however, despite the rest, were getting very poor, and the work of the men was doubled through having to drive and look after so many exhausted animals. The men behaved splendidly through all the hardships, often on scanty rations, and well deserved the thanks issued in general orders on the evening of 30th August.

The Cypress Hills country was well wooded, and the brush loaded with berries of all kinds. In those days it was also noted for grizzly bears, but although we saw many tracks we did not encounter any of the beasts. Our line of march skirting the Cypress Hills took us not far from the site in after years of the town of Maple Creek, and we little thought that only ten years would elapse before a great transcontinental railroad – the Canadian Pacific – would traverse a country that then for hundreds of miles was without a human habitation, that had pasturage for millions of buffalo, and was the hunting- and battle-ground of the wildest tribes of Indians in the North-West.

At the Cypress Hills we were nearly three months out from Dufferin, and seven hundred miles from that point. We had yet to travel far, our stock was daily diminishing, that left was daily growing weaker. Provisions were growing short, and but for the buffalo we should have been in a bad way. We killed the first buffalo on 1st September. Most of us joined in the hunt; guns popped in every direction. I remember seeing one man riding alongside an old bull, in his excitement beating him with the butt of his empty gun, until someone came to his assistance and brought down the game. We killed four, and the skins were carefully removed. The meat made a welcome addition to our bill of fare. From this point on we had no dearth of fresh meat. The farther west we travelled, the more plentiful became the buffalo. There were places where, as far as the eye could reach, untold thousands were in sight, the country black with them. They had eaten the grass short, making feed very scarce; the lakes were fouled by them. These immense bands were moving north, and there seemed no end to them; they were easily approached, and we killed many from the saddle without going off the line of march.

The buffalo sheds his coat in summer, and the robe is of little value; his winter coat is prime, thick and warm.

From the Cypress Hills Colonel French directed the march northward toward the junction of the Bow and Belly rivers, the point at which Colonel Robertson Ross and Palliser's map indicated the location of Fort Whoop-up. We arrived there on 9th September.

The following is taken from Colonel French's report to the Government in '74:

We were at last at our journey's end, the Bow and Belly rivers. Three deserted log huts without roofs were the only forts visible. Here we were supposed to find luxuriant pasturage, a perfect garden of Eden, climate milder than Toronto, etc. As far as our experience goes, that vicinity for sixty or seventy miles in every direction is little better than a desert; not a tree to be seen anywhere, ground parched and poor, and wherever there was a little swamp it had been destroyed by buffalo. A reference to my diary will show what a very serious position we were now in. We had come a distance of seven hundred and eighty-one miles from the Red River, and after the first eighteen had not seen a human habitation except a few Indian wigwams. It was now the middle of September, and the appalling fact was ever pressing on my mind that on the 20th of September last year the whole country from the Cypress Hills to the Old Wives' Lakes was covered with a foot of snow, several oxen and horses having been frozen to death. All over the country there is very little wood, and snow would hide the buffalo chips available. From what I heard of the fertility of the soil on the Bow and Belly rivers I had hoped that the horses and oxen with a few weeks' rest in the vicinity would have pulled up greatly in condition, but in reality the force had to leave there as quickly as possible to prevent their actually being starved to death. In fact several of the oxen did die of starvation, but the mistake is readily accounted for. Those who travelled along the base of the Rocky Mountains reported on the fertility of the soil on the headwaters of the Bow and Belly rivers, and somehow these reports came to be applied to the whole course of the rivers.

On the 11th the force moved up the Belly River but could find no ford at first, the water being either too deep or too rapid. Pushing on sixteen or eighteen miles we found a ford. I sent out two reconnoitering parties from this point, one up the Belly River, and the other up the Bow River, and made arrangements to send Inspector Walsh and seventy men and fifty-seven horses through to Edmonton. The Edmonton party forded the river on the 14th; on the 13th the Belly River party returned, having travelled about thirty miles west without finding road, trail or grass, but buffalo moving south in thousands. Inspector Denny's party did not return until late in the afternoon of the 14th. They had been up the Bow River for about eighty miles, and gave a dreadful account of the country; neither wood nor grass, country very rough and bad hills ahead. Mr. Levaillee (who was in charge of the party of half-breeds selected by His Honour the Lieutenant-Governor to accompany or precede the force with Indian presents) was with Mr. Denny and placing great reliance on his judgment I asked him if the party could get through to Edmonton. He stated it would be almost impossible to take the horses through, and that we would certainly lose most of them if we tried. With much reluctance I had to counter-order the Edmonton party, and instructed Inspector Walsh to follow the main party south to the Three Buttes.

North-West Mounted Police officers at Fort Walsh, Saskatchewan, 1879.
Sir Cecil Denny back row, right.

IV

Whoop-up and the whisky traders

As Colonel French states in his report, I was sent up the west side of the Bow River with three half-breeds, mounted on tough little Indian ponies, to see if any sign of a trading post existed on that river, or if I could discover any Indians or traders. We made a start at daybreak. We killed a buffalo during the morning, and on striking a small creek with some firewood, cooked the best pieces for breakfast. We took a further supply of the meat for future use.

During that afternoon, while riding along the bank overlooking the river, we saw two Indians on foot coming from the prairie, and making for a deep gully running to the stream. We tried to cut them off in order to interrogate them, but they were too quick for us; they disappeared down the ravine before we could overtake them. We rode toward the gully, but when within one hundred yards of the edge were confronted by a line of some fifty Indians, all armed, their guns pointed towards us.

With our rifles ready we kept moving in a circle and making signs to them. There seemed no danger of their being able to overtake us, as so far as we could see they had no horses.

The half-breeds spoke to them in Cree, but their answers were not understood.

At length they lay down under the bank, their heads and the muzzles of their guns only showing, but they did not fire. One man stood up and went through a pantomime of signs which my half-breeds could not understand. The latter were thoroughly scared and insisted on retiring; these were Sioux Indians, they said, who would kill us if they had a chance.

The Indians seemed uncertain what to do, thinking perhaps that another party might be behind us. One waved what appeared to be a scalp. They were evidently a war party. I much wished to get near and speak with them, but on the half-breeds riding off and leaving me there was no alternative but to follow, and I had to ride hard to overtake them. They were on the back track for camp, and it took all my persuasive powers to induce them to resume the journey up the river, which we eventually did, making a wide detour round the gully in which the Indians lay hidden.

We heard afterwards that this was a party of Assiniboines, afoot on the war-path. They had been one hundred miles up the Bow River from the point where we had met them, and had attacked a party of white men who were camped in the valley with two or three wagon-loads of goods for trade with the Blackfeet. They attacked at night, stole all the horses, killed one man, captured and burned the wagons, and destroyed the goods they were unable to take with them. They were later attacked in turn by a large party of Blackfeet, but got away after losing all their horses. One of the white men, Tony La Chappelle, resided for many years afterwards at Fort Macleod, opened a store there, and did well. Their indecision was no doubt lucky for us; they were doubtless at a loss to know what kind of a party we were, and my red coat must have puzzled them considerably.

After this we travelled at night, thinking the Indians might follow us, which indeed they did for at least a day as we found by their tracks on our return. We went about forty miles farther up the river, or at least ninety miles from our starting-point. No sign of any trail or habitation was seen, and we might have gone another hundred miles without meeting any; this, of course, we learned afterwards. No timber lined the Bow River as far as we went, and the country was broken and hilly.

We were witnesses of a thrilling scene on this journey – thousands of buffalo swimming the Bow, at this point a considerable stream, and very swift. We killed another buffalo, our meat supply being low. We returned to camp on the third, travelling mostly at night, in hard and long rides of at least fifty miles. The Indian ponies we rode were very tough and enduring. The last night thousands of buffalo passed us on a stampede, going south. The ground shook beneath their tread, and we were fortunate not to be in their path.

On our arriving in camp Colonel French decided to move the whole force to the Three Buttes, or Sweet Grass Hills, in clear view eighty miles to the south. We should remain in camp there while the Commissioner and Assistant Commissioner went on to Fort Benton, Montana, some hundred miles from the Sweet Grass Hills, to communicate with Ottawa and procure provisions and information. We left Belly River 15th September in a snowstorm, arriving on Milk River at the boundary line just north of the West Butte, after a most dismal journey, on the 18th, many horses giving out for want of feed. The weather continued cold, with occasional storms. We pitched the tents at the foot of the Butte on the site of an old Boundary Survey camp. Here we found a few stores left by the last party, including a gallon of syrup and some sugar. These luxuries almost started a war; we had not seen anything of the sort for weeks. We also found good coal and indications of minerals. In after years this became an active and important mining camp.

At this point it was decided that 'D' and 'E' troops, with the Commissioner, should return east, gathering up en route the stock and stores left on the way, and taking the best of the horses. These two troops wintered near Fort Pelly, on the North Swan River, and built Swan River barracks. We saw them off on 21st September;

Colonel French, returning from Fort Benton, caught them up some distance to the eastward. The remaining three troops, 'B', 'C' and 'F', were to remain at the Sweet Grass Hills until the return of Colonel Macleod, and we should then proceed westward to do the work originally planned. Colonel French and Colonel Macleod left for Fort Benton on 22nd September; we remained with a few crippled horses, many wagons, the two guns and miscellaneous stores. Thousands of buffalo around us were a guarantee against starvation. Inspector Winder was in command.

On 29th September word came from Colonel Macleod at Benton that we were only forty miles from Fort Whoop-up. We were instructed to move camp about fifteen miles west, a well-beaten trail leading to that notorious rendezvous from Benton. This trail had been continuously used for several years by the traders going back and forth, and was here clearly defined. The news was most welcome. The weather had grown cold, and the prospect of wintering in the vicinity of the Sweet Grass Hills was the opposite of cheerful. The messenger from Benton said the country to the west was well wooded, with many rivers and quantities of game. He also disabused our minds concerning the desperate characters of the whisky traders and Indians.

The traders were few, most of them having returned to Benton for the winter with their annual summer accumulation of robes and other furs. They also had warning of our advent, consequently it was not to be expected we should catch many of them with whisky. The Indians, also, were amicable. They had an abundance of game, and were trading with the whites without friction. Moving camp occupied two days. Our horses being few and in miserable condition, several trips were required to complete the shift. Sugar, tea and other commodities had long since been consumed, but we had plenty of antelope and buffalo meat.

At this Sweet Grass camp the first party of traders passed with loads of buffalo robes, no doubt spoils of the whisky trade, going south. We searched their wagons, but found no liquor. They were objects of great curiosity to us – the first of the far-famed whisky traders we had yet seen. Our new camp was established on 2nd October. The weather turned wintry, and we suffered from the cold; buffalo chips, our only fuel, gave little warmth. We hunted continuously. The buffalo on one occasion came almost up to camp; one man killed six.

Colonel Macleod arrived from Benton on 4th October. He was accompanied by Charles Conrad, of the firm of I. G. Baker & Company, and by Jerry Potts, a noted guide. Potts was engaged at $90.00 per month in that capacity, his duties including also those of interpreter. He knew the country and the Indians thoroughly. The half-breed guide and his fellows who had accompanied us from Dufferin had returned with Colonel French. Nothing could have induced them to go farther west; however, we were well rid of them. I. G. Baker & Company was a prominent Montana firm. Charles Conrad for several years had a post on Sheep Creek, where he traded liquor with the Indians, but had given it up some time previous to our arrival. The firm consisted of himself, his brother W. G. Conrad and I. G. Baker, the chief partner, who now resided in St. Louis. The latter was an old man, and the originator of the firm. He had traded at the pioneer stockade fort of Benton in the wild days of the sixties. In '74 I. G. Baker & Company did considerable contracting for the different United States military posts scattered over northern Montana. At this time Benton was a town of only a few hundred traders, hunters, miners and gamblers, with a few stockmen.

I. G. Baker & Company and T. C. Powers & Company, another equally wealthy firm, owned and operated several steamboats plying on the Missouri between Bismarck, near the Northern Pacific railroad and several hundred miles down the river, and Benton. The boats occasionally ran as far as St. Louis, and even New Orleans. All supplies for Fort Benton and supplies for the Mounted Police for years afterwards came in by this river route, and were then freighted to Fort Macleod across the plains.

While in Benton the Commissioner had contracted with I. G. Baker & Company to furnish all requirements of the force in the south for a year, and a loaded bull team was now on the way out. These bull trains were an institution peculiar to the plains. Each team of twelve or fourteen yoke of oxen hauled three enormous canvas-covered wagons. There were often as many as eight teams of twenty-four wagons to a train. Loads ranged from seven thousand pounds up, or ten to twelve tons to a team. Their rate of travel was slow, ten to fifteen miles a day, but nothing stuck them. A driver went with each team; a night herder and cook completed the outfit. Three or four horses tied to the wagons when on the move were used for night-herding the cattle. The drivers walked alongside the teams during the day, their heavy bull whips exploding as they swung them in reports like pistol shots.

On 6th October Colonel Macleod issued orders to break camp, and three troops, with Charles Conrad and Jerry Potts, moved on. The programme was first an advance on and investigation of Fort Whoop-up, then a move farther west to some point to be selected and the establishment of a permanent post. I was left at the camp with my troop horse, many wagons, the nine-pound guns, and loads of ammunition, for none of which transport was available. I had, besides, several sick men, a corporal, and a few others – about twenty in all. My instructions were to await the arrival of the bull teams, to join them, attach wagons and guns to the train wagons, and have accommodation made for the sick men. We were to proceed thus until we came up with the main body.

Jerry Potts was a Piegan half-breed, and on good terms with all the Blackfoot tribes. A better man for his duties could not have been selected. He did excellent service all the years he remained with the police, which was until his death in 1899 at Fort Macleod, the point to which he had guided us in the fall of 1874. The weather remained cold but fine. We enjoyed the rest in camp. If time lagged we hunted buffalo and antelope, which surrounded us in thousands, to break the monotony.

While in camp here a trader from Fort Benton – John Glenn – passed on his way to locate wherever the force determined to make headquarters. He was an enterprising man; immediately upon hearing of the arrival of the police loading a wagon with canned goods, sugar, syrup and a general assortment of articles they were likely to buy, and following promptly on their tracks. His expectations were fully realised, anything in the way of luxuries we had so long been without bringing the price he asked no matter how exorbitant, and in this venture he laid the foundation of the modest fortune he afterwards accumulated. The men in my party, clubbing together, bought a sack of flour, a barrel of syrup, and much canned fruit. Prices were: flour, $20 per sack; syrup, $3 per gallon; other articles in proportion. These unusual luxuries were quickly disposed of; cooking went on continuously until they were gone.

The bull trains arrived a week later, our loads were attached, the sick men made as comfortable as possible in the wagons, and we broke camp again. The men who were well had to walk, but as the weather was cold, travel slow, and the daily distances covered short, this was no particular hardship. We were three days in reaching the St. Mary's River, where we camped not far from Fort Whoop-up. It had been searched by the troops who went ahead, but no whisky discovered. On our way to the fort we passed a dead Indian lying by the side of the road. He was an Assiniboine, and had been killed by the Blackfeet. The body had shrivelled like a mummy's in the dry air; he was minus his scalp, which the Blackfeet had doubtless taken. We remained long enough to put the poor body underground.

Whoop-up was a stockade fort, about a hundred yards square, the dwelling-houses facing inward. The bastions at the corners were loopholed, and the fort was the proud possessor of two old-fashioned brass field-guns, which I doubt could be fired without danger of bursting. Only three or four men occupied the fort, D. W. Davis, afterwards Member of Parliament in the Dominion House, being in charge. He was very hospitable, showing us over the fort, and later providing a good dinner, with fresh vegetables from his own garden. The trading room was full of goods for Indian trade. Coal, from a fine open seam near the fort, was used in the stoves. The Galt coal-mines and the present city of Lethbridge are only seven miles below the site of old Fort Whoop-up. The men in the fort all had Indian wives. acquired by purchase, probably for whisky. The women were pleasant-featured and of good physique, dressed in calico, and respectable in appearance. No Indians were camped near Whoop-up; having heard of our approach they had moved out on the plains. The traders had also been warned, and if they had liquor it was hidden, which accounted for Colonel Macleod and his command finding none. We crossed the St. Mary's River a few miles above Whoop-up, following the old trail towards Old Man's River some twenty miles away.

A happening when pulling up the hill on the north side of the St. Mary's River furnished a lively interlude of fun and excitement. One of the trail wagons loaded with empty shells for the big guns upset, scattering the harmless missiles in all directions, and sending the teamsters panic-stricken for cover. It was a long time before they would return. Meanwhile the team, left to itself, swerved, over-turning a loaded wagon in which the night herder was sleeping. We expected to find him dead or gasping under the sacks of flour, sugar and cook stoves resting on him, but upon digging him out found him none the worse. The delay necessitated camp for the night.

We crossed Belly River at Slide Out, a name bestowed by the traders and retained to the present day. The Rocky Mountains, in sight since we left the Sweet Grass Hills, seemed quite near and majestic in their winter mantle. The Porcupine Hills, north of the Old Man's River, had also been visible for several days. These were the hills recommended by Colonel Robertson Ross in his report as a suitable location for a military establishment, to enforce the law on the plains.

We arrived at the Old Man's River the fourth day from the Sweet Grass Hills, and found the force comfortably settled in camp on the south side near a heavy growth of woods extending for miles up and down either bank. We had a hearty welcome, and were glad to be at our journey's end. The location chosen looked beautiful to us after the long and weary march. And beautiful indeed it was, with the lofty barrier of snow-draped peaks to the west, the timbered range of the Porcupines to the north, and the Old Man valley as far as the eye might reach lined with sheltering woods. Buffalo in bands dotted the prairie to the south. Our tired horses and oxen, freed at last from the wearing drag, grazed unworried; the many tents of the force gleamed white among the trees. The scene was one of peace and loveliness, the atmosphere homelike and restful. I was glad to learn that our stay here was to be permanent, and that a log fort was to be built at once. Indeed, the men had already started to fell cottonwood trees for logs.

No Indians had as yet visited us, but the time had not been wasted, as there were two prisoners in camp, Harry Taylor and a Spanish negro, captured the previous day by Inspector Crozier some miles up the river while endeavouring to escape south with several hundred buffalo robes and a quantity of whisky. The liquor was spilled, the robes, wagons and teams were confiscated, and the men fined $25.00 each, or in default sentenced to serve six months' imprisonment, with confiscation of their goods. Taylor paid his fine, but the negro, Bond, was unable to do so. He was confined under guard in a tent, and on completion of the fort, in the log guard-room, from which during the winter he made a bold escape. He was fired on by the sentry, but though wounded was not stopped. His body was found by Indians the following spring about thirty miles south.

Taylor became a well-known citizen, and after following various lines of business settled down as a hotel keeper at Macleod, dying there many years ago. The long march from Dufferin, lasting over four months, was ended, and we were at last definitely established in the new country, with the work for which the North-West Mounted Police force was created lying clearly before us. In closing this chapter I quote the conclusion of Colonel French's report to the Canadian Government:

> *I feel, sir, that in the foregoing report, I have but very inade-*
> *quately represented the doings of the force. The broad fact is,*
> *however, apparent – a Canadian force hastily raised, armed*
> *and equipped, and not under martial law, in a few months*
> *marched two thousand miles through a country for the most*
> *part as unknown as it proved bare of pasture and scanty in the*
> *supply of water. Of such a march under such adverse condi-*
> *tions, all true Canadians may well be proud. To the*
> *Government of the Dominion my heartfelt thanks are tendered*
> *for having placed me in a position which entitled me to claim*
> *that I was a member of a corps which performed one of the most*
> *extraordinary marches on record.*
>
> *(Signed)* G. A. FRENCH, N.W.M.P.

V

Fort Macleod: A Merry Christmas — a black New Year

The weather was now cold, cottonwood timber suitable for building was abundant, and after a few days' rest the men were all busy felling trees and cutting them into twelve-foot lengths as material for the proposed fort. Time pressed, for the season was late, and construction was rushed. Horses as well as men required shelter. In trenches three feet deep logs planted upright formed the walls, cross-logs the beams, and poles covered by a foot of earth the roofs. Clay served as plaster for the walls, inside and out. Windows and doors brought in by the bull teams were put in place, and the barracks was complete. Of lumber only enough for doors was available; the floor was bare ground.

The completed fort was in the form of a square, two hundred feet to a side. Other buildings similarly constructed were run up, two long buildings on each of three sides, the stables on the fourth. The men's quarters and saddle-rooms were on the east; officers' quarters and orderly-room on the west; stores, hospital, guard-room and latrines on the south; and the stables, blacksmith's shop and other saddle-rooms on the north. All buildings faced inward, their back walls the walls of the fort. A large gate at either end opened upon the square.

With every one engaged, the fort was soon finished. Plastering in low temperatures with clay softened by water and put on with bare hands, was frigid work. While the force was thus employed, I. G. Baker & Company's men were at work on similar structures for a trading post near the fort. Their store was soon finished and stocked with merchandise – canned fruit, clothing, groceries, guns, ammunition, Indian trade goods and anything likely to find sale with the police. Prices were high; a dollar a can for fruit or vegetables, for example. As we had received no pay since leaving Dufferin, all purchases were made on credit. Orders were taken on the men's pay, and when money at last came little was left to them after their accounts had been settled.

Patrols were sent out to look for whisky traders on their way south, trying to evade the police. There were a number of captures. The offenders were heavily fined, their liquor spilled, and their robes, teams and wagons confiscated. The Indians soon began to come in and set up large camps near us. Councils were held. They were told the reason for our coming into the country, and without exception declared themselves well pleased at seeing an end put to the whisky trade. Hundreds of Blackfeet, Bloods and Piegans visited us while the fort was building. They were in those days a fine lot of men, for the most part friendly. They owned hundreds of horses, lodges of tanned buffalo skins, often fancifully painted, and quantities of buffalo robes for trade. With plenty of meat in their lodges, no happier people might be found anywhere. They gave us valuable assistance in locating the whisky traders and in suppressing the traffic.

The Blackfoot nation in 1874 numbered eight thousand. Of our civilisation they knew nothing. They lived in summer on the plains, and in winter in camp on the wooded river-bottoms. Their tents, floored with buffalo robes, were warm and comfortable. Buffalo meat was their staple food; they ate little flour. They were extremely fond of tea and drank great quantities. Tobacco they generally mixed with dried red-willow inner bark or the leaf of a small shrub with a red berry, plentiful on the hillsides, called by them ah-so-kin-oky. This leaf gave the tobacco a very aromatic flavour.

The women did all work in camp, setting up and striking lodges, cooking, tanning robes, sewing, etc., while the men loafed, ate and smoked, or boasted of past exploits and planned raids against their enemies. They were continually at war with the Crees in the north, and with many tribes to the south in Montana, and summer or winter would travel hundreds of miles on horse-stealing expeditions, often returning with large herds of stolen animals. Years were required by the police to put an end to these forays, a custom of generations, and almost a part of their religion. It was meritorious to steal, and the murderer was acclaimed as a brave. The more horses stolen and the more enemies slain, the happier would be his state in the happy hunting grounds of the next world.

Prior to our arrival a few Catholic priests had at intervals visited the plains Indians, but missionary effort had been confined almost altogether to the Crees. In the north, in the shadow of the Rockies, the Rev. George McDougall had in 1871 established a small mission among the Stony Indians on the Bow River, and named it Morley; after his death this was carried on by his son John. Another son, David, had opened a store there, his trade being almost exclusively with these Indians. They did good work, but it was a mistake to suppose that the character and habits of the red men could be changed in a few short years, and that a wild people could be made to comprehend the laws of the white man and conform to them. The Mounted Police in their dealings with these people wisely from the beginning took this into consideration; and while the law was enforced, for several years the chiefs were often consulted as to the penalties to be imposed for offences, which among white men would have been punished by imprisonment. Thus by degrees the Indians came to understand our laws and to accept them.

At the time of our arrival there were no cattle in the country, except for a few domestic cows and work oxen belonging to the Hudson's Bay Company, and some half-breeds along the North Saskatchewan.

In the Indian camps near the fort during this first winter there was continual dancing. At these dances tea, mixed with black tobacco, was the standard beverage. The tobacco ingredient seemed to act as a stimulant. A tragedy occurred at one of these dances, several of us being present at the time. An old Indian, jealous of a young buck who was dancing with his young and comely squaw, left the tent, and returning cut a hole in the skin covering, poked his rifle through it, and shot the woman dead. She fell across the fire close to where we sat, and for a time it looked as if a bloody fight would follow. The man was captured, and handed over to us. Afterwards he was sent to Winnipeg for trial, and sentenced to some years' imprisonment. He subsequently returned and purchased another wife. The plains Indians in the early days were extremely jealous of their women, much more so than the Crees, and their punishments for infidelity were most cruel. Death was often the penalty, but more frequently mutilation – the nose cut off close to the face. An Indian wife was a chattel to be bought and sold for a certain number of horses. The more women could be purchased, the more buffalo robes would be tanned and traded. I have known Blackfeet with as many as twenty, or even thirty, women so acquired.

The Indian dead were left in the forks of trees or in lodges along the river-bottoms, most of their possessions beside them for use in the hunting grounds for which they were destined. Horses were also killed to accompany them. Indian names were given to many of the police. Colonel Macleod became Stamixotokan, or Bull's Head, from the ring he wore which had on it this crest. Most of us were named for some part of our dress or some peculiarity. I owned a beaver coat, and thus became Kis-ta-ke-ot-sokas – Beaver Coat.

We spent our first Christmas in Alberta in the new fort. At a grand dinner prepared by our chef and attended by all, buffalo hump was served in place of roast beef, but we had real plum pudding. A dance followed, our partners half-breed girls. With the exception of the McDougall family at Morley, there were no white women in southern Alberta at that time. A small village had sprung up near the fort; two or three stores, a billiard-room, an ex-police-man in a barber's shop; another in a shoe store. These buildings were all log, built chiefly by old traders who settled down to legitimate business once the whisky trade was ended. In spite of all we had heard against them, we found them a very decent lot of men. They were of all nationalities, and either miners, traders or hunters. There were, of course, bad characters among them, and they were all gamblers. The harder cases did not remain long, as law and order was not to their taste. Our guard-room was full of prisoners, one or two charged with murder. The guard-room was poorly equipped, and many men who could ill be spared were required to guard the prisoners. Winnipeg was an eight-hundred-mile journey across the plain; they could not be sent there until spring.

The villagers were most hospitable, and did what they could to entertain us. More or less bad whisky circulated during the winter at five dollars per bottle, but alcohol and Jamaica ginger were the chief refreshments. Several cases of whisky were unearthed by the Indians, and a general carouse ensued with resultant casualties. Our time was fully occupied. Long trips and many arrests were made, and the liquor traffic was in a fair way to being suppressed. Most of our horses were sent south in charge of Inspector Walsh to winter at Sun River, Montana, as it was too late to put up a supply of hay near Fort Macleod. Small quantities were purchased at twenty dollars a ton from a trader a few miles down the river, but we depended on purchased Indian ponies for use on our various journeys this first winter. They were hardy, serviceable animals, and would find their own feed under the snow by pawing in the coldest weather.

Sub-Constable McKernan, who died only a few years ago in Edmonton, accompanied Inspector Walsh to Montana. He was one of the 'originals' of 1874.

A small police detachment was stationed some eighteen miles down the Old Man's River at an abandoned liquor trading post, named Fort Kipp after the original builder. It was the customary log structure, surrounded by a stockade. An officer named Brisbois was in command. Two of his men had spent Christmas on leave at Fort Macleod; they left to return to Kipp two days before New Year. On that day word was brought to the fort that a Baker Company bull team, loaded with supplies and mail for us, had arrived at Whoop-up, but would be at least a week in reaching Macleod. We naturally were most anxious to get this mail at once, since no letters or papers had reached us since leaving Dufferin in June; particularly we wished to have it by New Year. I therefore asked permission of Colonel Macleod to ride to Whoop-up, pick up the letters, and return by that time.

The colonel hesitated, but being himself anxious to hear from the Commissioner, he at last consented. I started on the evening of 31st December, riding a tough little Indian pony, with the intention of staying overnight with the detachment at Kipp and returning to Macleod the following day. Snow on the ground made the trail faint. I had made about half the distance when a sudden change of the wind, bringing a north-west blizzard, decided me to turn back. The temperature fell to twenty degrees below zero, I found it impossible to make headway with the wind and snow full in my face, and I had difficulty in keeping my eyelids from freezing together. The slight trail was soon blotted out. I had no alternative but to turn my back to the storm and trust to the horse to find the way to Fort Kipp. Luckily I was wearing a warm buffalo coat, but even this and my buffalo skin moccasins did not prevent me suffering considerably, and I only saved myself from freezing by dismounting at intervals and running beside the horse. In doing so, however, I was in danger of leading the horse away from the point for which he was making. I could see only a few yards in any direction through the blizzard.

Darkness came on, and I did not dare leave the saddle, to the pommel of which I fastened the reins, letting the horse have his head. Fortunately he had been bred in the vicinity, and was wonderfully intelligent; he never went out of a walk, but kept plodding along hour after hour through the storm. Around midnight it cleared somewhat, and I could see dimly ahead what I took for the steep bank of the river. I trusted to the horse and he plodded on. The storm thickened again, and for another hour nothing was visible.

Then suddenly I found myself surrounded by lighted windows. Without my realising it the horse had walked through the open gate of Fort Kipp, and stopped in the middle of the square. It was fortunate I had put my trust in his intelligence; otherwise we should no doubt have been lost and I have perished.

Fort Kipp that night was a welcome haven. The comfortable rooms, with their blazing log fires and a warm meal, soon put my blood again in circulation. I inquired of Inspector Brisbois if the two men, Baxter and Wilson, who had been in Macleod on leave, had returned. His reply being that he had not seen them, we concluded they had taken shelter at a small trading post some ten miles up the river, and would come in the following day.

Next morning was clear, and I rode to Whoop-up, and returned to Kipp in the afternoon with the letters. Here I learned that the horses ridden by the missing men had come into the fort, riderless, soon after I had left, and a party accompanied by Indians had been sent out to search for them. Just before I started for Macleod the poor fellows were brought in, one frozen stiff, the other, Wilson, still breathing, but with arms, legs and most of his body frozen also. I took a fresh horse, and rode as fast as the snow would allow to Macleod, and on my reaching there Dr. Nevitt raced to Fort Kipp, only to find on arrival poor Wilson dead.

The search party had followed the trail of the unfortunate men's horses to where they had wandered in a circle, and then lain down, soon to freeze in that bitter north wind. Shortly after this sad occurrence another man named Parks, ill from the exposure and hardship of the march, died in the rude hospital at the Fort. These three deaths cast a gloom over us all, and our first New Year in the West. The bodies of Baxter and Wilson were brought to Fort Macleod and buried with military honours by their comrades, with whom they were great favourites.

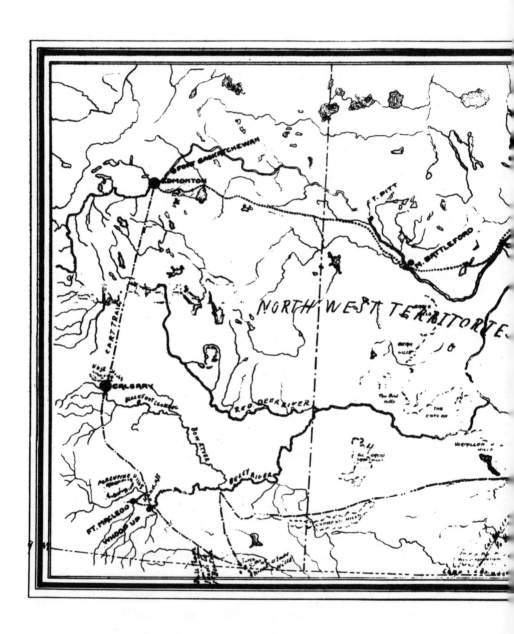

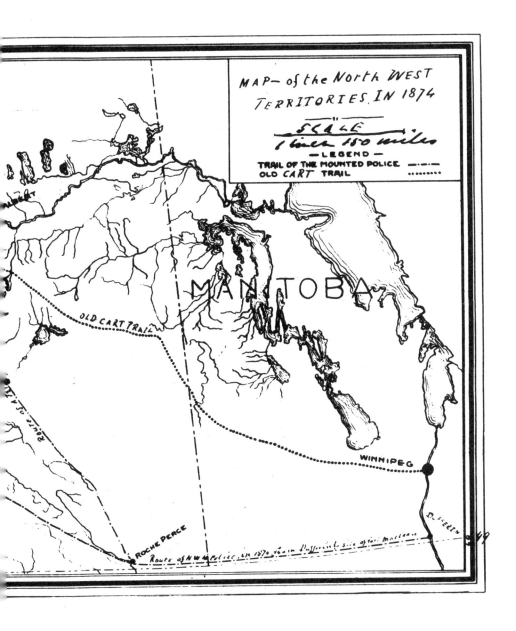

MAP — of the North WEST
TERRITORIES, IN 1874

SCALE
1 inch 150 miles
— LEGEND —
TRAIL OF THE MOUNTED POLICE ——·——
OLD CART TRAIL ··········

MANITOBA

OLD CART TRAIL

WINNIPEG

ROCHE PERCE

Route of N.W.M Police in 1874 from Dufferin to line of Fort Mcleod

D. FERIN

VI

An interrupted card game and a slump in spirits

January and February of 1875 were cold and stormy The work the men were called upon to do was hard and new to them. On our arrival we were almost without clothing, and we had no prospect of obtaining any until the following summer, when supplies reached us via the Missouri River from the east. The Assistant Commissioner purchased quantities of tanned buffalo skins from the Indians, and our two tailors were kept busy day and night fashioning pants and coats of these skins. They formed the principal wear for the first police at Macleod. Our chief tailor, J. Stuttaford, worked indefatigably, and if the men were clothed and spared much suffering much of the credit was due to him.

Buffalo coats and moccasins were warm, but jacket and trousers of the same material were stiff and clumsy to work in. Also, traders about the fort had fired the men's minds with stories of the wealth to be made at mining in Montana, the high wages prevailing, and in comparison with which their police pay was a mere pittance. These things caused considerable dissatisfaction and grumbling, which culminated in the desertion with their arms, one night in February, of some twenty men. No doubt the traders helped them with horses to escape. They were pursued, but crossed the Line before being sighted. The American authorities, however, recovered and returned their arms.

These desertions made the duties doubly hard on the men remaining. There could be no relaxation in the task of rounding up whisky traders, and the large number of prisoners necessitated strong guards, leaving few to do the other work. We were but a handful in an almost unknown country, charged with the control of thousands of warlike Indians, of whom as yet we knew but little. The responsibility upon our commanding officer, Colonel Macleod, was heavy, and must have given him hours of great anxiety, but the firmness and justice with which the Indians were treated, and the fact that what we promised we performed, combined with their recognition of the great benefits to them of the suppression of the liquor traffic, established a confidence not to be gained by force or threats. On many occasions officers, accompanied by two or three men, went into Indian camps of several hundred lodges and made arrests for crime, or put a stop to drunken orgies, without encountering opposition or resistance, although the tribes had it in their power at any time to wipe out the whole force had they felt so inclined.

Trips to different points to gather in illegal traders continued in all weathers – journeys made, it must be remembered, in a wide territory, without trails or roads, and without assistance to our small force. Transport there was none, blankets and provisions, usually pemmican, being carried on pack-horses. We camped in the open, tents being too cumbersome to carry, and because of desertions the work was made more arduous, while the scarcity of clothing was an added hardship. Little wonder if more or less dissatisfaction was at times voiced. On parade, in our uncouth garments, we were a motley crew.

About the fort, too, there was constant activity; timber to be felled, hauled out and cut up, buffalo hunted for meat, buildings to be repaired. The sod-covered roofs collapsed, the earthen floors were cold and damp – these combined miseries were enough to sap the morale of any body of men, and no praise can be too high for those who endured them during that long and trying winter of 1874 at Macleod. Also, some allowance may be made for the deserters.

A brighter side of the picture was that the Indians were most hospitable. If in our many expeditions we came upon them we were always made welcome, the best they had was placed before us, shelter from frequent storms given us in their lodges. Their cooking was primitive, and their utensils the simplest – wooden bowls for plates, fingers for forks, buffalo horns their cups. Their meat was usually boiled, but there was always plenty of it, and as has been said, we were always welcomed.

Throughout the winter we had abundant meat. Elk and deer were numerous along the river. Hunters armed with long-range rifles, lying in some gully near a herd of buffalo, killed at unbelievable distances as many as were needed. Then wagons brought in the meat. The animals covered the prairie in immense numbers. At times one might travel over miles of territory and, as far as the eye could reach, see nothing but buffalo, or ride at an easy lope through countless thousands streaming ahead and behind. It is hard to realise that in a few years the great herds were gone, but the slaughter was tremendous. Fifteen thousand robes were shipped by I. G. Baker & Company from Fort Macleod to Benton – the number traded from the Indians during the winter and spring of 1874–5.

Many white hunters also brought in robes and wolf skins. Thousands, too, were killed by the Indians, not only for meat, but for their tents, which they renewed annually. A tent required ten to thirty skins for the making. Enormous numbers died from wounds and were eaten by wolves. The half-breeds were also a factor in the destruction, slaughtering whole herds for portions only of the meat, the remainder being left to rot on the prairie. The wolves contributed also to the slaughter, as when we arrived the large grey prairie species ran in packs, and were often found near the buffalo herds, pulling down wounded animals and killing young calves. An attempt was made, when the first North-West Council was formed a few years after our arrival, to enforce a law against the killing of buffalo calves, but the country was so vast and the more pressing duties of the small force were so arduous, that it had little effect.

Fur trading was profitable. The large grey wolf pelts brought two to three dollars; buffalo robes about the same. Beaver were numerous on the rivers and creeks, and many skins were traded. At old Fort Macleod an Indian brought in the only white beaver skin I ever saw, and presented it to Colonel Macleod, who had it made into a pair of gauntlets which he wore for many years.

Towards the end of the first winter the Benton firm of T. C. Powers & Company opened a general store in Macleod. By this time there were in the village three stores: the Baker Company, with Charlie Conrad in charge; T. C. Powers, with T. Boggy as store-keeper; and Tony La Chappelle, an ex-whisky trader, who sold tobacco, candy, etc., and had also put in two billiard tables. An old Hudson's Bay Company boat-builder, W. Gladstone, ran a carpenter's shop; Dan Horan, an ex-policeman, a shoemaker's shop; and Dick Kennefick, also an old trader, a blacksmith's shop. Other small stores blossomed, and one or two gambling places. These were countenanced, as there seemed no law applicable to them. Faro and poker were the games favoured, and the stakes were considerable. These places were closely watched by the police, and no serious disturbances occurred. The shooting and hold-ups common in such places in the western United States Territories were unknown. From the start the gamblers held for the police a healthy respect. The two principal characters operating these concerns were Ace Samples and Poker Brown, both quite decent fellows with Indian wives. Samples in later years opened a ranch-house and stopping-place at High River, but both he and Brown eventually returned to Montana. Samples was a noted pistol shot, deriving his nickname, 'Ace', from his ability at twenty-five yards to hit the ace of any card four times out of five. He had, it was said, killed more than one man across the border, but he never exercised his skill along this line while in southern Alberta.

A Catholic priest, Father Scollen, came to Macleod, and remained the winter. He spoke both Blackfoot and Cree, and was of great assistance to us. We had engaged a second guide and interpreter, Munro, thoroughly familiar with the country north. He stayed with the force for many years. Formerly with the Hudson's Bay Company at Fort Edmonton, on hearing of our arrival he came south in February, and offered his services, which were accepted.

With Sergeant Francis and three men I made a three-day journey to a stream at the foot of the mountains, later named Lee Creek, where we had information that a trader from the south was dispensing whisky to the Indians camped nearby. The weather was bitterly cold, and the snow deep. A pack-horse carried our bedding, a small tent, and a few provisions. We camped the last night with the Indians – Piegans. We had a good lodge and many robes, some freshly killed venison, and were very comfortable.

The trader had moved up the north branch of the Old Man with his team and a quantity of robes purchased for alcohol. We confiscated and spilled a five-gallon can of this liquor in the Indians' possession. By the exercise of a little diplomacy an Indian was secured to guide us to the trader's camp next evening. The man himself was absent, but a search uncovered ten gallons of alcohol, which we destroyed, two hundred robes, and a hobbled horse.

Leaving two men at the camp, with the sergeant, one man, and the Indian, I followed the tracks of the fugitive's mount. They led due north, and it became apparent that he had had warning of our approach, and made a hurried departure. Why he had not destroyed the liquor we could not understand. In below-zero weather he took great chances, travelling, as far as we could see, without blankets and riding bareback. All that day we pushed on without coming up with him, and spent a miserable night, *sans* tent or covering, but, dry wood being plentiful, comforted by a rousing fire. We supped on dried meat but missed our tea. Towards morning snow began to fall, and but for the Indian, who though uncommunicative seemed to know where he was heading, we should never have been able to follow the trail that day.

As night came on we rode down to a heavy patch of wood on the river bottom, and stumbled upon a large log house. We had not heard of anything of the kind in this vicinity, but in view of the time we had been in the country this was not strange. Several sleighs lay about, and a band of hobbled horses grazed in the open not far away. Smoke rose from a stove-pipe projecting through the roof – the men, whoever they were, were at home.

Leaving the Indian and the sub-constable on guard outside, Francis and myself pushed in the door and entered. Three men and two Indian women looked up and stared. The former were drinking and playing cards. Had they not been taken by surprise, they

Bull-teams at Fort Benton, 1874

would no doubt have offered resistance. One was Wetherwax, connected with a wholesale liquor firm in Benton, and another Diamond R. Brown, so called. The third man's name I have forgotten. The man whose trail we had followed stated that he had known nothing of police in the vicinity, but had ridden over to this resort for supplies he was in need of. They were all placed under arrest, and on searching the house we found a large stock of liquor, hundreds of robes and furs of various sorts. The liquor we destroyed, and getting the horses together we loaded as many robes as they would hold on the sleighs, and with their horses in the harness and the owner driving, we returned as quickly as possible to the camp we had left the day before. On arriving we loaded another sleigh, slept at the camp and left next day for Fort Macleod, feeling well pleased with our success. It had been a hard trip, and I have given these details as an illustration of the kind of work the North-West Mounted Police did during that first winter, and indeed until a much-needed respect for law and order was developed in the country.

We were three days in reaching Macleod. The prisoners were tried by the Assistant Commissioner, and fined $250 each, their robes, teams, and sleighs confiscated. Two were unable to pay their fines, the result being that they joined the other culprits in the guard-room. The third man, Wetherwax, was most defiant, threatening dire consequences to follow an appeal he should make to Washington. He failed to impress Colonel Macleod, who told him to pay his fine or go to jail, and so far as an appeal to Washington was concerned he was welcome to go the limit. He spent a week in the guard-room; then as hard labour was the lot of all prisoners – wood-cutting, stable-cleaning and other jobs – he paid his fine and was released. He remained in the country, opening a small store in the cabin in which he was arrested, but later returned to Fort Benton. We saw him there in visits we paid to that town in after years, engaged in the wholesale liquor business. He bore us no grudge, and seemed glad to see us. These whisky traders, as I have said before, with few exceptions, were not a bad lot, and many in time became good law-abiding citizens. The squaws we found in the cabin returned with our Indian guide to the Piegan camp.

In February 1875, in a second large mail from the east, via Fort Benton, Colonel Macleod was directed to proceed as soon as possible to Helena, Montana, to meet Lieutenant-Colonel A. G. Irvine, who was travelling by the Northern Pacific and Utah Northern to Corrin, about two hundred miles south of Helena, and the nearest railroad point. From Corrin his journey would be by stage-coach. Lieutenant-Colonel Irvine had been appointed Inspector in the Mounted Police, and on arriving in Helena was to institute proceedings to procure the extradition of the men who committed a cold-blooded Indian massacre, which, since the boundary between the United States and Canada had been fixed, was found to have taken place on the Canadian side of the Line, near the Cypress Hills. Colonel Macleod on arriving in Helena was to lend his assistance in the matter, and on its conclusion return with Colonel Irvine to Fort Macleod.

Spring was approaching, whisky-trading had been largely stamped out, the Indians were moving to the plains for their summer hunt, and Colonel Macleod decided that the trip to Helena should be made in March. With Sergeant Cochrane, Sub-Constable Charles Ryan, and Jerry Potts, I was detailed to accompany him.

We left Macleod on the 15th of that month, with saddle- and pack-horses, blankets, tea, bacon and hard biscuits, but no tent, behind us a formidable undertaking successfully launched. We had made a march that should for all time be memorable, we had built a fort, routed the law-breakers, and won the confidence of the wild tribes of the plains, and while in the course of our duties we had endured much hardship, it had been endured in the right spirit and with little grumbling or complaint. We could look back upon our work since leaving Dufferin in the previous June with satisfaction, and to the future with confidence. All, however, rejoiced that spring would soon be with us, and that the first and hardest winter ever experienced by the North-West Mounted Police was now almost over.

VII

A battle with Boreas

The first night out from Macleod we spent at Whoop-up with Dave Akers, the man then in charge. As we were leaving the next morning Akers pointed out two rainbow-like halos around the sun which he called sun dogs, and predicted a blizzard within twenty-four hours. This was the first time our attention had been drawn to this celestial portent, but we were to remember it in after years, for we noted particularly on this journey that it nearly always was the forerunner of a storm of some kind, usually a blizzard or, if not, extremely cold weather. However, his predictions did not trouble us as we rode – depending entirely upon our guide, for there was no trail – during a fine clear but cold day, toward the Milk River and to the boundary line, our proposed camp for the night.

We passed many buffalo herds, and during the morning the colonel took a fancy to test the speed of his horse in chasing one of the great brutes. He followed an old bull for a good mile before overhauling him, but had no idea of killing the animal. As he drew alongside the bull suddenly swung his massive head in a vicious lunge at the horse. The sharp horn caught the stirrup leather, ripping it clear away from the saddle, and almost unseating the colonel, missing his leg and the horse only by a hair. This was enough for Colonel Macleod. He dropped behind, leaving the bull to lumber on unmolested. It was not safe to trifle with those mighty beasts. One thrust of a horn might disembowel a horse, or toss both horse and rider skyward.

'Colonel, I guess you leave dem ol' buffalo bull alone after dis, hey?' said Jerry Potts.

As it was now about noon we dismounted and turned the horses out on their picket-ropes to feed, dug some buffalo-chips from under the snow for a fire, and while the colonel's saddle was being repaired we lunched. We had made, the guide said, about half-way to Milk River. The sun had disappeared in mist, and it began to look as if Akers's prediction was promptly to be fulfilled. We hurried along. As night came on the storm which threatened broke. A bitter wind blew out of the north, and before we rode down the steep banks of Milk River we were enveloped in a blinding blizzard.

The outlook was not cheerful. No wood was to be found. On the advice of our guide we unsaddled and stowed the packs under a snowbank on the north side, which gave us some protection from the piercing wind. With our hunting knives we dug a deep hole in the bank, into which we all crowded. We were in for real trouble, as the guide said these blizzards sometimes lasted for days. To attempt to return in the face of the storm would have been madness – courting death. We afterwards learned that a temperature of sixty-five degrees below zero had been recorded during this blizzard, the worst seen in Montana in many years. That night and the following – we were stormbound here for thirty-six hours – were, I think, the worst in the experience of any of us. There was no grass, and had there been we should not have chanced losing our horses by turning them loose to graze. Buffalo swarmed down into the river-bottom, and even close to the horses, which for the day and two nights we remained, bunched together at the ends of long picket-ropes. We took two-hour shifts at holding the halter ropes and keeping the buffalo from crowding in on our animals. This seems almost incredible, but the fierceness of the blizzard and intense cold had driven all fear from the beasts, and they huddled together for warmth and shelter. Our snow-cave was damp and chilled us to the bone. We slept little, but ate at intervals, and the bacon, bolted uncooked, no doubt helped to pull us through.

The storm continued, and on the second morning we decided, the guide agreeing, that to remain longer meant death by freezing for both men and horses. The poor beasts had stood for a day and a half without food or covering in that terrible weather. The snow which blanketed them had been some protection, but they were in evil case and we could only trust to Jerry Potts to guide us to Rocky Coulee, twenty-five miles south, where he said there would be shelter if no wood. It was miserable work saddling and packing the horses with our numbed fingers on the morning of the 9th, and a more forlorn company it would be hard to imagine as we moved off afoot, dragging the horses, through the storm. Jerry Potts led, but at a distance of only a few feet or we should have lost him in the smothering white blank. Walking brought some warmth to our stiffened frames, and after a time we mounted, and made better progress.

We had gone some way when we missed Ryan, and I rode back, while the party waited within hail, to search for him. I found him sitting on the snow holding his horse.

'What's the matter?' I asked.

'We'll never get through, Mr Denny. You and the colonel go on; I can't make it any farther.'

I learned that he had endeavoured to mount, but was unable to do so. His buffalo-skin breeches had frozen stiff, and he was unable to bend his knees. I lifted him, and helped place him in the saddle, and we rejoined the party.

The storm persisted, and we plodded on without resting. Our guide was a marvel. He rode steadily ahead, with short stops at intervals when he seemed almost to smell out the trail, for nothing was to be seen in any direction. Toward evening the storm abated somewhat, and we saw directly ahead a deep gash, and rode down into Rocky Coulee, our objective, just as it became dark. Here we spent another miserable night in the open. The colonel, Jerry, Ryan, and myself lay close together for warmth under our buffalo robes, while Sergeant Cochrane held the horses bunched under a bank not far away. I should have gone out during the night to relieve him, but that the colonel stopped me. In getting from under the robes, the snow covering us would have fallen in and flooded our bed. So we lay, sleeping little, through the long and wretched night.

The sun shone brightly next morning, but it was still very cold. Cochrane and the horses were completely covered with snow, but he said he had been warm and comfortable through the night. We saddled up and, postponing breakfast, started again on foot, leading the horses. We hoped to reach the Marias River in a few hours. Here, we had been informed, were stationed a company of American soldiers in some log buildings, on the look out for illicit traders on their way across the Line into Canada with contraband arms and liquor.

We rode down the hill to the Marias in the early afternoon, and towards the quarters of the detachment. They saw us coming and, mistaking us for whisky traders, rode out to make a capture. Discovering their mistake, they invited us in and spared no effort to make us feel at home and comfortable. We certainly were a forlorn and bedraggled lot. We had all suffered more or less from frost bites, and our horses could barely stagger. The commanding officer, Captain Williams, was kindness itself. We did yeoman justice to an enormous meal of fresh buffalo steak and hot tea, and after a comfortable night, much refreshed, were able to continue our journey next day to Fort Shaw. Captain Williams furnished us with fresh mounts, and also sent two of his men with sleighs to carry our baggage.

Our own horses were completely used up. Three died a few days after we left the Marias. Fort Shaw was only fifteen or twenty miles away, and we arrived early. Built of adobe or sun-dried bricks, Fort Shaw was at that time the largest American post in western

Montana. General Gibbon, the commanding officer, had under him some four hundred men, cavalry and infantry. He was an old Civil War veteran, with a record of much service in the Indian wars. Many of his officers had with them their wives and families. The life was monotonous, their only duties having to do with depredations committed on the settlers by Indian war parties. Montana in that day was the home of many warlike tribes – Gros Ventres, Sioux, Assiniboines and Blackfeet – who looked upon the Long Knives (their name for United States soldiers) as their enemies. Warfare between them was continual. The soldiers never went except in force into an Indian camp, and many a poor fellow caught alone was tortured and barbarously mutilated. This was the condition existing on the American side of the Line, between the United States authorities and the western Indian tribes. What a contrast to that in the North-West Territories of Canada, where the Indians welcomed our residence among them, and looked upon us as their friends and deliverers from the many evils they had suffered at the hands of unprincipled white men.

After two days' rest, Colonel Macleod and party again set out for Helena, General Gibbon being kind enough to send an escort and supply the transport. I remained at Fort Shaw, the general hospitably placing a room in his house at my disposal. I was suffering from snow-blindness, a most painful affliction, and was laid up for ten days, while the general and other officers did everything possible for my relief. General Gibbon had known President Lincoln well, and I have often regretted having been unable at the time to preserve in writing the many interesting stories he told me of the martyred war president.

On recovering from my eye trouble and frozen foot, through the kindness of the general I was taken to Helena in a six-mule ambulance. I was sorry to say good-bye to such friends, and the cordial goodwill shown us, and the help rendered us at Fort Shaw, will never be forgotten.

While I was recuperating at Fort Shaw, the weather cleared, and became warm and spring-like. The journey to Helena through beautiful Prickly Pear Canyon was most interesting. The road crossed the summit of the Rocky Mountains to reach Helena, lying in a lovely valley in the heart of the range. The capital of Montana was then a thriving mining town of some three thousand inhabitants. Placer mining in the adjacent gulches was still the leading activity, water being brought to the workings by flumes several miles in length. Accommodation at the hotels where we put up was very good. Helena boasted two banks and several opulent business houses. Drinking and gambling houses made up the eastern section. The Chinese, also, formed a separate community. They worked the old placer diggings, and made them pay. Gold was discovered here in 1856. A prospecting party had worked all summer without success, and their supplies and hopes had about reached zero. They determined upon one last effort, and their luck turned. They struck it rich. They named their location Last Chance Gulch, and there the town of Helena sprang up.

At the time this is written Helena, the capital of the rich state of Montana, is a city of some 15,000 people, on the main line of the Great Northern and Chicago, Milwaukee and St Paul railroads. The placer diggings have long since been worked out, but there are quartz mines operating in the vicinity. The city is also the centre of a rich farming and stock-raising district. Our stay in Helena was made pleasant by the courtesy of leading businessmen and visiting United States Army officers, who went out of their way to entertain us. The surveyor-general of the territory, Mr Smyth, showed us the sights, not forgetting Chinatown and the dance and gambling houses. We remained some weeks, and met most of the men who had deserted from Macleod in the winter. After great hardships they had arrived in Helena, only to find their dreams of wealth easily acquired not up to expectations. The majority of them called shamefacedly on Colonel Macleod, and begged to be taken back in the force. A few of the best were re-engaged.

Colonel Macleod purchased wagons, horses and needed supplies and instructed me to take the guide and return with these to Macleod. With the men re-engaged he awaited the arrival at Helena of Colonel Irvine.

The return journey was pleasant. Spring had arrived and the only difficulties we met were in fording the rivers, where high water and running ice made the crossings dangerous. We found the guard-room at Macleod full, many more arrests among the whisky traders and Indians having been made in our absence. The Indians as a whole had given no trouble. Much work had been done. The men's quarters and the stables had been enlarged and better roofs provided. Considerable lumber had also been whipsawed by half-breeds who had come down from the north and settled near the fort.

Colonel Macleod arrived shortly after us, but remained only a week before returning to Helena. Colonel Irvine had changed his route. Instead of coming via the Utah Northern to Corrin, he would travel by steamer up the Missouri to Benton, and the first boat would not arrive until early in June. It was August before Colonel Macleod and Colonel Irvine actually arrived. Colonel Irvine at once proceeded overland with escort and transport to Winnipeg, taking with him all prisoners who had been sentenced to lengthy terms.

NWMP scouts at Fort Macleod, Alberta, 1890. Sir Cecil Denny middle row, left. In the foreground are the Indian scouts Black Eagle and Elk Facing the Wind.

VIII

Establishing Fort Walsh

S oon after the spring break-up Inspector Walsh came in from the Sun River camp with the horses in good condition, and was instructed to take his troop, 'B', to the Cypress Hills and construct a fort similar to that at Macleod. The site selected lay in the centre of the hills, two hundred miles to the east, and not far north of the American boundary. This region was infested by whisky traders. It was a favourite hunting ground for many Indian tribes, and they were continually coming into conflict. Horse stealing was rife. Briefly, it was about as lawless a section as could be found in the territory. It was to put an end to this state of affairs that Fort Walsh was established in the summer of 1875. Major Walsh and his troop soon stamped out the whisky trade, and did much to gain the goodwill of the various Indian tribes that were accustomed to visit the fort.

A small village sprang up, and the firm of T. C. Powers & Company opened a general store. All supplies came in by way of Benton and bull teams. In the north Inspector Jarvis and 'A' troop passed a busy winter at Edmonton, living in the old Hudson's Bay fort, then in charge of Chief Factor (later Senator) Richard

Hardisty. They made numerous hard trips in pursuance of their duties, and gained much useful information. The Cree Indians and half-breeds along the Saskatchewan proved friendly. Inspector Jarvis was visited by a party of Canadian Pacific Railway engineers under Mr. E. W. Jarvis, who had crossed the mountains from the west through the Yellowhead Pass in search of a route for the transcontinental road. The route at that time had not been definitely settled.

A troop, under Inspector Jarvis, built the fourth North-West Mounted Police establishment on the present site of Fort Saskatchewan, twenty miles down the Saskatchewan River from Fort Edmonton. Colonel Steele (afterwards Major-General Sir Sam Steele, and at the time sergeant-major of 'A' troop) describes the building of Fort Saskatchewan in his book, *Forty Years in Canada.*

July 1875 was a month to become memorable in Canadian North-West history, for on a day in that month the Hudson's Bay Company steamer *Northcote* arrived at Fort Edmonton on her maiden trip, the first boat to navigate the Saskatchewan. She brought for 'A' troop the first mail of any consequence to reach it since camp was struck at Dufferin more than a year before.

In the spring of 1875 orders were issued that one troop from Macleod should proceed north to the Red Deer River, about two hundred miles, and there await the arrival of General Selby Smyth, the imperial officer in command of Canada's Militia forces, and an escort from 'A' troop at Fort Edmonton. General Smyth was the first man to make a tour of the North-West Territories under police escort. The route was Winnipeg to Swan River, to Fort Carlton, to Edmonton, to the Red Deer River, whence he would be escorted by 'F' troop to Macleod. Thence he was to return east via Fort Benton, the Missouri River, and the Northern Pacific Railroad. Inspector Brisbois was in command of 'F' troop. I was the other officer. Colonel Macleod would accompany us. The troop was full strength and had one hundred good horses, with wagons for all supplies, tents, forage and troop baggage, as the programme was that after meeting the general at the Red Deer and escorting him to the Bow River, a site was to be selected at some suitable point on that stream, and a fort built for permanent occupancy by this troop.

The Bow River was hunting and winter camping headquarters of the Blackfeet and the Sarcees. Occasionally the Crees in large camps from the north met there whisky traders from the south, who slipped into the country without our being aware of it at Fort Macleod. With a frontier extending for hundreds of miles open to them they could choose their own point at which to cross into the territories, dispose of their liquor, and be back over the Line again before men could be sent to Bow River to deal with them.

We did not start on the Red Deer trip until 18th August 1875, shortly after the return of Colonel Macleod with Colonel Irvine from Helena. The attempt to extradite the men wanted for trial in connection with the Cypress Hills massacre failed, as it could not be proven that it had occurred on the Canadian side of the Line.

Colonel Irvine had been appointed Assistant Commissioner of the Police, vice Macleod, appointed stipendiary magistrate. Upon the resignation a few months later of Colonel French, who returned to England, Colonel Macleod was appointed Commissioner of the Force. On Lieutenant-Colonel French's arrival in England he was decorated with the C.M.G., and appointed Inspector of War Stores at Devonport and the Channel Islands. Later he organised the defence force of Queensland and, returning to England, was appointed, first, Commandant of the School of Gunnery at Shoeburyness, and then of Artillery in Bombay, India. He was sub-sequently in command of the troops in New South Wales during the Boer War, and organised the whole force sent to Africa from that state. General – at that time Sir George – French died in London in 1921 at an advanced age, after a life-time of distin-guished service to the Empire, not the least valuable being the organisation of the North-West Mounted Police in 1873 and 1874.

When 'F' troop left Fort Macleod, Inspector Winder remained in command with one troop of fifty men and a busy time ahead in improving the fort and in patrols. Through Government contracts for supplies at very high figures, the American firms in business in Macleod became wealthy in a few years, and it seemed a pity that this money, amounting to millions, should go out of Canada, as it did for nearly a decade.

Previous to our leaving Macleod the first cattle – a few cows – were brought into that district by Joe McFarland, who located a ranch some three miles below the fort on the Old Man's River.

We crossed the Bow River about half-way between the Blackfoot Crossing and the site of the present city of Calgary, having as guide J. Munro. There were no trails. The Bow was very high and about two hundred yards in width. We swam the horses and improvised a boat by tying together a couple of wagon boxes, wrapped around with wagon covers coated with axle grease. In this contraption we ferried everything over. The boat was buoyant and carried a good load, but even so the crossing occupied two days. As the weather was warm, the hours spent in cold water did not bother us.

Some forty miles north of the Bow River the prairie ended and the wooded country began. The travelling was heavy without roads, and with many swamps and small creeks to cross. Ducks and geese were plentiful and we lived mainly on them. The mosquitoes were frightful, driving the horses wild and almost ungovernable. Smudges were kept burning all night to give the worried brutes the protection of the smoke. They needed watching to prevent their standing in the fire and injuring their hoofs. To our relief as we neared the Red Deer the pests became less numerous.

We were six days from the Bow to the Red Deer River, and we went into camp on the south side. A half-breed occupied a cabin on the north side, and as he had a boat we made visits to his camp. We also met here Ad McPherson and Jack Norris, two white traders from Edmonton. We had a regular course of mounted drill in this Red Deer camp in anticipation of an inspection on meeting General Smyth. We noticed trees along this river scarred as much as thirty feet up in the spring floods by ice jams, the river in some

Fort Macleod, Alberta, Barracks of N.W.M.P., 1877

years overflowing its banks and covering the valley with many feet of water.

Word came that General Smyth, with the police escort, would cross the Red Deer at a ford forty miles above our location, so we struck camp and moved up the river to that point. The travelling through swamp and thick brush, plagued by flies and mosquitoes, was terrible, and we were with difficulty able to control the horses. We arrived just a day ahead of General Smyth's party, which also had had a very hard journey. Their horses were in a bad way from hoof disease, caused by almost constant travelling through mud and water. It was necessary to leave many behind.

We came here upon many indications of coal in seams along the river bank, and were told by Cree Indians that not far from us there was a seam that had been burning for as far back as they had record. However, we had no time to verify the story.

General Smyth inspected our troop at the camp, and complimented us on our appearance. He then proceeded south with escort. Accompanied by Colonel Macleod, he crossed the Bow River at the same place and in the same manner as we had, visited Fort Macleod, and from there returned east, via Benton and the Missouri River.

'F' troop, with the guide Munro, then moved south to a point already selected at the junction of the Bow and Elbow rivers. A bull train with supplies and extra men had already left Fort Macleod to meet us here, and I. B. Baker & Company had contracted to cut and raft timber down the Elbow River for a fort to be built at a point to be selected by us near where that stream entered the Bow.

IX

Fort Calgary on the map

We crossed the Bow River a little above the mouth of the Elbow, finding a good ford at this place. The view from the hill on the north side of the Bow, when we reached it at the beginning of September 1875, amazed us. Before us lay a lovely valley, flanked on the south by rolling hills. Thick woods bordered the banks of both streams; to the west towered mountains with their snowy peaks; beyond the Elbow stretched another wide valley, and heavy timber farther west along the Bow. Buffalo in large bands grazed in the valleys, but of man we saw at first no sign. Indeed, toward the south no human dwelling existed nearer than Fort Macleod, though at Morley to the west the Rev. George McDougall had established a small mission among the Stony Indians. In fact, except for roving bands of Indians, all this vast country, for a thousand miles to the east at Winnipeg and two hundred miles to Edmonton in the north, at that time was utterly uninhabited. Our first sight of this enchanting spot was one never to be forgotten, one to which only a poet could do justice. It was by far the most beautiful we had seen since our arrival in the West, and after our trying journey we felt that we were amply repaid for all we had undergone. The knowledge that a fort was to be built here, and that it would become our permanent residence gave us all the greatest satisfaction.

A small tent near the mouth of the Elbow River, a white speck in the distance, at length attracted our attention, and we wondered what solitary individual could be sheltered there. We found afterwards that it was occupied by Father Doucet, a Catholic priest not long out from France, who had been sent from the mission at St. Albert south to the Bow River to study the Blackfoot speech, it being the intention to open a mission at Fort Macleod to which he would be appointed. His only companion was an Indian boy, and he was delighted to see us. He had been living lately on poor fare, and did ample justice to our Government rations.

We pitched camp near the mouth of the Elbow, and as it would be some time before the fort was built, placed the tents in excavations dug two or three feet deep. Some of the men, desiring more substantial shelter, built small huts. By a bull train which arrived a week or so after us we received our winter clothing, and a number of small sheet-iron stoves. As fuel was abundant near at hand, we were soon very comfortable. There was plenty to be done – besides a fort to build, dry firewood for winter to be cut, run down to the boom we stretched across the Elbow River, hauled out on the bank and stacked.

Some of I. G. Baker's men who had arrived with the bull train cut hundreds of spruce and pine logs for the fort, and drove them down to this boom. We chose a site for the fort on a plateau of high ground at the forks of the two rivers. In trenches three feet deep we set upright twelve-foot pine logs side by side to form the stockade and the outer walls of the buildings, which faced inward. The men's quarters were on one side of the square, store-room and shops opposite; on the north, stables for fifty horses, and on the south, officers' quarters and guard-room. The pole roofs were covered with earth, and the log walls mudded with clay. The whole formed a square of one hundred and fifty or two hundred feet, with a gate at either end.

At first, having no lumber, the floors were bare earth, which when continually moistened became as hard as brick. Large stone fireplaces were built in all the rooms. This work was done by John Glenn, who had taken up a ranch at Fish Creek, a little to the south, the preceding fall. He had put up considerable hay, and this we purchased, securing a sufficient supply to feed the horses for the winter.

No Indians visited us until we had been a month in camp, but quite a number of half-breeds from Edmonton arrived with their Red River carts and built cabins on both sides of the Elbow, so that before winter a little settlement had sprung up. The half-breeds did considerable freighting for us to Fort Macleod, and in the following year took a quantity of flour and other supplies from the fort to Inspector Jarvis's troop at Fort Saskatchewan. The average load was five hundred pounds per cart. I. G. Baker's men also erected a building on the flat for a general store, and several log houses for residences, and the enterprising ex-whisky trader, Harry Taylor, already referred to, brought a billiard table all the way from Fort Benton, and built a hall, which was also used for dances. He sold home-made beer, candies, etc. From Morley the Rev. George McDougall visited us, and erected a small church, the first place of worship in Calgary, a little west of the fort, in which he held services upon alternate Sundays.

In the previous year a small Hudson's Bay Company store had been built on Ghost River, not far from Morley, and this was moved down and rebuilt on the east side of the Elbow. John Bunn was in charge, and Angus Fraser was storeman. They had an assortment of goods which would be a curiosity today – flintlock muskets, Hudson's Bay hooded duffle capots, pig-tail tobacco sold by the fathom, carrot tobacco in three-pound rolls, the heavy Hudson's Bay knife which could be used as a hatchet when required, and many other articles now as rare as the dodo, but which had been traded by this company for generations.

After the two stores were built the Indians began to come in with large quantities of pemmican and some fall robes. Buffalo robes are prime only during the winter, and these came in later. Both stores did a good business, and in the spring fifteen thousand buffalo robes were shipped south by bull teams through the firm of I. G. Baker & Company alone. How many went from the Hudson's Bay Company north I do not know, but certainly a large number.

David McDougall of Morley also took considerable fur, traded from the Stony Indians, to Winnipeg in the spring, fur in the main of the finest description, trapped by these Indians in the mountains. He journeyed across the plains with carts, returning with goods for another year's trade. D. W. Davis, whom we first met in charge of Fort Whoop-up when we visited it on arriving in the country, was now with I. G. Baker & Company in charge of their men building the fort. He later assumed the management of the store built for that firm with a large stock of general merchandise. Sergeant Kinghorn, who took his discharge after our arrival at Bow River, engaged with this firm.

The fort was finished at Christmas, and we were glad to move into it, as our camp outside was getting decidedly cold. We found the remains of an Indian and also those of a white man lying near the Elbow River. They had been killed in a drunken fight the previous year. Many such relics had been seen by us since our arrival, and were mute evidence of the lawlessness that had prevailed previous to our advent. Now all was changed. The Indians of different tribes could camp near each other in safety; the liquor smugglers had given up their sinister trade, only a few of the more daring now and then trying to evade the police. Selling whisky to Indians had become too risky a business to follow, and those who still took chances dealt only with the whites and half-breeds.

I rode down to Fort Macleod a week before Christmas, leaving all well at Bow River. The fort had not been officially named, although Inspector Brisbois, without the Commissioner's authority, had named it Fort Brisbois in all his official correspondence. Things had been going on well at Macleod. Better roofs had been put on the buildings. The Commissioner, Colonel Macleod, had brought up

Mrs. Macleod and Inspector Winder and Sub-Inspector Shurtliff had also been joined by their wives, so that there were now three ladies in barracks. Sub-Constable Gallagher had left the force and started to farm nearby. His wife had also come up. These ladies all came by way of the Missouri River to Fort Benton, and then made the long journey across the plains to Macleod. It was quite an undertaking for women unused to the hardships of the West, and proof of great courage on their part. An old trader named Fred Wachter, but nicknamed Dutch Fred, had begun farming on Belly River, and made a small fortune out of the vegetables which he sold to the police for several years. He shot and killed his partner a year later, and was tried for murder, but as there were no witnesses and he pleaded self-defence, he was acquitted. Joe McFarland and Henry Olsen brought in the first cattle, a few cows, located a few miles down the Old Man's River, and did very well in after years. Sub-Constables Bell and Patterson left the force this year, and located on Belly River, residing there for many years until the death of Bell. Patterson, I believe, still owns the farm. He was for a time member for Macleod in the Provincial Legislature.

Inspector Jarvis's troop at Edmonton had received no pay for a long period, and the Commissioner instructed me to return to Bow River and proceed as soon after Christmas as possible to Fort Saskatchewan with the money. I returned to Bow River on Christmas night, and found a Christmas dinner in full swing. It was given by the non-commissioned officers, and all civilians of the village were invited. Everyone had a good time, and a dance followed in the Taylor billiard hall. The ladies, who attended in numbers, were the half-breed belles, well dressed and some very, very good looking. Many of these old-time dances held at Macleod and other posts were far ahead, in the way of fun and hearty exercise, of the prim and select affairs usual after the country became settled.

In 1875 the first domestic cattle came into the country south of the Saskatchewan River. Thomas Lee, who gave his name to Lee's Creek, was the pioneer cattleman in the Pincher Creek district. In the same year a man named Armstrong with his family and another named Morgan arrived from Montana and located on the Old Man's River above Fort Macleod. This was known as Mrs. Armstrong's ranch; she did a profitable dairy business, receiving as high as seventy-five cents per pound from the police for butter. Also in 1875 a man named Shaw drove a herd of cattle through the Rockies by the Kootenay Pass, and wintered near Morley. His stock was principally beef steers, which were readily disposed of at the police post on Bow River. The remnant of his herd he took to Edmonton in 1876.

The Commissioner in 1875 established a farm at Pincher Creek, Sub-Inspector Shurtliff being placed in charge. All the mares brought in from the east were sent here, and a stallion was purchased, the idea being to breed horses for the force. Grain was also grown. The farm did not prove a success, however, and was sold after a few years, with a band of young breeding cattle purchased for the Blackfeet which they had refused to take after the treaty of 1877. So long as the buffalo remained the plains Indians would not eat beef; it was 'bad medicine', they said. Pincher Creek was the name given this place by the police detachment sent there in 1875; they unearthed at this spot an old pair of rusty steel nippers. The name stuck.

While the buffalo roamed the plains it was useless to let range cattle run; the bulls would attack and kill the domestic steers, and the cows were carried away in the great migratory herds; therefore such cattle as were brought in during the first five or six years of the police regime were generally herded along the river bottoms.

Shortly after Christmas I left for Fort Saskatchewan, taking with me the guide Munro and Constable Johnstone, and the pay for Inspector Jarvis's troop. I expected to return with a prisoner. We used single-horse flat-sleds; with plenty of buffalo robes they were comfortable to ride in. We carried oats for the horses, and the necessary camp utensils, but no tent, since the country was wooded and we could build brush shelters. The trip occupied six days owing to the deep snow after passing the Red Deer River. We had below-zero temperatures, but, well-clothed and running much of the time, we did not mind it. In the absence in those days of a road to Edmonton, we had to depend altogether on our guide. The territory north of the Red Deer then abounded in big game and we saw many deer, moose and caribou. We saw no buffalo, although a few bands were reported by Indians to be ranging along the Peace River. We remained overnight at Fort Edmonton, enjoying the hospitality of Chief Factor Richard Hardisty, the Hudson's Bay Company officer in charge.

The fort was heavily stockaded, with bastions at the corners, and was built of squared pine logs. It comprised a number of buildings, including stores, warehouses, the chief factor's residence and the officers' quarters. It was well stocked with trade goods. A few half-breeds lived in cabins, and some Cree Indians in lodges near the fort. Heavy timber covered the whole country beyond. A number of visitors with dog trains had recently arrived, and the howling of the dogs housed inside the stockade at night made sleep impossible for us, but did not seem to trouble the company's people, who, no doubt, were accustomed to it from childhood.

Mrs. Hardisty and her sister, Mrs. Wood, were here at the time, and we were able to give them news of their father, the Rev. George McDougall, at Morley, and also letters from Mr. McDougall and their brother John.

One of the warehouses was stacked to the roof with pemmican in sacks of one hundred and fifty pounds. On the opening of navigation these would be sent to northern posts on the Peace and Mackenzie rivers.

The chief factor expressed himself as much gratified over the change in the country since our arrival, and the truce between the different Indian tribes, which enabled them to carry on their vocation of hunting without fear of attack, and he gave us due credit for this, as well as for ending the lawlessness that had prevailed prior to our advent. He pointed out to me logs of the fort both inside and out pitted by bullet-marks made at times when bands of Indians engaged in drunken warfare. A small brass field-gun of ancient pattern in each bastion commanded the outside walls. In the front gate was a small log-shuttered window, through which goods had in the old days been passed in exchange for furs when some southern tribe, such as the Blackfeet, came to trade. On these occasions should any Crees be camped near, they were likely to take shelter in the fort until the departure of their hereditary enemies, who were eager for their scalps. Peace and contentment had now supplanted all this.

Piles of dried and frozen fish for dog feed were also stored in the fort, and quantities of dried buffalo meat taken in trade during the summer. Numerous large flat-bottomed boats, called 'bateaux' by the half-breeds, were under construction, and would be used to transport furs, pemmican, etc., to Hudson Bay in the spring. These scows were of several tons' capacity. By way of the Saskatchewan they journeyed from Edmonton to Lake Winnipeg, and via the Nelson River to the bay. They returned to Edmonton from York factory with fresh stocks of supplies and trade goods just before winter set in, the round trip occupying from the break-up of the river in the spring to its closing again in the fall. Hardy crews of Indians or half-breeds manned what was called a brigade, numbering twenty or more boats. Portages were frequent, and on the return journey against the stream the boats were towed for hundreds of miles by gangs of men with 'tracking' lines, working in relays of a few hours each. These voyageurs were a stalwart type, peculiar to the service of the Hudson's Bay Company, certain families having followed the calling for generations. They were inured to water, in which most of their summer working-hours were spent, and were satisfied with gaudy scarfs and blankets, tobacco, and a little flour and sugar, or other goods occasionally, as pay for their work. Game and fish were plentiful everywhere en route, so that they had always an abundance of good sustaining food. The winters they spent about the different Hudson's Bay Company posts in dancing and feasting, and in drinking when they could procure liquor. Occasionally they went south to hunt buffalo.

X

Tobacco with the compliments of the Sioux

At Fort Saskatchewan we remained several days. The fort had been built that summer, and was patterned after Macleod and other forts. The troop had comfortable quarters, having been able to procure shingles for roofing the buildings, thus escaping the discomfort we experienced at Macleod and Bow River, where the earthen roofs leaked badly, both during and after rain. Troop 'A' had passed a quiet winter. They had not been required to make the long hard journeys after smugglers which fell to the lot of troops in the south, while, since the country was wooded, they had always good fires to brighten their camps when on patrols. No whisky traders had come so far north, and their work was chiefly the apprehension of those guilty of petty crimes among the Crees and half-breeds.

They had several prisoners in their guard-room, one of them, George Godin, or Kis-ka-was-is (his Cree name), who some years previously had killed his wife in a most atrocious manner, and most brazenly defied such authorities as were in the country before the arrival of the police. The case had been mentioned several times in reports sent east by Sanford Fleming, C.E., Colonel Robertson

Ross, and, others. He had been held in jail by Inspector Jarvis pending an opportunity to send him south for trial at Fort Macleod. I took him with me on my return to Bow River. He was a sullen brute, and I took no chances with him, handcuffing him at night to Constable Johnstone, and putting him in leg irons during the day to forestall any attempted break by him for liberty. The journey south took the usual six days' heavy travelling, the snow being very deep.

We found the Commissioner, Colonel Macleod, and Colonel Irvine, who had been appointed Assistant Commissioner, awaiting us at Bow River. They had two dog trains, and were on the way to visit Fort Saskatchewan, but required the guide Munro to accompany them. On my arrival the question of a name for the Bow River fort came up, and after many had been discussed Colonel Macleod mentioned an old castle in the Isle of Mull that once belonged to the Macleod clan, and was called Calgary, which he stated meant in Gallic, 'Clear Running Water'. This so appropriately fitted the waters of the Bow and Elbow rivers that it was immediately adopted by us all, and that night it came out in orders that in future the fort should be known as Fort Calgary, subject to the approval of the Minister of Justice. This approval was afterwards given. And so the name of Calgary came into being.

It was never spelled with two r's as often stated. Stories without number have been written as to how the place was named, not one being correct. I therefore have given a detailed account of its christening, having been one of three who decided on the name in February 1876. The original correspondence between Ottawa and Colonel Irvine relative to the general order is now in the possession of the city of Calgary.

The half-breed murderer, Kis-ka-was-is, was tried, sentenced to hang, and sent down to Stony Mountain Penitentiary. He was, however, reprieved owing to the intercession of the Catholic Church, and afterwards returned to Edmonton. He was later re-arrested for horse-stealing, escaped, and still later was arrested in Montana for a murder there, and sentenced for the second time to hang. He again escaped, turned up on the reserve west of Edmonton, was recaptured, and returned to Montana. He eventually died in jail, thus ridding the country of about the worst character it was ever my lot to come across.

Inspector Brisbois resigned from the force this spring, and I remained in command of 'F' troop at Fort Calgary during the summer of 1876. Mail was now carried monthly between Fort Benton, Macleod, and Fort Walsh, and travel between these last posts was frequent. Walsh was a very important post, owing to the number of United States Indians who hunted near there upon what was jealously regarded by the Canadian tribes as their special preserve. The Sioux and Assiniboines were the principal offenders, and had always been deadly enemies of the Blackfeet. This situation was the cause of much anxiety to the police, and the fact that thousands of Sioux and Cheyennes were at war with American troops in the Blackhills country south of the Missouri River, and not far from the Canadian boundary, added greatly to their worries. Our force was so small and the duties so arduous that we had little rest from patrols to Indian camps, often several hundred miles away. Summer or winter, there were innumerable journeys to Fort Walsh, to Edmonton, and to other parts of Alberta where trouble was reported. We had become accustomed to the work by this time. I doubt if a hardier or more courageous body of men ever existed than that first small force of Mounted Police who patrolled the plains in the early seventies and eighties.

In the year 1876 control of the North-West Mounted Police was transferred from the Department of Justice to that of the Secretary of State, and Lieutenant-Colonel Macleod succeeded Lieutenant-Colonel French as Commissioner of Police. The two troops were moved from Fort Pelly to strengthen the force at Fort Walsh and Fort Macleod. The massing of the force at these posts near the frontier no doubt secured tranquillity in that section of the territory, and prevented the American Indians from using Canadian soil as a base of operations for prosecuting the war with the United States troops.

N.W.M.P. Officers at Fort Walsh, 1876

The following extract is taken from Comptroller Fred White's report to the Hon. R. W. Scott, Secretary of State in 1876:

On the 22nd August the following report of Sub-Inspector Denny was received from the Assistant Commissioner:

'According to orders received on 8th July, to proceed to the Blackfoot camp for the prisoner Nataya, I left Bow River on the above-mentioned date, and found the Blackfeet camped about thirty miles above the mouth of the Red Deer River, being about two hundred miles north-east of Elbow River.

'After having secured the prisoner I was detained in camp by a council called by the principal Blackfoot chiefs, who invited me to their meeting. They told me they were very glad I had arrived, as at that time they were in a very unsettled state owing to communications that had passed between the Blackfoot nation, including the Blood and Piegan Indians, and the Sioux from across the Line. About a month ago the Sioux had sent a message to the Blackfoot camp, with a piece of tobacco, which the Blackfoot chief showed us. The message told the Blackfeet from the Sioux that the tobacco was sent them to smoke if they were willing to cross the Line and join the Sioux in fighting the Cree Indians and other tribes with whom they were at war, and also the Americans whom they were fighting at the same time. The Sioux promised to give the Blackfeet, if they would join them, plenty of horses and mules they had captured from the Americans.

'They also told the Blackfeet that they had a number of white women whom they had taken prisoners. These they also promised to the Blackfeet if they would join them. They also told the Blackfeet that if they would come and help them against the Americans, after they had killed all the whites, they would come over and help the Blackfeet to exterminate the whites on this side. They also told them that they knew that the soldiers on this side were weak, and it would take but a short time to capture

any forts they had built here, as they had taken many strong stone forts from the Americans with small loss to themselves. The Blackfeet had sent an answer to the Sioux a short time before I arrived to the effect that they could not smoke their tobacco on such terms, and that they were not willing to make peace with the understanding of helping them to fight the whites, as they were friends and they would not fight against them. The messenger from the Blackfeet to the Sioux had just returned when I arrived at their camp, with the answer the Sioux had sent.

'They said that as they would not come and help them against the Americans, they would come over to this side and show the Blackfeet that white soldiers were as nothing before them, and that after they had exterminated the soldiers and taken their forts, they would come against the Blackfeet.

'In consequence of this message the Blackfeet nation, when I reached their camp, were in a state of uncertainty, not knowing how to act. Crowfoot, the head chief, was authorised by the nation, many of whom were present, to ask me whether in case they were attacked by the Sioux, without themselves being the aggressors, and they called upon us, the Mounted Police, to help them, would we do so? I told them that if the Sioux crossed the Line and attacked the Blackfeet without cause we were bound to help them, they being subjects of the country, and having the right to the same protection as any other subjects.

'Chief Crowfoot told me in these words:

"We all see that the day is coming when the buffalo will all be killed and we shall have nothing more to live on, and then you will come into our camps and see the poor Blackfeet starving. I know that the heart of the white soldier will be sorry for us, and they will tell the Great Mother, who will not let her children starve. We are getting shut in. The Crees are coming into our country from the north and the white men from the south and east. They are all destroying our means of living, but *still, although we plainly see those days coming, we will not join the Sioux against the whites, but will depend upon you to help us".*

'The chief then told me that the Blackfeet had told him to tell me that as we were willing to help them, they would in case of being attacked, send two thousand warriors against the Sioux.

'I thanked them for this offer, and told them I would inform you of all they had told me, and that as long as they were quiet and peaceable they would always find us their friends and willing to do anything for their good. They expressed great satisfaction with all I had told them, and promised to do nothing without letting us know and asking our advice.

'I distributed some tobacco among them, and told them to let us know of any movement of the Sioux to the north. I left them on Friday last, camped all together about thirty miles above the mouth of the Red Deer. I brought the prisoner with me without any trouble and arrived here this day.'

A copy of this report was forwarded by His Honour the Deputy Governor to The Right Honourable the Secretary of State for the Colonies, from whom the following reply was received by His Excellency the Governor-General:

'I have the honour to acknowledge the receipt of the Deputy Governor's despatch No. 21 of 26th August, enclosing a report of Sub-Inspector Denny of the North-West Mounted Police, giving an account of a recent visit to the camp of the Blackfeet Indians. I have read Mr. Denny's report with much interest, and have communicated a copy of it to the Queen.

'Her Majesty has commanded me to instruct you to inform the chiefs of the tribe that Her Majesty has heard with much satisfaction of their faithful conduct in declining to take up arms with the Sioux Indians, and has been much gratified by this evidence of their loyalty and attachment. You will further apprise them that the Great Mother desires to assure them that she has always taken, and will continue to take, a lively interest in all that concerns their welfare and trusts that nothing *may at any time occur to disturb the friendly relations between her Indians and her white subjects.'*

Instructions have been given to communicate this message from Her Majesty to the Indians.

The spring of 1876 saw more cattle and horses brought into Alberta from Montana. Jim Christy and George Emerson came with separate herds. The horses – Christy's – were first to be offered for sale or trade. He found a good market among the white settlers and police, who paid on an average $100.00 per head. The horses were about fifteen and a half hands, tough and used to ranging out in the winter, and the best ever procured for police purposes. George Emerson, an old Hudson's Bay Company ex-employee of 1869, brought in the cows, which he readily sold to the settlers beginning farming and stock-raising in southern Alberta. About thirty men left the force this spring, many locating land with their North-West Mounted Police script in the Macleod and Pincher Creek districts. Emerson kept some of his cows, and located near Calgary, went into dairying and sold butter and milk to the police there. Considerable business was done at Macleod this year. I. G. Baker & Company shipped forty thousand buffalo robes and wolf skins, the proceeds of their winter's trade there and at Calgary. W. F. Parker, ex-sergeant of the police, also took up a farm near Macleod, and purchased a herd of cattle from J. Healy at Whoop-up.

A French-Canadian named Beaupré located at Pincher Creek, and Jim Votier, an old trader, near Fish Creek, so that this year may be said to have seen the beginning of farming and stock-raising in southern Alberta.

In the Edmonton district, too, agriculture had made progress, except at St. Albert, where, owing to the destruction of crops by hail, the inhabitants were likely to suffer during the winter. It became necessary therefore to consider relief measures to prevent distress and the breaking up of the settlement. Instructions were accordingly given to the officer commanding the police at Edmonton to invite the clergy of the several denominations to co-operate with him in extending aid so far as the surplus supplies of the force there would permit, payment at cost price, plus expense of transport, to be obtained where possible, and in the alternative the best security available to be taken for ultimate payment in furs or money.

A report of the Assistant Commissioner regarding the killing of the buffalo reads:

> *The country between Cypress Hills and the Rocky Mountains, which has hitherto been claimed by the Blackfeet as their hunting ground, has this year been encroached upon by other Indians and half-breeds, causing much irritation among the Blackfeet, who have called upon the police to protect them in maintaining their rights to their territory, saying that if they were not restrained by the presence of the police they would make war upon the intruders. The correspondence on this subject has been submitted to the Lieutenant-Governor of the North-West Territories in order that it may receive the consideration of the North-West Council in connection with the adoption of rules for hunting and for preserving the buffalo from extinction.*

A law was passed by the North-West Council prohibiting the killing of buffalo calves, but it was never more than a dead letter, being found impossible to enforce. The multitudinous duties of the police, the vastness of the country, and the thousands of Indians continually engaged in hunting made such a law absurd on the face of it.

The foundation of what was to become the coal city of Lethbridge was laid when an old miner named Nick Sheran opened the first seam and for several years supplied the police at Fort Macleod with coal hauled by bull teams and displacing wood as fuel. Others secured it at the mine mouth for $3.00 per ton. He also loaded any bull teams returning empty to Fort Benton and found there a ready market. Sheran worked his mine for several years, and made considerable money. He was drowned in the Old Man's River while bathing. The wife of Joseph McFarland, the first settler near Macleod in 1874, was his sister.

Toward the end of the bitter winter of 1875–6, the Rev. George McDougall, with his sons John and David, came down from Morley to secure a supply of buffalo meat, and camped on Nose Creek, north of Fort Calgary. The minister left camp alone one morning to hunt. A blizzard came up during the day, and he never returned. The police searched for several days and picked up the horse, but it was a week before the body was recovered. The minister had let his mount go, wandered round on foot, and succumbed to the intense cold. This was the first death at Calgary since the arrival of the police, and it cast a shadow over the New Year.

Sergeant-Major Clyde and myself, with Mr. Bunn of the Hudson's Bay Company, had a narrow escape while looking for Mr. McDougall. The weather had turned quite mild after a period of the severest cold, and we were ten miles up the Bow River, without overcoats or moccasins, one afternoon, when one of the sudden changes peculiar to the region occurred. From bright sunshine and a summerlike western breeze, the wind swung swiftly to the north, and a fierce blizzard swept down upon us. We rode for our lives, but it became so thick that we missed the fort. However, we struck the river a mile or so above it, and luckily recognised the locality. We arrived at the fort chilled to the bone. A very little more exposure would have made our case much worse. As it was we were all nipped, my boots were frozen stiff, and feeling only returned to my feet after I had held them for a long time in a basin of snow. But the lesson was not lost upon us and we were careful ever afterwards not to take such chances, however alluring the weather.

XI

The Blackfoot Treaty of 1877

In 1877 the Comptroller of the North-West Mounted Police reported as follows:

In consequence of the manner in which the Blackfoot Indians had scattered over the plain during the early winter and spring, it was found impossible until the month of August to communicate to them the message [referred to in the previous chapter] expressing Her Majesty's appreciation of their conduct in rejecting the overtures from the Sioux Indians of the United States to join in a war of extermination against the white population. Assistant Commissioner Irvine, who conveyed the message to the Indians, reports that Her Majesty's expression of approval was received by them with the liveliest feeling of satisfaction and gratitude. They expressed their unaltered loyalty to the British Crown, and repeated their willingness to fight in its defence if they were ever required to do so. At the time of these expressions of loyalty from the Blackfeet, the United States newspapers were announcing the probability of the Northern Indians, who were represented as being ready for revolt, joining Sitting Bull and other hostiles in a devastating Indian war.

In the spring of 1877 the Commissioner received word at Fort Macleod that the Government intended that summer to make a treaty with the Blackfeet and other tribes of plains Indians, give them reservations and such Government allowances as might be deemed necessary; that Governor Laird would proceed to Fort Macleod from Battleford, the treaty would be negotiated at the Blackfoot Crossing, and all tribes coming under that treaty were at once to be notified.

This was no easy task. The Indians were widely scattered, hunting buffalo, and it was not until July that all was in readiness and the ground laid out at the Crossing for the majority of the two troops stationed at Macleod and Calgary to proceed with their transport and camp equipage to that place. Inspector Crozier had charge of the preparations.

The Comptroller's report to Ottawa reads as follows:

> *An escort consisting of one hundred and eight police, one hundred and nineteen horses, and two nine-pounder guns was detailed to accompany the Lieutenant-Governor of the North-West Territories during the making of the treaty in September with the Blackfeet and other Indians, known as Treaty Number Seven. The Commissioner, Lieutenant-Colonel Macleod, had previously sent out messengers to warn the Indians of the time and place of the meeting. A detachment of police was on the ground to be occupied by the various tribes. The officers of the force also paid the Indians after the treaty had been completed. The treaty was made at the Blackfoot Crossing of the Bow River, about ninety miles from Fort Macleod. Not a single casualty occurred nor yet was there disturbance of any kind amongst the Indians or traders, which was very remarkable when the large number of Indians of different tribes camped so close together is taken into consideration. It is estimated that the Indians had not less than fifteen thousand horses and ponies with them. His Honour the Lieutenant-Governor of the North-West Territories*

expressed his unqualified satisfaction with all the arrangements that had been made, and the services performed by the police.

I left Calgary with a detachment of 'F' troop for the Crossing on the 14th of September, and on arriving found most of the Indians already collected. The valley at the Blackfoot Crossing on the south side of the Bow River where the treaty was held is of considerable extent, being about three miles long by one in width, with plenty of timber along the river, and good feed for horses on the hills to the south and in the valley itself. There must have been at least a thousand lodges in camps on both sides of the river, as they had all by this time come in. They were plentifully supplied with meat, having only just left the large buffalo herd down the stream to the east. Their horses, herded day and night, covered the uplands to the north and south of the camp in thousands. It was a stirring and picturesque scene; great bands of grazing horses, the mounted warriors threading their way among them, and, as far as the eye could reach the white Indian lodges glimmering among the trees along the river-bottom. By night the valley echoed to the dismal howling of the camp's curs, and from sun to sun drums boomed from the tents. Dancing, feasting, conjuring, incantations over the sick, prayers for success in the hunt or in war, all went to form a panorama of wild life vastly novel and entertaining, and seen but once. Never before had such a concourse of Indians assembled on Canada's western plains; never had the tribes appeared so contented and prosperous.

The tribes represented were Blackfeet, Bloods, Piegans, Sarcees and Stonies. Many Crees had been drawn by curiosity to the treaty ground; half-breeds also who hoped to derive some gain from the annuities to be paid the Indians. Traders from both the north and south displayed their stocks in tents and were already doing some trade in robes, for although the summer pelts had no value, there were still many hundreds in camp from the last winter's hunt. White men from Montana had brought in bands of horses for trade. A fair-sized horse fast enough to run buffalo would always fetch a good price from the Indians.

Governor Laird and Lieutenant-Colonel Macleod had been appointed Commissioners to make the treaty. The Governor had arrived at Macleod, and some of his observations on the police, and on work done by them, published in his report to the Government, are well worth quoting. Regarding his journey south, he says:

> *After we crossed the Red Deer we met a few Crees and half-breeds, and several hunting parties of Blackfeet. The former generally use carts in travelling, but the Blackfeet and their associates are always on horseback.*
>
> *The Crees appeared friendly, but were not so demonstrative as the Blackfeet, who always rode up to us at once with a smile on their countenances and shook hands. They knew the uniforms of the Mounted Police at a distance, and at once recognised and approached them as their friends. I cannot speak too highly of the kind manner in which the officers and men of the Mounted Police at Fort Macleod treat their Indian visitors. Though the Red Man is somewhat intrusive, I never heard a harsh word employed in asking him to retire. The beneficial effects of this treatment, of the exclusion of intoxicants from the country, and of impartially administering justice to whites and Indians alike, were apparent in all my interviews with the Indians. They always spoke of the officers of the police in the highest terms, and of the commander of that force, Lieutenant-Colonel Macleod, especially, as their benefactor. The leading chiefs of the Blackfeet and kindred tribes declared publicly at the treaty that had it not been for the Mounted Police they would all have been dead ere this time. In the village of Macleod I found excellent stores, supplied with almost every article of dry goods, hardware and groceries that any inland community requires. Notable among these were the stores of I. G. Baker & Company and T. C. Powers. There is also a good blacksmith's shop in the village, in which coal is used from Belly River. I was told by the proprietor of the shop*

that the coal answers tolerably for blacksmith purposes, and in the fort it is extensively used for fuel. It burns nearly as well in a stove as some varieties of Pictou coal.

The land round the fort, and indeed the whole distance between the Bow and the Old Man's rivers, is well adapted for grazing, and where cultivation has been fairly attempted this season, grain and vegetables have been a success. In short, I have little doubt that this portion of the Territories before many years will abound in herds of cattle, and be dotted with not a few comfortable homesteads.

I had ridden from Fort Calgary to Fort Macleod at the beginning of September and while there the Commissioners received instructions regarding the holding of the treaty at the Blackfoot Crossing. I was instructed to proceed with all speed to Calgary with orders for Inspector Crozier (who had taken command of the post) to go with 'F' troop to the Blackfoot Crossing and lay out the camp. I left Macleod on horseback at daylight of September 5th, and arrived at Calgary at 6 o'clock the same evening, about as long a day's ride as I ever made; a hundred and six miles without roads and with several rivers to swim or ford. Two days later we were on the way to the Blackfoot Crossing with the troop, leaving a sergeant and three or four men in charge at the fort.

I. G. Baker & Company and T. C. Powers were both occupying large hastily-built stores with log walls and canvas roofs, well stocked with goods. The Hudson's Bay Company was also represented. Chief Factor Hardisty and his family had come down from Edmonton, and his brothers-in-law, the Rev. John and David McDougall, from Morley, the former to act as interpreter and advisor to the Stony Indians. They camped apart from the Blackfeet, with whom they were not on very good terms. Governor Laird, with the police commissioner, Colonel Macleod, and police escort of sixty men, arrived from Macleod after some days and went into camp. A large council tent was also erected.

Several days were occupied in preliminaries and in discussions between the different chiefs and officers and the Governor. More than once it looked as if all chance of concluding a treaty would have to be abandoned, the Indians threatening to leave the ground. The chief cause of this delay was old jealousies existing not only between different tribes but among individuals. The adjustment of these matters called for the exercise of tact and diplomacy and the patience shown by the Commissioners was beyond all praise. However, after a week of parleying and negotiation, the terms were finally agreed upon and the following day, the 22nd September 1877, set for the signing of the treaty by the different chiefs and witnesses. The Commissioners' interpreter was an old Hudson's Bay Company ex-employee named Bird, who had left the Company many years previously and taken a Blackfoot wife. Aided by the Rev. Father Scollen, he did very well. The report of the Commissioners reads:

> *The Indians, comprising the tribes of Blackfeet, Bloods, Piegans, Stonies and Sarcees, at this treaty surrendered to the Government of Canada for Her Majesty the Queen and her successors for ever all their rights, titles and privileges whatsoever to the following lands: Commencing at a point on the International Boundary due south of the western extremity of the Cypress Hills; thence west along said boundary to the central range of the Rocky Mountains, or to the boundary of the Province of British Columbia; thence north-westerly along the said boundary to a point due west of the source of the main branch of the Red Deer River; thence south-westerly and southerly following on the boundaries of the tracts ceded by the Treaties numbered Six and Four to the place of commencement; and also all their rights, titles and privileges whatsoever to all other lands wherever situated in the North-West Territories, or in any other portion of the Dominion of Canada. To have and to hold the same to Her Majesty the Queen and her successors for ever.*

And Her Majesty the Queen hereby agrees with her said Indians that they shall have the right to pursue their vocation of hunting throughout the tract surrendered as heretofore described, subject to such regulations as may from time to time be made by the Government of the country, acting under the authority of Her Majesty, and saving and excepting such tracts as may be required or taken up from time to time for settlement, mining, trading, or other purposes of Her Government of Canada, or by any of Her Majesty's subjects duly authorised therefor by the said Government.

It is also agreed between Her Majesty and her said Indians that reserves shall be assigned them of sufficient area to allow one square mile for each family of five persons, or in that proportion for larger and smaller families, and that said reserves shall be located as follows:

The reserves were then described. They included some of the choicest lands and were granted to the tribes for ever. Though not thought so at the time, it was a generous settlement, for with the advent of railroads and population, the lands became valuable. The treaty continues:

In view of the satisfaction of Her Majesty with the recent good conduct of the said Indians, and in extinguishment of all their past claims, She hereby, through her Commissioners, agrees to make them a present payment of twelve dollars each in cash to each man, woman and child of the families here represented.

Her Majesty also agrees that next year, and annually afterwards for ever, She will cause to be paid to the said Indians in cash, at suitable places and dates, of which the Indians shall be duly notified, to each Chief twenty-five dollars, each Minor Chief (or Councillor) not exceeding sixteen Minor Chiefs to the Blackfoot and Piegan and Blood Indians, and four to the Sarcee band, and five Councillors to the Stony Indian bands, fifteen dollars, and to every other Indian of whatever age five dollars; the same, unless there be some exceptional reason, to be paid to the heads of families of those belonging thereto.

Further, Her Majesty agrees that the sum of two thousand dollars shall hereafter every year be expended in the purchase of ammunition for distribution among the said Indians. Provided that if at any future time ammunition becomes comparatively unnecessary for said Indians, Her Government, with the consent of the Indians, or any of the bands thereof, may spend the proportion due such bands otherwise for their benefit.

Further, Her Majesty agrees that each Head Chief and Minor Chief, and each Chief and Councillor duly recognised as such, shall, once in every three years, during the term of their office, receive a suitable suit of clothing, and each Head Chief and Stony Chief, in recognition of the closing of the Treaty, a suitable medal and flag, and next year, or as soon as convenient, each Head Chief, and Minor Chief, and Stony Chief shall receive a Winchester rifle.

Further, Her Majesty agrees to pay the salary of such teachers to instruct the children of said Indians as to Her Government of Canada may seem advisable, when said Indians are settled on their reserves and shall desire teachers.

Further, Her Majesty agrees to supply each Head and Minor Chief, and each Stony Chief, for the use of their bands, ten axes, five handsaws, five augers, one grindstone and the necessary files and whetstones.

And further, Her Majesty agrees that the said Indians shall be supplied as soon as convenient, after any band shall make due application therefor, with the following cattle for raising stock; that is to say: For every family of five persons and under, two cows; for every family of more than five persons and less than ten persons, three cows; for every family over ten persons, four cows; and every Head and Minor Chief, and every Stony Chief for the use of their bands, one bull. But if any band desires to cultivate the soil as well as raise stock, each family of such band shall receive one cow less than the above-mentioned number, and in lieu thereof, when settled on the reserves and prepared to break up the soil, two hoes, one spade, one scythe and two hay-forks; and for every three families, one plough and one harrow; and for each band enough potatoes, barley, oats and wheat (if such seeds be suited to the locality of their reserves) to plant the land actually broken up. All the aforesaid articles to be given once for all for the encouragement of the practice of agriculture among the Indians.

LIEUT.-COL. G. A. FRENCH,
FIRST COMMISSIONER OF
N.W.M.P., 1874

LIEUT.-COL. J. F. MACLEOD,
SECOND COMMISSIONER OF
N.W.M.P., 1876

LIEUT.-COL. C. IRVINE,
THIRD COMMISSIONER OF
N.W.M.P., 1880–6

THE HON. DAVID LAIRD,
FIRST LIEUTENANT-GOVERNOR OF
NORTH-WEST TERRITORIES

NWMP, including Indian scouts, at Fort Macleod, Alberta, 1890. Sir Cecil Denny on the left.

XII

The Blackfoot Treaty – continued

The Indians then agreed to strictly observe the treaty and to conduct themselves as good and loyal subjects of Her Majesty the Queen.

They promise they will in all respects obey the law, that they will maintain peace and order between each other and between themselves and other tribes of Indians, half-breeds and whites, now inhabiting or hereafter to inhabit any part of the ceded tract, and that they will assist the officers of Her Majesty in bringing to justice and punishment any Indian offending against the stipulations of this treaty, or infringing the laws in force in the country so ceded.

In witness hereof Her Majesty's said Commissioners, and the Indian Head and Minor Chiefs, and Stony Chiefs and Councillors, have hereunto subscribed and set their hands, at the Blackfoot Crossing of the Bow River, the day and year herein first above written.

Signed by the Chiefs and Councillors within named in presence of the following witnesses the same having been first explained by James Bird, Interpreter.

A. G. Irvine, Asst. Com., N.W.M.P.
W. Winder, Inspector, N.W.M.P.
L. N. F. Crozier, Inspector, N.W.M.P.
E. Dalrymple Clark, Lieut. and Adjt., N.W.M.P.
Constantine Scollen, Priest
J. McDougall, Missionary
Jean L'Heureux
Mary J. Macleod
Julia Winder

(Signed) David Laird, Lieutenant-Governor of North-West Territories and Special Indian Commissioner.

A. Shurtliff, Sub-Inspector, N.W.M.P.
C. E. Denny, Sub-Inspector, N.W.M.P.
W. D. Antrobus, Sub-Inspector, N.W.M.P.
Frank Norman, Staff-Constable, N.W.M.P.
Julia Shurtliff
E. Hardisty
A. McDougall
E. A. Barrett

Witness to the signatures of Stamixotokan and those following,
(Signed)
Charles E. Conrad.
Thomas J. Bogg.
James F. Macleod, Lieutenant-Colonel, Commissioner, N.W.M.P., and Special Indian Commissioner.
(All Indians mentioned below placing their marks.)

Chapo-Mexico, or Crowfoot. Head Chief of the South Blackfeet.
Matose-apiw, or Old Sun. Head Chief of the North Blackfeet.

Stamixotokan, or Bull Head. Head Chief of the Sarcees.

Mekaste, or Red Crow. Head Chief of the South Bloods.

Natose-Onistors, or Medicine Calf.

Pokapiw-otoian, or Bad Head.

Sotenah, or Rainy Chief. Head Chief of the North Bloods.

Takoye-Stamix, or Fiend Bull.

Akka-Kitcipimiw-otas, or Many Spotted Horses.

Attistah-macan, or Running Rabbit.

Pitah-Pekis, or Eagle Rib.

Sakoye-actan, or Heavy Shield. Head Chief of the Middle
  Blackfeet.

Zoatze-Tapitapiw, or Sitting on an Eagle Tail. Head Chief
  of the North Piegans.

Akka-Makkeye, or Many Swans.

Apenako-sapop, or Morning Plume.

Mas-gwa-ah-sid, or Bear's Paw.

Cheneka, or John.

Ki-Chi-pwot, or Jacob.

Stamix-osok, or Bull Backfat.

Emitah-Komotziw, or the Captive or Stolen Person.

Apawawakosow, or White Antelope.

Makoye-kin, or Wolf Collar.

Aye-Stipis-simat, or Heavily Whipped.

Kissoum, or Daylight.

Pitah-otocan, or Eagle Head.

Apaw-Stamix, or Weasel Bull.

Onistah-pokah, or White Calf.

Netah-kitei-pi-mew, or Only Spot.

Akak-Otos, or Many Horses.

Stokimatis, or The Drum.

Pitah-Annes, or Eagle Robe.

Pitah-Otsikin, or Eagle Shoe.

Stamixo-tapka-piw, or Bull Turn Round.

Maste-Pitah, or Crow Eagle.

James Dixon.
Abraham Kechepwot.
Patrick Kechepwot.
George Moy-any-men.
George Crawler.
Ekas-kine, or Low Horn.
Kayo-okosis, or Bear Shield.
Ponokah-stamix, or Bull Elk.
Omaski-sapop, or Big Plume.
Onistah, or Calf Robe.
Pitah-siksinum, or White Eagle.
Apaw-onistaw, or Weasel Calf.
Attista-haos, or Rabbit Carrier.
Pitah, or Eagle.
Pitah-onistah, or Eagle White Calf.
Kaye-tapo, or Going to Bear.

The number of Indians paid at the treaty was something under five thousand, and the amounts paid as follows:

Head chiefs, 11 at $25	$ 275
Minor chiefs, 42 at $15	630
Men, women and children, 4771 at $12	57,252
Total number – 4,824	58,157

The Lieutenant-Governor commented upon the carrying out of the treaty as follows:

Not in regard to the payments alone were the services of the officers most valuable. With respect to the whole arrangements Lieutenant-Colonel Macleod, my associate Commissioner, both in that capacity and as Commander of the Police, was indefatigable in his exertions to bring the negotiations to a successful termination. The same laudable efforts were put forth by

Jerry Potts, Guide and Interpreter

Major Irvine and the other officers of the force, and their kindness to me personally I shall never fail to remember.

On Sunday the Indians fought a sham battle on horseback. They wore only the breech-cloths. They fired off their rifles and sent the bullets whistling past the spectators in such close proximity as to create most unpleasant feelings. I was heartily glad when they defiled past singly on the way back to their lodges and the last of their unearthly yells died away in the distance.

Monday, Tuesday and Wednesday were occupied in paying off the different tribes. They were paid by Inspector Winder, Sub-Inspector Denny, and Sub-Inspector Antrobus, each assisted by a constable of the force. It was hard work to find out the correct number of each family. Many after receiving their money would return to say that they had made a wrong count. One would discover that he had another wife, another two more children, and others that they had blind mothers and lame sisters. In some cases they wanted to be paid for the babies that were expected to come soon. On Wednesday the Chiefs presented an address to the Commissioners expressing the entire satisfaction of the whole nation with the treaty, and of the way in which the terms had been carried out. They tendered their well wishes to the Queen, the Governor, Colonel Macleod and the Police Force. They spoke in the most flattering and enthusiastic manner of the Commissioner, Assistant Commissioner, Officers, and the force in general, and said it was their firm determination to adhere to the terms of the treaty and abide by the laws of the Great Mother. Potts, the interpreter of Fort Macleod, said he never heard Indians speak out their minds so fully in his life before.

The Blackfeet, Bloods and Sarcees first took a reserve in common on both sides of the Bow River for many miles above and below the Blackfoot Crossing. Their relations were not amicable and next year the Bloods were transferred to a new location on the Belly River and the Sarcees to the Elbow River above Calgary. The Blackfeet remained at the Crossing. The Piegans had located in the Porcupine Hills above Macleod, and the Stonies at Morley.

The sham battle given by the Blackfeet at the treaty was, as the Governor stated in his report, to say the least, unpleasant. He was not told of the uneasy feeling prevailing. The Indians had been in a state of excitement all the morning, and while we were attending to our duties five or six hundred mounted warriors, stripped with the exception of a blanket round the loins and in war-paint and feather head-dresses, staged a mounted war-dance round our camp. These men, armed with loaded Winchesters and on the dead run, circled the tents, their rifles exploding and the bullets whistling over our heads. Their blood-curdling whoops accentuated the unpleasantness.

They were only half in fun, and had fear been shown by us it is hard to tell what would have occurred; the sham battle might easily have become one of grim earnestness. We went on quietly with our duties however, and after a time the braves tired of their warlike demon-stration and returned to their camps. Nevertheless this caused us, while it lasted, considerable uneasiness. Many of the Indians, we knew, were dissatisfied that a treaty had been made at all and a few unruly spirits might in a reckless moment have started a massacre, out of which none of our small party could have escaped.

The payments commenced on Tuesday. The money had been brought by I. G. Baker & Company from Fort Benton in both American and Canadian bills in denominations of from one dollar to twenty, and as the Indians knew nothing about money it was most difficult to make them understand values of the different bills that they received. Tickets were issued to each head of a family, with his name and number of men, women and children paid, these tickets to be presented at the next payment. It was very difficult to obtain the names and numbers in each family, as the Indians themselves, then and for many years afterwards, would not tell their own names and it was generally necessary to ask a second Indian the name of the first.

They also had some superstition about giving their numbers which made our work long and arduous and called for the exercise of much patience. The payments were made by the police officers and required nearly a week, but at last all details were satisfactorily concluded and our success celebrated in a dinner that night in the officers' mess-tent, at which the ladies present on the grounds, the Hudson's Bay Company officials, and other traders were guests. There were many speeches and the evening passed very pleasantly.

The traders were given a week from the conclusion of the payments to finish trading, when they were to move off. The police of course remained to see that all went on quietly and also to protect the Indians, as money was new to them and some of the trading gentry were not above cheating. An Indian would come to us to count his change after the purchase of a horse or article, and frequently we found that he had been given the labels off fruit jars or cans as money, being none the wiser. We had then to hunt up the culprit and deal with him. The money taken in by the traders at this treaty was the foundation of wealth for many of them, particularly those dealing in horses.

The Indians built a medicine lodge before they broke up and made braves. This practice has ceased for many years, but at that time it was an annual custom. Torture was always inflicted. Slits were cut in the flesh of chest or shoulders, and wooden cleats inserted under the raised muscles. From these, rawhide lines ran to the top of the medicine pole, and the Indian, putting his weight against them, danced round the pole until the muscles broke under the strain and released him. Or a buffalo skull might be hung from his back while he danced until freed. Or he might be tied to a horse and dragged. Great endurance was often shown, and the greater the fortitude displayed the higher became the standing of the brave in the tribe.

Owing to the presence in Canada of their enemies, the American Sioux, against whom they were planning to send war parties, the making of braves was popular among the Blackfeet at the time of the treaty negotiations.

XIII

Sitting Bull crosses the line

The weather turned cold, and a considerable fall of snow made life under canvas far from comfortable before we left the Blackfoot Crossing. Toward the end of the last week, word came that the American Government was sending General Terry as commissioner to treat with Sitting Bull at Fort Walsh for his surrender to the United States. The Sioux chief had crossed over with many thousands of his followers into Canada after the annihilation by the Indians, on the Little Big Horn in Montana, of General Custer and his command, and the pursuit of the hostiles by General Miles and his army. Colonel Macleod was to proceed immediately to Fort Walsh with a suitable escort to meet General Terry at the boundary and represent the Canadian Government. Major Crozier returned to Calgary with 'F' troop and Governor Laird across the plains to Battleford.

The following is taken from the *Sessional Papers*, Ottawa, of 1878:

> *During December 1876 United States Indians numbering about five hundred men, one thousand women and one thousand four hundred children, with about three thousand five*

hundred horses and thirty United States mules, crossed the Line and camped at Wood Mountain, south-east of the Cypress Hills. They informed the officers of the Mounted Police who visited them that they had been driven from their homes by the Americans, and had come to look for peace, which they had been told by their grandfathers they would find in the land of the British; that their brothers, the Santees, had found it years ago, and they had followed them; that they had not slept soundly for years, and were anxious to find a place where they could lie down and feel safe.

Parties of observation were immediately sent out by Inspector Walsh, commanding at Fort Walsh, and the Indian camp was observed by the erection of outposts convenient distances apart. The police took possession of all firearms and ammunition held by the parties for the purpose of trade, and sales have since been made by permits granted by officers of the force.

Towards the end of May, Sitting Bull, with one hundred and thirty-five lodges, crossed the Boundary and joined the other United States Indians in Canadian territory. On 2nd June the officers of the force held a council with Sitting Bull and other chiefs and headmen of the United States Indians, which resulted in promises on the part of the Indians to observe the laws of the White Mother, which were explained to them.

At this council the chief of the Teton Sioux said it took them twenty-five days to make the trip from Powder River to where we saw them; that they were harassed by the troops until they got close to the Missouri, which they crossed west of Fort Peck, and they were so closely pressed they could not hunt and were obliged to kill their horses for food; they had lived on horse flesh for ten or fifteen days. They claim the Sioux are British Indians; that sixty-five years ago was the first their fathers knew of being under the Americans. Their fathers were told at that time by a chief of their British Father (it was a father, they say, they had at that time) that if they did not wish to live under the

Americans they could move northward and there they would again find the land of the British. Why the White Father gave them and their country to the Americans they could not tell.

From childhood they were instructed by their fathers that properly they were children of the British. They were living with strangers, but their home was in the North; further, that in their tribe could be seen medals of their White Father (George IV), given to their fathers for fighting the Americans, and although the British gave them and their country to the Americans, they never made peace with them; they always intended moving to the country of their fathers.

They were informed that their arrival would be reported to the White Mother, the Great Chief in this country, and if they obeyed the words given them, they and their families would sleep in peace.

The following is an extract from Assistant Commissioner Irvine's report to the Secretary of State, Ottawa, in May 1877:

I have the honour to report for your information that I have just learned from Fort Walsh that Sitting Bull, with one hundred and fifty-five lodges of hostile Sioux, have crossed to the Canadian side of the Line, and are moving along the White Mud River. Inspector Walsh has had an interview with Sitting Bull, Bear's Head and several other chiefs. They asked for ammunition, and Inspector Walsh informed them that they would be permitted to have sufficient to kill meat for their families, but cautioned them from sending any across the Line.

They claim that their grandfathers were British and that they had been raised on the fruit of English soil. Inspector Walsh explained the law to them, and asked Sitting Bull if he would obey it. He replied that he had buried his arms on the American side of the Line before crossing to the side of the White Mother. He also said he had been fighting on the defensive, that he had come to show us that he had not thrown this country away and that his heart was always good, with the exception of such times as he saw an American.

On the 30th May Commissioner Lieutenant-Colonel Macleod recommended that an attempt should be made to induce the United States Indians in Canadian territory to re-cross the Line. Subsequently the United States Government appointed a commission to negotiate with Sitting Bull and other United States Indians with a view to inducing them to return to the United States. Unfortunately, the efforts of the Commissioner were not successful.

A portion of Lieutenant-Colonel Macleod's recommendation to the Hon. Alexander Mackenzie, Premier of Canada, is as follows:

I am of the opinion that the presence of these United States Sioux in our territory is a matter of very grave importance. There is not much reliance to be placed on their promises and they have not been on friendly terms with the Blackfeet or Crees for years back. The Blackfeet, I know, are anxious about the invasion of their country. They say that before our arrival they were always able to keep them out, but they now wish to be friends so long as they keep away. While at Swan River I heard that the Crees are very suspicious of the Sioux who had crossed the Line. I think therefore that an attempt should be made at once to get these Indians – who are now in a very impoverished condition – to re-cross to the United States side. The longer it is delayed the more difficult it will be to accomplish.

The following extract from a letter to Colonel Macleod from the Hon. David Mills, Minister of the Interior, dated Ottawa, 24th August 1877, informs him of the appointment of a commission by the United States Government to interview Sitting Bull, on receipt of which Colonel Macleod left for Fort Walsh in the beginning of October:

The Government of the United States has appointed General McNeill of the City of St. Louis, and General Terry, who is in active service in the Federal Army; commissioners to negotiate with Sitting Bull and others of his band with a view to inducing them to return to the United States. I informed the United States Government during my visit to Washington that should they decide to send these commissioners you, or some other officer of the police force in the North-West, would meet them at the boundary with a suitable escort, accompany them to the Sioux lodges, and afford them all possible protection while they remained in Canadian territory.

The Government are most anxious that the United States commissioners should succeed in inducing the hostile Sioux who have come into our territory to return again to the United States. It is feared that should they remain in Canada they will be drawn into hostile conflict with our own Indians, that on going upon the hunting grounds of the Blackfeet and Assiniboines, or Crees, they will excite the opposition and resentment of these tribes, and that ultimately, from a failure of the means of subsistence and from other causes, they will become a very considerable expense to the Government of Canada. It is not at all improbable that they may also be disposed to make hostile incursions into the United States and in this way become a source of international trouble.

These Indians while engaged in hostilities with the United States were reported to be guilty of acts of such barbarous cruelty that should they again return for the purpose of scalping women and children, their conduct would not fail to excite the indignation of the Government and people of the United States against this country. It is, therefore, important that you should use your influence to promote as far as you well can the object of the United States commissioners in securing the return of these Indians to their own reservations.

The United States commissioners arrived at the boundary line in the middle of October. General Terry and General McNeill were accompanied by their staff; also a strong escort of United States cavalry. We met them with twenty-five men, and it was a continual surprise to the American officers with what a handful we managed to control and keep quiet the thousands of the most warlike Indians on the continent, there being only about sixty men all told at Fort Walsh.

The American cavalry escort remained in camp at the Line near the Sweet Grass Hills, while we escorted General Terry and staff to Fort Walsh. The Sioux, several thousand strong, were camped not far from the fort when we arrived, and were far from being in a peaceable mood, and the responsibility for the safety of the American officers rested heavily on the shoulders of the small police detachment.

The following day was set for the interview, and that night the Sioux warriors held a war-dance outside the fort, and several of us, with our Sioux interpreter, went out to see it. The Indians in their war-paint danced round the fire and were hideously ornamented and painted. One chief was most conspicuous for his get-up. He was naked except for the breech-cloth round his middle, his body blackened and ribs painted white, while his face was that of a devil. He wore a long feather head-dress and a pair of buffalo horns on each side of his head. From his coup-stick (a long rod wrapped with raw hide, an oblong stone at the end), hung many scalp locks, and as he recounted his deeds of valour he pointed to these grizzly trophies and told how he had used this stick upon American soldiers at the Custer fight, knocking them off their horses and then dispatching them. This Indian was Rain-in-the-Face, who was credited with killing General Custer, against whom he had an old grudge. Rain-in-the-Face and others harangued the Indians, urging them to attack the fort and kill the American officers. It would be easy they said, to destroy the buildings and all in them. This army of savage warriors could most certainly have done it, but the older chiefs opposed them and spoke for peace. Where, they asked, were

Sitting Bull at Fort Walsh, 1877

they to go if they were at war with the whites on both sides of the boundary? In the end their wise counsel prevailed.

The Sioux camp was well off for food. The buffalo were near and meat was plentiful. Of tea and tobacco they also seemed to have a good supply. They were well armed, had quantities of ammunition and appeared content and disposed to remain quiet at least for the winter.

After being searched for firearms, the following morning the chiefs were admitted to the fort. In the orderly-room General Terry and his staff, with Colonel Macleod and the police officers, awaited them. The chiefs shook hands with our officers but haughtily ignored the Americans. General Terry then announced the terms of the United States Government if they chose to re-cross the border and surrender. They would be required to give up their arms and to leave their former homeland of the Dakotas for the Indian Territory in the south.

When he had finished, Colonel Macleod informed them that as

trespassers on Canadian soil they could not look for assistance from the Queen's Government. They would not be forced to return to the United States, however, so long as they were peaceable and obeyed the laws.

Sitting Bull was spokesman for the Indians. He began to recount their grievances but was at once checked; such a recital might easily start trouble. They were told to answer briefly 'Yes' or 'No' whether they would surrender or the contrary. They then refused the terms of the United States Commissioners and begged to be allowed to remain in Canada. After some more talk the council closed and the Indians returned to their camp.

That afternoon a detachment of police escorted General Terry's party back to the boundary. The Americans thoroughly appreciated our work for them and again expressed astonishment that so small a force could control such a vast country and the thousands of warlike red men who roamed its plains and valleys. It was a great relief to us to see them safely over the Line and away. Our responsibility was heavy. A constant watch was necessary to anticipate any hostile move and we had all felt uneasy.

Except for scalps, clothing and guns, the Sioux had few trophies from the Custer fight. General Custer's watch we secured and sent to Mrs. Custer. His horses had been drowned while crossing the Missouri River. The clothing was of little use to the Indians, whose dress was limited to breech-clout and buffalo robe. They were a splendid-looking lot of warriors and without doubt the wildest and most warlike on the continent. They remained on the Canadian side, camped near Wood Mountain, until 1882, when, the buffalo having disappeared, they were forced to surrender to the American Government. During their stay in Canada they were the cause of some trouble and much anxiety, and it was a matter for congratulation that so small a body as was the force in those early days was able to hold them in check, especially when it is remembered that this was only one of countless duties it was called upon to perform in all parts of the North-West Territories.

XIV

Farming and stock-raising follow the law

S ince it was in that year that the western Indians deeded their lands to the Canadian Government, 1877 has constituted an important milestone in the development of the West. Previously the whole vast country was technically Indian property, and this was ceded for promises of support when hard times should come. The North-West Council in this year passed its first ordinances, among them those protecting the buffalo, prohibiting gambling and regarding prairie fires. It may easily be understood, considering the territory to be covered and the small force available for the purpose, that to put these laws into effect would be most difficult.

Upon the conclusion of the treaty and the departure of the traders, the Indians moved out to the plains to hunt. The Commissioner had left for Fort Walsh and the police detachments for Forts Macleod and Calgary. The Rev. John McDougall returned to Morley with the Stonies and a band of horses he had purchased from a trader named Ursinger, the second lot taken into that district from the plains. This year John Miller brought the first range cattle into Alberta. They were turned loose on the prairies to rustle for themselves. Another herd was imported by Joe McFarland and

Olsen of the Pioneer Ranch near Macleod, but later moved to the country north-west of the Cypress Hills, in the vicinity of the present city of Medicine Hat.

The first Canadian not an ex-member of the Mounted Police to start farming near Fort Macleod was W. J. Hyde, who in this year located on Willow Creek above the fort. He later was joined by Dug Allison, an ex-policeman. George Emerson and Tom Lynch drove in more cattle, which they sold to settlers, among them J. B. Smith, J. Murray Bell and Patterson. Prices, as they go today, were low, a cow and a calf bringing about twenty dollars and yearlings ten. Jim Christy brought in another lot of horses, which he soon disposed of. The police generally bought from him and the type of animal he dealt in was well suited to the purposes of the force. Lynch and Emerson went into the livestock business quite extensively and sold cattle in considerable numbers, principally young breeding stock, to settlers now taking up land in southern Alberta. Captain Winder and Inspector Shurtliff were among the purchasers, their brand being the original 'Slippery' Moon, why so called I do not know.

J. C. Nelson, with A. P. Patrick as assistant, was the first Dominion land surveyor to set up an instrument for the Government in Alberta. He came in during 1878 and surveyed in the vicinity of the junction of the Red Deer and Bow rivers. They were stopped by Cree Indians of Big Bear's band, and the police at Fort Walsh were obliged to take a hand before they continued their work. Wandering Spirit, who seven years later was to be the ringleader in the Frog Lake massacre and who had pulled up some of the survey stones, was arrested and tried at Fort Walsh, but was let off with a warning, the Indians being told that this section of the country was outside their territory.

By 1878, a dozen or more homesteads had been taken up in Alberta, chiefly on the Old Man's and Belly rivers and at Pincher Creek. One or two ranchers had settled on High River, Ace Samples the first, while a man known as Buck Smith built a cabin on Sheep

Creek. The summer of this year saw most of the country towards the Cypress Hills burnt over by great prairie fires, and the feed being destroyed the buffalo moved south, many Indians following them. During 1878 and '79 numbers of range cattle had been branded and turned loose to graze and the ranchers began to complain of cattle killing by the Indians. Some of these pioneer ranchmen, indeed, went back to Montana, though they returned a year or so later. There was no doubt truth in these charges, as the buffalo were becoming scarce, the great herds that had moved south never again being seen on the Canadian plains. The cattle promised the Indians at the treaty were delivered from Montana in the fall of 1878, but the Indians being either out on the plains or across the Line, there were none to look after them and they were driven to the police farm at Pincher Creek and there herded until the Indians occupied their reservations. It became apparent in 1879 that the day of the buffalo was over, although for a few years afterwards small bands of stragglers drifted north into Canada.

The Indians made longer and longer journeys to the south to hunt them, some far down the Missouri River, where they frequently came into bloody contact with American Indians. The main herd of such buffalo as remained was now surrounded by the southern tribes, including some from Canada, in the territory from Milk River south, to the Little Rockies and the Bear Paw Mountains, and crossing the Missouri River to the Judith Basin, and the state of the Canadian Indians who had not followed the buffalo south was one bordering on starvation.

The cattle for the Indians were herded at the north end of the Porcupine Hills by a man named Jim Scott and two helpers, no police being available for the purpose. A few were still stationed at the Pincher Creek Farm, but as it was found that the place could not be worked to advantage, it was soon afterwards sold. A considerable number of the horses kept there for breeding purposes were lost or stolen and but few were recovered.

The summer of 1878 was unusually wet. Rain fell almost

continuously for weeks. Rivers everywhere were in flood, and at the numerous crossings of the streams we encountered on our journeys accidents were frequent. Swimming was often the only means of passage, and more than one man was drowned at these treacherous places. The bank of the Old Man's River whereon stood Fort Macleod, was turned into an island; what had been a dry, low-lying gully on the south side became a river needing to be bridged. The current undermined the bank of the main river on the north and it fell in, sweeping away several log houses.

Macleod had become of some proportions. More stores had been opened and the fort had been much improved. Boards and shingles had replaced mud roofs and floors. Previous to 1878, lumber had been whipsawed by the half-breeds, a tedious process. A small saw-mill was imported from Benton and set up on the flat a mile or so above the fort, and hundreds of spruce logs were cut and driven down to it from the hills some miles away. A quantity of lumber was sawed but the high water carried away the boom and with it most of the logs. Thereafter this mill was for the most part idle, and a scarcity of lumber existed until a second mill was built some years later farther up the river by the Galt Company. This was when that company opened the coal mines at Lethbridge in 1884, and established the mill for the purpose of building scows to carry coal down the river.

At Calgary, Fort Walsh and Fort Saskatchewan the barracks had been made more comfortable, but all lumber used was whipsawed. About these forts also clustered villages of some size. The experiment had been made of bringing in eastern horses via the Missouri River for the use of the force, but they were found far less service-able for police purposes than those bred in the country. These stood the hard winter journeys without grain and kept in good condition on the wild grasses, while the Canadian horses, used to stabling and good food, generally became useless or died from hardship. The expensive journey by steamboat up the Missouri River, too, almost doubled their original cost. Good horses of the class required by the police were now purchasable at seventy-five to a hundred dollars, and many settlers went into horse breeding. The years 1878 to 1880 saw hundreds ranging on Willow Creek, High River, and Sheep Creek. The country was open and they were rounded up twice a year like the range cattle.

In the fall of 1878, Fort Walsh became headquarters of the police. The buffalo having disappeared entirely from the Macleod country, Indians in large numbers, Sioux, Assiniboines, Salteaux, Blackfeet, Sarcees and Crees, hunted in the Cypress Hills. These tribes had been in many cases hereditary enemies one of another, but were now at peace. Buffalo were few, and in their common poverty old enmities were forgotten. Raiding parties crossed the Line and returned with stolen horses. The American owners usually followed and reported their losses at the fort. Scouting by the police ensued and the stolen property almost invariably was restored to the rightful and gratified owners. Much of our time was taken up by these claimants, who were charged nothing for these services and who were accorded the same treatment as our own people, although there was no reciprocity in such matters.

The states along the border made their own laws and had omitted to provide one which would allow them to act in a like neighbourly manner in cases where the circumstances were reversed and horses stolen in Canada were taken across the Line.

In July the second treaty annuities were paid to the many Indians gathered in the Cypress Hills. The Blackfeet, however, were notified that they must assemble at the Blackfoot Crossing for their money. Colonel Macleod proceeded there to make the payment, which passed off quietly, although it was thought there might be trouble with these Indians, who were now much worse off for food and robes for trade than in previous years. I accompanied the Commissioner, and when we had finished at the Crossing I was instructed to go to Morley to pay the Stonies.

The Blackfeet and the Sarcees were the only two tribes to be paid at the Blackfoot Crossing. The Bloods and Piegans refused to go there and the former were paid at the Belly River, where they were afterwards given their reservation, and the Piegans at Fort Macleod. The latter tribe was allotted a reserve the next year in the Porcupine Hills west of Macleod. The Blackfeet, and particularly the head chief, Crowfoot, tried our patience considerably. At first he refused the payment. He resented strongly the Bloods and Piegans being paid apart from the Blackfeet. He also professed not to understand why the sum to be paid this year was only five dollars to each Indian, instead of the twelve dollars paid the year before. I never saw Crowfoot, who was generally a most reasonable Indian, so obstinate. He was aggrieved that the allied tribes of the Blackfeet were separated; he wished to be recognised as supreme chief of the confederacy. However, after much time wasted in talk, the payments were concluded, I went to Morley, paid the Stonies, and returned to Calgary to take charge of that post for the winter.

With respect to the circumstances of the Indians at this time, due to the sudden disappearance of the great buffalo herds, I quote from the report for 1879 of the Commissioner, Colonel Macleod, to the Minister of the Interior, an office then held by Sir John Macdonald, who lately had become Premier of Canada and had transferred the Mounted Police to the Interior Department, so that they should be under his supervision:

> *I ventured in my last annual report to express a fear that the large herd of buffalo after being driven south, with so many Indians behind them, would never return in anything like the number of former years. I little thought the prophecy was to be so literally fulfilled. Unfortunately such has been the case. Once during the summer a very large band crossed the Line, east of the Cypress Hills, and smaller bands have come into the country, in some instances making their way north to the South Saskatchewan. The main herd, hemmed in by nearly all the Indians of the North-West and Montana, remained south of the Milk River, about the 'Little Rockies' and the 'Bear Paw',*

extending, I believe, across the Missouri into the Judith Basin. During the spring and early summer the condition of our Indians was desperate in the extreme. Buffalo, their only source of supply, had moved south, and their horses were too weak to follow. The flour and beef supplied by the Government was sufficient for a time to ward off the impending famine and to supply a large number with enough to take them to the Milk River country. The great bulk of the Bloods and one large band of the Blackfeet, together with some North Piegans, the Assiniboines, and other Indians about Cypress, pursued this course as soon as they were supplied with food to take them to where the buffalo were. The larger portion of the Blackfeet remained with Crowfoot at the Blackfoot Crossing until after the payments and suffered the most dire distress for want of food throughout the summer.

The Canadian Indians who crossed the Line managed to secure a large supply of meat, but were after a time ordered off by the United States authorities. They came flocking into Fort Walsh and those who belonged to Treaty Number Seven made their way through to Fort Macleod, where they remained until they were paid at the end of September.

Under such circumstances I think it a matter of congratulation that the Indians throughout the Territories generally have behaved so well. They have, however, been accused of killing large numbers of cattle in the Bow River District and some in the neighbourhood of Fort Walsh. It is undoubtedly the case that they have killed some, but nothing like the numbers claimed. It is the opinion of many respectable stockmen that whites had more to do with it than the Indians. A great many cattle must have strayed back to Montana, and a great many more must have perished in the storms which passed over the country in March last. The fact that seventy carcasses were found in one coulee shows the damage to be attributed to this cause. When I visited Fort Macleod for the Blackfoot payments in September I was called upon by several stockmen who were then driving their cattle across the Line. I pointed out to them that if they herded their cattle in certain localities, it would be possible to do something for them, but as they turned their cattle adrift on the prairies, and only looked after them twice a year, they were themselves to blame if they lost a great many. To have done what they asked would have amounted to this: that the Police would have to act as herders over a country about one hundred miles wide, and over two hundred miles long, as the cattlemen who have squatted through this section are scattered over a country of that extent.

XV

Murder at Walsh: Constable Grayburn ambushed

During the summer of 1878, Edgar Dewdney was appointed Indian Commissioner, with Elliott Galt as assistant. He visited Fort Macleod and Fort Walsh during the summer and authorised the issuing of certain rations to starving Indians. This summer was also a very wet one and much sickness prevailed, principally typhoid fever, and several deaths from that cause occurred, both at Fort Macleod and Fort Walsh, among both whites and Indians. In July, E. H. Mansell and his brother George, purchased a band of several hundred head of cattle and went into the cattle business, starting their ranch near Pincher Creek, but left after a short time and drove their cattle into Montana. Other ranchers did the same, among them Mrs. Armstrong and Morgan, Patterson and Bell, and G. B. Smith. Mrs. Armstrong never returned to Alberta, being murdered in Montana in a most cruel and cold-blooded manner in the year 1880.

These cattlemen became nervous owing to the Indians of the North-West suffering for want of meat, and all losses of cattle were placed to the red man's account. Many who at this time went into cattle-raising were without experience, and seldom saw their cattle after turning them out. Those who had gone to Montana did not remain long, and on returning, following the example of the large cattle ranches then being established in the Territories, engaged experienced stockmen from Montana to manage their ranches.

At Calgary, where I was in command in the winter of 1879 and '80, Lynch and Emerson reported that twenty head of their cattle had been killed by Indians. In the spring that number bearing their brand were found together on Jumping Pond Creek, south of the Bow River. They were undoubtedly those whose loss was charged against the Indians.

In August 1879 occurred the first round-up in southern Alberta, sixteen cattle owners taking part. They were W. Parker, W. Winder, Shurtliff, Jack Miller, E. H. Mansell, T. Lee, R. Patterson, G. B. Smith, Joe McFarland, H. Olsen, Morgan, Sam Brouard, Bell, Day, Allison and W. Hyde. Many of these men in the course of years made money in the cattle business, owning individually thousands of range cattle and horses and leasing large tracts of land from the Government for grazing purposes. The men mentioned were the pioneers of what became the great stock industry of southern Alberta.

Eventually settlers came in and possessed the land, railroads were built, towns sprang up, and the great ranches became a thing of the past.

The mail routes of the southern half of the Territories had not been changed since the building of Fort Macleod and Fort Walsh. There were no post offices between the Rocky Mountains and the western boundary of Manitoba, a distance of at least seven hundred and fifty miles. Letters were posted in the Mounted Police orderly-rooms at Calgary, Macleod, Walsh and Wood Mountain, with United States postage stamps attached, as the nearest post offices were in American territory. The orderly-room clerks sorted and made up the mails, which were carried to their destinations by contract with the Mounted Police. The service was fortnightly, from Fort Macleod and Calgary to Fort Walsh, thence to Benton, in the years 1879 to 1880, and the mail was chiefly official. In the north, mail was carried by contract with the Post Office Department and picked up at Hudson's Bay Company and police posts on the way.

Recruits for the force came in via Benton and there was much travel between the North-West Territories and points in Montana. Although at that time Montana Territory had a considerable white population, it was made up in the main of cattle ranchers, miners, gamblers, traders, adventurers and 'bad' men who came and went. Lawlessness was rife and vigilance committees were formed, which dealt out summary justice to the tough element. Lynchings were frequent. It was said forty men were hanged by these committees for horse-stealing, murder and other crimes in the town of Benton and vicinity in less than three years. Benton boasted a sheriff and deputies, and as magistrate a man who led a Fenian raid on Canada in 1871 and had no love for a Britisher. He was said to measure the amount of any fine imposed by the amount of money in the possession of the prisoner.

In 1879 the pay of the force was reduced to fifty cents a day. Other changes were made. Inspectors were to be known in future as superintendents, sub-inspectors as inspectors, while military rank of the non-commissioned officers was confirmed by law. A chief constable was a sergeant-major and a constable a sergeant.

The sale of whisky to Indians had by this time been practically stamped out, although occasional instances cropped up of its being traded in the camps, but much liquor still found its way into the country for sale chiefly to settlers and to whites in the towns. Some now and then was disposed of even at a police post. The poorest quality, costing in Benton two dollars to three dollars a gallon, sold readily at Macleod or other posts for ten dollars per bottle. The vendors took great chances, penalties being severe. Fines ranged up to three hundred dollars for a third offence, with confiscation of horses, wagons and other outfit, but profits were so large that the traffic persisted all through the early years of prohibition in the Territories. It was impossible completely to eliminate the evil and liquor was always procurable at a high price in any of the small towns or settlements in spite of the constant patrol of the boundary line and the close watch kept on all suspected traders.

At Fort Macleod in the old days the vilest concoctions were sold, the favourite Jamaica ginger. A six-ounce bottle, compounded of alcohol and a few drops of ginger extract, cost a dollar. Red ink, Florida water, eau-de-Cologne and many other alcoholic fluids were used as beverages. Liquor permits for two and a half gallons were granted to persons recommended to the Lieutenant-Governor. The liquor was ostensibly for medical purposes, but the permit system was much abused. Men detected with quantities of liquor in their possession had permits to cover it in the names of different individuals and were therefore safe from arrest or prosecution. Gambling was openly practised, there being no law against it.

Until 1878, the police had drawn upon the buffalo for its meat supply, but in that year contracts were made with I. G. Baker & Company to furnish the force with domestic beef, and the firm drove in herds of range cattle and opened butcher's shops at the various posts. The contract price for the meat was fourteen cents per pound and they made enormous profits, the cattle costing them in Montana an average of around twenty dollars per head.

Since our arrival in the Territories in 1874, a number had died from one cause or another, but no man of the force had been killed or molested by an Indian. But the time came when this unclouded record was to be broken. In October 1879, a policeman was deliberately murdered near Fort Walsh. Four constables and a non-commissioned officer, in charge of the police horse herd, were in camp some three miles from the post. During the day one man was continually on herd; at night the horses were driven in to the fort and stabled. At the time of the murder, some Blood Indians who made themselves obnoxious by continual prowling and begging, were in camp not far from the police tents. On the fateful morning Constable Grayburn left camp to take his turn on herd and was followed by one of the Bloods named Star Child. This Indian was a vicious character who had given much trouble to the police, and Grayburn had shortly before had words with him.

When the time came for Grayburn to be relieved and he did not return to camp, search was immediately made for him. Hanging from a bush about a mile away, his companions found his cap, and, in the snow nearby, stains of blood. At the bottom of a gully a little farther on, the searchers came upon the body with a bullet hole in the back of the head. The horse, tied by the halter shank, lay dead at the foot of a tree. The animal had also been shot.

Word of the tragedy was sent to the fort and the body removed. A party was dispatched to make a thorough search of the Blood camp, suspicion centering on Star Child, but the Indian could not be found. It was subsequently learned that he had escaped to Montana. Efforts were made unsuccessfully to extradite him, but in 1881 he returned to the Blood camp near Fort Macleod and after repeatedly escaping arrest by his alertness, was captured. He was tried at Macleod for murder, but although morally certain of his guilt, in the absence of any evidence, the jury could do nothing but bring in a verdict of acquittal. A year or two later Star Child was arrested for horse stealing. This time he was less fortunate. He received a sentence of five years in Manitoba penitentiary. He died before completing his term.

In the fall and winter of 1879 the Canadian Indians were returning from the American side and their pursuit of the buffalo, now – except for a few scattered animals found on rare occasions up to 1884 between Wood Mountain and Battleford – gone from the North-West Territories for ever. The returning Indians were in dire distress and flocked to the different police posts for assistance. Mr. Dewdney, the recently-appointed Indian Commissioner, had arranged with I. G. Baker & Company to furnish flour and beef cattle for the relief of Indians who might be suffering for lack of food on their return, but the amount contracted for was limited, and when thousands of destitute turned to the Government in their only hope of succour, the resources of the police, who had to do their best to feed them, were taxed to the utmost. As soon as possible they were sent to their reserves and men were engaged by the Indian Department to look after them, but this could not be done until 1880. In the meantime their supervision fell upon the shoulders of the police and a most trying task it proved. Complaints of cattle-killing, calling almost daily for investigations, combined with the multitude of their other duties, made life a burden and gave the force little rest.

At Fort Calgary, where I commanded, as the summer advanced matters became serious. The Blackfeet were actually starving and had I not taken the responsibility of coming to their relief, an outbreak must certainly have occurred. It was pitiable to see parties of the less impoverished bringing their weakened fellows, some mere skeletons, to Fort Calgary for food. Some even ate grass along the road. I have seen them when a steer was shot, rush on the animal with their knives before it had ceased kicking, cut away the flesh and, maddened by hunger, devour it raw. The Blackfeet were most grateful for the succour extended to them at this critical time and I found in after years when acting as their agent that to their recollection of this incident I owed much of my success in dealing with them in more than one ticklish situation.

Following is a copy of my report to Colonel Macleod, at that time expected at Fort Macleod, although Inspector Winder, in command at the post, had authority to forward supplies to any Indian camp in need of food:

FORT CALGARY,
5th July 1879.

SIR,

As Mr. Merret leaves this fort today to proceed via the Crossing to Fort Macleod, I have the honour to report how the Indians are situated at this post and the Blackfoot Crossing, and the action I have taken in the matter of feeding them. On the arrival of word from the Crossing that there were nearly two hundred lodges there starving and waiting for supplies, I immediately despatched S. C. Christie to Fort Macleod, with a letter to you stating the condition of the Indians, and asking permission to purchase beef for them, but since that time the Indians have been coming in here in hundreds, always headed by a chief, for food, as they are actually dying of starvation. (I have already heard of twenty-one cases of death.) As they are and have been getting no assistance from any post, I took upon myself the responsibility of purchasing and issuing beef to them. For the last three days I have been obliged to issue beef at the rate of two thousand pounds per diem. I have advised the Indians not to move their camp up here from the Crossing, as I expected you would have been at Fort Macleod when Constable Christie arrived there, and that some of the Indian cattle would be sent to the Indians at the Crossing. I have told them all that as soon as you arrived at Macleod provisions would be sent to them, and in the meantime I would supply them with meat, which I have done, and am now doing. Until assistance arrives from Fort Macleod I can keep them in meat the way I am doing for a week or two, but of course the expense will be great. I am buying cattle from Mr. Emerson at the post at seven cents per pound. There is no doubt whatever that if I had not fed them, and do not continue to feed them, they will take the matter into their own hands and help themselves.

Crowfoot sent up word yesterday asking me to go down and talk to them in their distress. It is utterly impossible for me to leave here until the Blackfeet receive assistance from some other post. Crowfoot himself, I think, will be here tomorrow. All the other chiefs have been in with the exception of Three Bulls, who is at Cypress. The Blackfeet are utterly destitute, there being no buffalo in the country. I have had to send out meat to parties on their way in, who were eating grass to keep themselves alive.

The rush is not quite so great as it was, as I have established some order in the going and coming. Every party that comes in is headed by a chief, who sends a man some hours ahead to notify me of their coming so that I can have meat ready for them. I am keeping careful note of what I issue, and to whom, and in what quantity. I am paying the men from whom I purchase beef by voucher on I. G. Baker & Company. I am nearly out of flour, and can issue no more without running myself short. I am not only feeding the Blackfeet, but also the Sarcees and Stonies and some half-breeds.

I have advised the Blackfeet not to move up from the Crossing until I hear what is going to be done for them and when supplies will be sent. They are now within easy reach of this post, coming up from the Crossing in a day and going backwards and forwards with meat. I hope that I have your approval in the action I have taken, and trust to have full instructions before long as this is rather a trying situation.

I have the honour to be,
Your obedient Servant,
C. E. DENNY, Inspector.

To LIEUTENANT-COLONEL J. F. MACLEOD,
Commissioner, North-West Mounted Police,
Fort Macleod.

I had received orders from Mr. Dewdney, Indian Commissioner, in the spring not to ration Indians at Calgary, but of course such a state of affairs as I have described was not apprehended, and not long afterwards I received a letter from the Indian Commissioner thanking me for the action I had taken.

XVI

The Blackfeet settle for a dead Cree

The price of beef, seven cents a pound live weight, was in those days considered high. Cattle could be purchased in Montana at a very low figure, the ranges being overstocked. Yearling heifers were brought into Alberta and sold at ten dollars per head. In Montana they cost five dollars. Soon after this cattle and flour were purchased in large quantities and sent to the reserves, men were engaged as butchers and the police went to see that a fair issue of rations was made. From this year dates the issue of regular rations to the Indians of Treaty Number Seven which has continued in some measure ever since. Next year regular farm instructors were appointed, and in 1880 Norman Macleod, brother of the Commissioner, was named first Indian Agent over the whole treaty. On his resignation in 1882, I was offered and accepted the position, resigning my commission in the force for the purpose.

For a year or two the Indians continued to leave their reserves in large numbers in search of the vanished buffalo. It was hard to make them believe that they were gone for ever and for years they believed they would reappear. They had a legend that the buffalo came originally from a hole in the ground in the centre of a lake in the north and that on the advent of the whites they had re-entered it and would ultimately re-emerge. L. V. Kelly in his book, *The Rangemen*, says:

> *Across the boundary the slaughter of the hemmed-up buffalo continued, and the white and red hunters made huge kills. One hundred thousand buffalo robes were sold out of the Yellowstone valley from the winter hunt of 1880 and 1881, but never again would there be such a shipment, for the herds of millions had now dwindled to a few thousands, and the day of the buffalo was gone.*

In 1882 Sitting Bull and his hostile following were forced by the disappearance of the buffalo to surrender at Fort Buford on the Missouri River to the United States authorities, and this relieved us of endless responsibility and trouble. He was subsequently shot to death by Indian police of his own tribe. A perpetual supervision over them had been necessary since their arrival in 1876. The force at Wood Mountain, which had most to do with the Sioux, with Major Crozier in command, consisted of less than fifty men behind a flimsy wooden stockade that a war-party of Sioux could have taken in an hour.

Sitting Bull and his camp were beginning to feel the pinch of poverty with the growing scarcity of the buffalo and had become more persistent than ever in their demands, backed by threats, for rations from the police. Being as consistently refused, they were in a savage mood. They had always been enemies of the Canadian Indians, particularly of the Blackfoot confederacy.

The Blackfeet were frequent callers at our posts when near them, and individual hunters roamed the country on the lookout for any shaggy stragglers that might remain. A starving Blood Indian appeared at Wood Mountain making for the police post and ran upon the Sioux. Instantly they were in pursuit of their solitary enemy like a pack of hounds.

Crowfoot, Head Chief of the Blackfoot Nation

Sitting Bull, Chief of the Sioux

The Blood evaded them by hiding in the brush and managed to get into the fort at night, where he was promised protection. The Sioux on learning this flocked to the fort in hundreds, to find the gates closed against them. They demanded the surrender of the Blood; threatening if their request was refused to burn the fort and kill all behind its walls.

Preparations were made for defence and Superintendent Crozier went to the gate to parley with Sitting Bull. For an hour he argued with the chief, and when Sitting Bull suddenly attempted to force his way past him into the fort, the major seized the Sioux by the shoulders and flung him out. An immediate attack was anticipated, but the firmness shown by the police daunted even these fierce redskins and they returned to their camp sullen and vowing vengeance. That night the Blood was smuggled out, mounted on a good horse, and sent on his way. He reached Fort Walsh with his scalp intact, thanks to the courage of the Wood Mountain detachment and their commander.

In November 1880 Lieutenant-Colonel Macleod resigned from the force and the Assistant Commissioner, Lieutenant-Colonel Irvine, succeeded him. Colonel Macleod did not leave the country, however. Until 1886 he was stipendiary magistrate and that year was appointed judge.

During the winter of 1879 word was received at Fort Walsh that the Indian Star Child (suspected, as has been related, of the murder of Constable Grayburn), was in an Indian camp south of Fort Benton and I was given orders to proceed there and try to arrange with the Benton sheriff to have the suspect delivered to us at the boundary. I was instructed to offer up to five hundred dollars for this purpose. I was to meet at Benton, Lieutenant-Colonel Norman Macleod, Indian Agent and brother of the Commissioner, and the Commissioner himself.

I rode into Benton in the spring of 1880. The sum asked by Sheriff Healy for delivery of the Indian it was out of my power to pay and I awaited for some weeks the arrival of the Commissioner and Norman Macleod. This was my first visit to Fort Benton and I found it a busy place of round one thousand inhabitants. It was at the head of navigation on the Missouri and many steamboats discharged their loads there. A portion of the old fort, built of unbaked adobe bricks, still stood. There were handsome residences and business blocks. It was what was called a wide-open town. Water Street, facing the river, was lined with gambling houses, liquor saloons and dance halls, and the sidewalk and street were strewn with playing cards, thrown out as the easiest way of getting rid of them. Benton boasted a club, 'The Choteau', and our names were immediately enrolled. It had a very mixed membership, among those on the list being Colonel Donnely, of Fenian memory, whom we met. He was practising law in Benton, was justice of the peace, and not at all a bad fellow socially. He seldom referred to the little unpleasantness existing between himself and the Canadian Government. We also met the colonel and officers of the Seventh United States Cavalry, stationed at Fort Benton. Colonel Macleod proceeded with his brother to Fort Macleod, and Mr. E. Galt, Assistant Indian Commissioner, who had also arrived, returned with me to Fort Walsh. After inspecting the Indian camps in the vicinity, we went on to Macleod, whence I returned to my post at Fort Calgary.

In the spring of 1881 I travelled to Fort Saskatchewan with the pay for the division there and remained a few days at Edmonton. Not much in the way of building had been done in the future Alberta capital at that time. A few lots had been cleared and laid out and Donald Ross had built a small hotel. John A. McDougall, who had arrived in 1876, was in business as a trader. The Hon. Frank Oliver came up in the same year but did not remain. He returned in 1880 and began publication of the *Edmonton Bulletin*. The first Methodist Church had been built by the Rev. George McDougall in 1871 and a large block of land was owned by the church.

The Canadian Pacific Railway survey ran not far south of Edmonton and it was confidently expected the road would follow the survey. In consequence Edmonton saw a boom in the sale of its town lots at Winnipeg in the years 1881 and '82, the first purchased by the Hon. Frank Oliver and J. A. McDougall.

Bishop Grandin, of St. Albert Mission, desiring to visit the Macleod district and establish a mission in the south, expressed a wish to accompany me on my return. I was glad of his company and we made a very pleasant journey to Calgary. He was met at the Red Deer River by a large number of half-breeds and we remained over Sunday. The bishop held service and talked with many of the half-breeds. Father Scollen met the bishop at Calgary and went with him to Fort Macleod, where they established the first Catholic mission in southern Alberta. It became in time a strong and wealthy community. Bishop Grandin was a most zealous missionary and had seen hard service for the Church. He was for many years in the Mackenzie River district. Some of his experiences in that far north region were most interesting. He always thought there were great possibilities in the country. He was wearing a ring in which was mounted a very large and perfect emerald that he had found on the Mackenzie and had had cut and set while on a visit to France.

The force at Calgary had been reduced, as the Indians were getting rations on their reserves and it was the intention to move most of the men to Forts Walsh and Macleod.

The Indians still looked for buffalo where none existed and the Blackfeet lodges were at or near the Crossing. A large camp of Crees arrived from the north and camped not far away. The two tribes were far from friendly; in fact, word reached Calgary that a Cree had been killed during the summer by a Blackfoot and that the Crees were about to attack the Blackfoot camp and avenge his death. I therefore started for that point with what men could be spared, which was six, including Corporal G. C. King and Interpreter Munro. An American officer, Captain Williams, who had come from Montana after some army mules taken by deserters from his regiment, had been staying with me for a short time. He asked permission to accompany us to the Crossing, and I was glad of his company. We rode light, with a spring wagon for bedding and provisions, and made the Crossing late that night. We stopped near the river and in the morning found a Blackfoot camp of about a thousand Indians on the edge of the bluff, overlooking the river. The Cree camp, nearly equal in size, was about three miles distant.

The Blackfoot chiefs came down to see me, bringing many complaints against the Crees. I asked if it was true that a Cree had been killed. They admitted the killing, but alleged provocation. I demanded they give up the slayer, but found that he had left the camp the day after the occurrence and gone no one knew where. I then told them to pitch a large lodge somewhere between their camp and that of the Crees. Meanwhile I would go over to the Cree camp and try to persuade their chiefs to meet the Blackfeet, when I hoped they would arrange a peace. The Blackfeet agreed to this proposal and also promised to talk reasonably and endeavour to settle their differences.

I rode with the interpreter to the Cree village and found them more amenable to reason than I had anticipated. In fact they were feeling far from comfortable. They were in the Blackfoot country, a long way from their friends and more likely to be attacked by their hereditary enemies in the circumstances than to attack them. They were much incensed, however, over the killing of one of their number, but at last consented to accept a payment from the Blackfeet in settlement and agreed to meet their former foes next day in council. When the matter was adjusted they would move camp to the Cypress Hills, as advised, and join others of the tribe there.

This reply, which I brought to the Blackfeet, satisfied them. I found that in my absence they had brought a supply of dried meat and put up a lodge for us. We had no tent and this was most welcome. It was intended as evidence of great friendliness on their part.

Next morning, with the interpreter and Captain Williams, I went to the Blackfoot camp and was shown the tent pitched for the council. We seated ourselves at the head of it and awaited the arrival of the chiefs. After a short interval the head Blackfoot chief,

Crowfoot, arrived and with great ceremony passed round the fire and shook hands with us, at the same time throwing down a fine dressed buffalo robe before me. I told the interpreter to tell them that I had not come to take presents but to settle the matter in dispute between themselves and the Crees. Munro advised me to take the robe as it was given as a token of their good-will towards us. I therefore threw the robe behind me.

Soon afterwards no less than thirty-three more chiefs, Cree and Blackfoot, arrived, and each as he entered threw down a robe as Crowfoot had done. This was embarrassing as, having taken the first, I could not, without affronting the other chiefs, refuse the rest. I had, therefore, thirty-four robes piled at my back. A little later we felt grateful to the chiefs. We were short of bedding and the weather turned cold before we returned to Calgary. I distributed the robes among the men, who were delighted to get them.

Following a solemn smoke all round I advised the Blackfeet to settle with the family of the slain Cree in the usual Indian fashion by payment of so many horses. For several hours, however, we were obliged to listen while they aired their grievances against each other and the talk at times waxed loud and heated, but in the end the opposing tribes came to an agreement. The Crees promised to move the following day and the Blackfeet to give up the murderer should he come into camp. I got them to shake hands all round, and after seeing the Crees out of camp we returned to our lodges tired but well satisfied with the day's results. Our success in settling such matters among our Indians astonished Captain Williams. He said on his side of the Line it would have taken a regiment of cavalry and a war to have done what we accomplished with a handful of men.

We remained at the Crossing for two days and saw the Crees well started on their way east before returning to Calgary.

In the fall of 1881 I left Calgary for Fort Walsh. Sergeant Johnston remained in charge of Fort Calgary, the only persons besides him there being G. C. King, now manager of I. G. Baker &

Company's store, and the Hudson's Bay Company trader, A. Fraser, and his man. I took with me all 'F' troop with the exception of the sergeant and after a few days at Macleod went on to Fort Walsh. While we were at Macleod a bad fire broke out which burned down the quartermaster's stores and some stables, causing considerable loss. The village of Macleod had not grown. Much of it had slipped into the Old Man's River and the Commissioner had recommended that the fort be moved and rebuilt in a more secure situation.

NWMP camp and pack train party on the way to Peace River, Alberta.

XVII

Belly River claims a victim

few more settlers came in in 1880 and several time-expired police also went into farming and stock-raising. In 1881 the first Government leases were granted in southern Alberta; large tracts for twenty-one year periods at the nominal rent of one cent per acre. The Oxley Ranch Company, a group of rich English shareholders headed by Lord Lathom and Staveley Hill, Q.C., M.P., was organised. On its one hundred thousand acre lease on Willow Creek were placed several thousand head of cattle. The Cochrane Company, under Senator Cochrane's direction, secured a large lease west of Calgary, but later moved south of the Belly River. They brought from Montana ten thousand head of cattle. The Waldron Ranch, another English interest, took over from Dr. McEachern, Dominion Veterinary head, a large lease in the Porcupine Hills. The Allans, of Allan Steamship fame, established themselves on High River under the name of the North-West Cattle or Bar U Company. Although most of these leases were granted late in 1880, or early in '81, it was a year before the major-ity were in operation. All stock was purchased in Montana and, in general, experienced cattlemen were engaged in the south to manage these large concerns. The Government, to encourage the cattle industry, removed the duty on cattle imported from the United States. Smaller ranchers also drove in stock, among them John Quirk, who with his family and herd located on High River. Lynch and Emerson made more importations. Some they sold, but eventually they themselves settled down to ranching on High River. Many who had left the country a year or two earlier now returned to engage extensively in stock-raising.

The summers of 1880 and '81 were very wet, the rivers high, and the losses in the herds from Montana in crossing them quite heavy. At Macleod the river banks were continually crumbling, buildings were swept away, and it became apparent that, to escape a like fate, the fort must soon be moved.

Captain Winder left the Mounted Police in 1881 to establish a store at Macleod and a ranch on Willow Creek. Fred Stimson came in to manage the Bar U ranch and Inspector James Walker left the force to take charge of the Cochrane ranch. He drove twelve thousand head of cattle over from Montana in 1882 and ranged them some twenty miles west of Calgary. The following winter, which was unusually severe, the cattle died by hundreds and the river was polluted by the carcasses. After this disastrous start the Cochrane Company moved what remained of their herd to a new lease between the Kootenay and St. Mary's rivers, where they were most successful.

The route of the Canadian Pacific Railway had been changed and the road was under construction on its present location. Much disappointment was felt in the north over the change, the original survey crossing the Rockies over much lower and easier paths than that finally selected. There were various explanations, but no doubt pressure exerted by the wealthy cattle companies in the south was responsible for the shift. The Edmonton district had few settlers at the time and their representations counted for little against those of these powerful interests.

Colonel Macleod left Fort Walsh in the summer of 1880 to take up his duties as stipendiary magistrate at Fort Macleod and, having obtained a month's leave of absence, I took the opportunity of travelling with him. As he had a four-horse team and spring wagon, I was able to take my baggage and ride my troop horse. The Indian Agent's son, Norman, Guide Jerry Potts and two constables were the others in the party.

Nothing happened until we reached the Belly River at Whoopup. Here we found the stream very high and just managed to cross without swimming. After dinner we went on to Slide-out, the second crossing of the Belly. It was then about six o'clock and the Colonel having taken my horse, I rode in the wagon. He and Jerry had crossed the river on the ford without difficulty and I told Constable Hooley to drive in after him. When we were nearly halfway over, however, the Colonel called to me to return to the south bank, camp, and come over in the morning. He and Jerry Potts were going on to Macleod, nine miles north.

I was loath to do this, having made a good start, but orders were orders. We spent a most unpleasant night in the open. Mosquitoes were bad and sleep was almost impossible. Two of the horses, although hobbled, crossed the river, and in the morning we could see them grazing on the other side.

A little after daylight I sent the driver, Hooley, over after them and instructed him to pay particular attention to the ford so that he should know his way when we started to cross. He got over safely and brought back the horses. I saw that the water was about breast-high on them and that the current was swift. Hooley pronounced the ford all right and said we would have no trouble in crossing. We loaded the wagon and drove in.

A log house owned and occupied by two ex-police ranch men, Bell and Patterson, stood on the opposite side, but the hour being early they were still in bed.

We had reached the middle of the river when the lead team balked. I took the reins of the team, the driver attending to those of the wheelers, and we succeeded in starting them all together, when I handed the reins I had back to the driver. But we had gone only a few steps when the leaders stopped a second time, swerving downstream and dragging the wheelers after them. Over went the wagon, throwing me among the floundering horses. How I escaped injury is a miracle, but half-drowned I managed to reach the shore. Climbing the bank, I saw that young Macleod and Constable Stewart had both jumped and were also safe. Team and wagon were drifting down the centre of the river. The driver had dropped the reins and was hanging to the side of the seat in water to his waist. The horses, entangled in the harness, were crazed with fear. The leaders had swung round and were frantically pawing on the team in the rear. The driver had completely lost his nerve.

'Mr. Denny,' he called, 'come and help me!'

I jumped into the river and swam towards him. I was nearing the wagon when suddenly it again turned over and man, horses and the vehicle itself disappeared. I swam over the spot and down the river for a quarter of a mile, but they did not reappear and, with my strength almost exhausted, I was forced to make for shore.

In the meantime the two young men had watched the tragic happening from the bank. I called out Bell and Patterson, borrowed two horses from them, and sent Stewart and Macleod to the fort for assistance. The ranchers and myself followed down the river and found the wagon attached to the four drowned horses on a sand-bar half a mile below the ford. We were obliged to wait until a detail arrived with a boat aboard a wagon before we could reach the wreck and with much difficulty disentangle the horses and bring harness and some recovered baggage ashore. We then went on down the river for several miles in hope of discovering the body of the driver, but as night came on we were reluctantly compelled to abandon the search.

Most of the baggage was never found but, oddly enough, not a thing belonging to Colonel Macleod was missing. Even his waistcoat, left on the driver's seat with his gold watch in the pocket, was recovered. I lost among other things a good part of my uniform, besides the three months' pay I had placed in the uniform case.

Poor Hooley's body was discovered, though not for nearly a

month, about twelve miles from the scene of the accident. It was buried at Macleod with military honours. This was one of the many fatalities that occurred in the North-West in crossing the dangerous streams before the day of ferries and bridges. These mountain streams are most treacherous. The rapid currents cause frequent shifting of the sand bars and where in one year a good ford might be found, in the next swimming might be the only method of crossing from one bank to the other.

The dissatisfaction of the Sarcee Indians over being placed on a common reserve with the Blackfeet came to a head when, four hundred strong, they moved up to Calgary and demanded to be fed there. The lone policeman on the ground at the time was Sergeant Johnston; the only other white men were G. C. King, manager of I. G. Baker & Company's store, Angus Fraser of the Hudson's Bay Company post, W. Smith and Walter James. The Sarcees, reduced in number through smallpox and warfare from a tribe of several thousand to one of perhaps six hundred souls, were the most difficult to handle of any of the plains Indians. They warred continually with other tribes, and though nominally allies of the Blackfeet, each camp was distrustful of the other.

The two stores were well supplied with goods and the Sarcees took advantage of the helplessness of the traders, demanding supplies and threatening if refused to help themselves. They beset the stores, shot off their guns and even built a fire in front of the Baker Company's place. Eventually they succeeded in so intimidating the men in charge that they were given what they asked. A messenger made a rapid ride to Macleod with the news and Inspector Crozier ordered me to proceed with a detail of eight men and a sergeant with all speed to Calgary. We were accompanied by the Indian agent. My instructions were to move the Sarcees from the place and punish any who had committed depredations.

We arrived at Calgary on the second day, greatly to the relief of the few settlers in the locality. The Indians we found had up till then confined their hostile demonstrations to threats and the firing of guns inside the stores. The traders, however, to avert possibly more serious trouble, had been coerced into making them many presents.

The agent held a council in the fort and, upon the Sarcees refusing to return to the Crossing, promised rations to them at Fort Macleod if they went there. This proposal they declined, demanding to be rationed at Calgary, which, in the absence of cattle or other supplies there, was out of the question. The agent went on to Morley to visit the Stonies, leaving the Sarcees to us. For three days we could do nothing with them and the possibility of their attacking us necessitated a strong guard night and day. No doubt they would have done so had we not shown a bold front. However, on the third evening they consented to move next morning but, their horses being very poor, asked help to transport their tents and effects. I promised them some carts, but at the same time told them that if they failed to move as agreed I would pull down and carry away their tents. This was a rather pretentious threat but it had to be made good. I engaged Sam Livingstone, a rancher up the Elbow River, to be on hand with a number of carts in the morning.

Early next day I went with all the men I could muster – thirteen I believe – to the lodges. We found no sign of movement. I lined up the men, rifles loaded, on the camp's outskirts and Sergeant Lauder and myself commenced to pull down the tents.

The Indians had been sulking inside. They swarmed out like a nest of hornets and for a time things looked sultry. But they cooled off when they found themselves facing the row of rifles with determined men behind them and they began hurriedly to pack their goods into the carts. One shot, fired from behind a lodge still standing, came unpleasantly close to Sergeant Lauder. No one had seen the skulker and as the Indians were now busily preparing for the trail, we paid it only passing notice. By afternoon they were moving. We kept with them until next day and then rode on. They arrived four days later and for the next year drew rations at Macleod. A separate reservation was then allotted to them on Fish Creek, about ten miles from Calgary. This they still occupy.

A death that cast a gloom over us for a long time occurred this fall. Captain Clarke, the adjutant of the force, lately married, died at Fort Walsh of gastric fever. Walsh was always an unhealthy post and there were many deaths from the same cause during the few years it was occupied. Captain Clarke was the first officer we had lost since coming to the country and he was most popular. The surgeons of the force, Kittson and Kennedy, were both clever men, but their skill could not save him. The monuments over the graves of Captain Clarke and the other men who died there were still standing near the ruins of old Fort Walsh a few years ago, although the fort itself and the buildings of the old village have long since disappeared. Most were burned by Indians some years after the place was abandoned.

XVIII

Lord Lorne sees the West

Lieutenant-Colonel Jarvis, who built Fort Saskatchewan in 1875 and had, since been in command there, in 1881 was transferred to the command at Fort Macleod in succession to Captain Winder, resigned.

We were notified from Ottawa that year that it was the intention of the Marquess of Lorne, Governor-General of Canada, to visit the North-West Territories during the summer. Superintendent W. M. Herchmer commanded the escort for Lord Lorne from Fort Ellice to Qu'Appelle, Carlton, Battleford, Crossing, Calgary and Macleod, and from Macleod to Fort Shaw, Montana. A detachment under Superintendent Crozier then took over the duties on the return journey through the United States. The escorts travelled a total of two thousand one hundred miles at the rate of thirty-five miles per day. The efficiency of this bodyguard and the manner in which the men performed the arduous duties inseparable from such a trip won the highest appreciation of His Excellency, who, in parting with the escort at Fort Shaw, addressed them as follows:

Your force is often spoken of as one of which Canada is greatly proud. It is well that this pride is so fully justified, for your duties are most important and varied. Your work is not only that of military men, but you are called upon to perform the responsible duties which devolve upon you in your civil capacities, your officers in their capacity of magistrates and other duties which they are called upon to perform, even that of diplomacy. The perfect confidence in the maintenance of the law prevailing over the vast territories, a confidence most necessary with the settlement now proceeding, shows how thoroughly you have done your work. You have been subjected to the most severe criticism during the long march on which you have accompanied me, for I have on my personal staff experienced officers of the three branches of the Service, cavalry, artillery and infantry, and they one and all have expressed themselves astonished and delighted at the manner in which you have performed your arduous duties, and at your great efficiency.

In closing this mention of the Governor-General's visit it may be profitable to recall the fact that what was at that time a portion of the North-West Territories was named Alberta after Her Royal Highness the Princess Louise (Louise Caroline Alberta), born in 1848 and married in 1871 to the Marquess of Lorne, later Duke of Argyll. The incident is preserved in the following lines by the distinguished husband of Queen Victoria's daughter:

In token of the love which thou hast shown
For this wide land of freedom, I have named
A province vast, and for its beauty famed,
By the dear name to be hereafter known.

Settlements had now begun to dot the whole of the North-West Territories from the North Saskatchewan to the International Boundary; the country was being occupied, not rapidly but slowly and surely. Commissioner Irvine impressed upon the Government the necessity of increasing the force. His recommendation was approved and in 1881 the force was enlarged to five hundred men. Since its organisation in 1874 the strength had never exceeded three hundred and it had long been evident that there were too few for the work expected of them, especially since the Indians were now for the most part settled on reserves, and settlers entering the country, compelling a constant extension of police duties. The force was divided among thirteen posts, namely: Fort Walsh, Qu'Appelle, Shoal Lake, Swan River, Fort Macleod, Blackfoot Crossing, Calgary, Pincher Creek, Blood Reserve, Battleford, Fort Saskatchewan, Prince Albert and Wood Mountain. These various detachments were in most cases long distances apart and their number made the strength of each necessarily small. The increase, therefore, was most welcome. The large herds of stock now ranging the prairie were a standing temptation to the Indians and a constant watch was required to prevent wholesale cattle killing. The following extract from the report of the Commissioner when recommending the increase illustrates the conditions prevailing:

Since the beginning of Treaty Seven in 1877, the Blackfeet, Bloods and Piegans have never been even temporarily assembled in Canadian territory up to their full strength. In 1877 it must be remembered that large quantities of buffalo were to be found in the country. The Indians were then self-supporting, almost rich, and certainly contented, and notwithstanding the fact that they were nothing less than savages, they were not dangerous. Now matters have completely changed. The savage nature alone remains, and they are partly dependent on the Government for a living. The yoke of dependence weighs somewhat heavily upon them. It is true, the policy of settling the Indians on reservations and instructing them in agricultural pursuits has been adopted, small bands have from time to time straggled in, found homes on the reserves and adopted the new mode of life, but the majority are fresh from south of the

International Boundary Line, where they have been employed in hunting buffalo. It must be remembered that these Indians have led a lawless and roving life, that they have been accustomed from infancy to regard other men's cattle and horses as fair plunder and that the habits of a lifetime are not easy to unlearn. It is not natural to suppose that they will at once settle down to a quiet and humdrum life and devote themselves heart and soul to farming. Discontent may, in fact possibly will, break out and the spirit of unrest show itself, particularly among the young men, which, if not suppressed in time, will result in periodical raids on the cattle and horses of the settlers. This would in a short time lead to acts of retaliation and a serious outbreak would follow as a natural consequence.

The number of Indians in the North-West Territories, all under the jurisdiction of the police, may be taken as twenty-seven thousand. The area of territory is some three hundred and seventy-five thousand square miles, almost equal to the area of France and Germany combined, or nearly twice that of Spain and Portugal.

The Hon. Edgar Dewdney was this year appointed to succeed the Hon. David Laird as Lieutenant-Governor of the North-West Territories. Mr. Dewdney was already Indian Commissioner and E. T. Galt assistant. In the late summer of 1881 the Crees and Assiniboines went south from Fort Walsh in the hope that there were still buffalo along the Missouri River. Although starving when they returned, it was with great difficulty that the majority were induced to go on the reserves near Fort Qu'Appelle. Big Bear, who had opposed the treaty, and his large following of Crees had for years been a source of trouble to the police at Fort Walsh. But in the spring of 1883 Big Bear signed at that place and moved with his band to the North Saskatchewan, only to create discord in that locality and join in the rebellion of 1885. The Commissioner states in his report: 'Big Bear was admitted to Treaty Number Six.' He adds: 'Big Bear, who has I think unjustly borne a bad character, will make one of the best chiefs.'

This prediction might have been realised but that age had stripped Big Bear of control over his band of miscreants, who murdered and pillaged at Frog Lake and Fort Pitt in 1885.

Fort Walsh was abandoned in 1883 and the force there under Inspector McIllree was moved to Fort Macleod.

I left the Mounted Police in 1882 and at his request drove with Lieutenant-Governor Dewdney from Macleod to Fort Walsh to take charge as Indian Agent of the Crees and Assiniboines at that place. I succeeded after tedious negotiations in persuading them to move to their different reservations, the Crees to the north and the Assiniboines to the east.

Trouble had occurred at the Blackfoot Crossing and I was ordered by Mr. Dewdney to Fort Macleod to take over Treaty Number Seven, which embraced the Blackfoot, Blood, Sarcee and Stony Indians. In this post I was the successor of Norman Macleod, who had resigned in 1882. The Blackfeet had only the previous year returned from a long sojourn across the Line and little or no work had been done on the reserve; the Indians for the most part hung round the Agency Buildings. The flour supply had sometimes run short during the winter and remembering their experience in starving previous to going south, they were afraid of a recurrence. Two years spent at horse stealing and trading for whisky in Montana was not calculated to make of the Blackfeet young men an altogether exemplary body, although they were more or less under control of the Soldiers' Lodge, organised while they were on the United States side.

XIX

'Dickie' (Dickens's son) tangles with Bull Elk

The Soldiers' Lodge was the cause of much trouble to the resident Indian Department employees. Guns had blazed in their proximity and one day a bullet whipped past a man employed by the butchers. This man, the Indian responsible – Bull Elk – declared, had sold him a beef head and then had delivered it to some other Indian. Inspector Francis J. Dickens, son of the novelist, was sent with a police detail from Macleod to arrest the offender, but the Blackfeet, for the first time since the arrival in the country of the police, offered resistance. Although the police were but a handful, vigorous efforts were made to take the Indian and it was not until he had been arrested by Sergeant Howe and Constable Ashe and forcibly rescued, and Inspector Dickens had been knocked down to the accompaniment of exploding Blackfoot guns, that proceedings were halted pending the arrival of reinforcements asked for from Macleod.

Major Crozier with all available men – twenty – started immediately for the Crossing. He found the Indians upon his arrival greatly excited. Bull Elk, they declared heatedly, would not be given up. The situation was serious. Swift, uncompromising action was demanded if the prestige of the police among the Indians was not to be permanently impaired.

Superintendent Crozier informed Crowfoot that he intended to make the arrest and that unless Bull Elk was surrendered by the following day he would be taken by force. Meanwhile one of the Indian Department buildings was converted into a temporary fort, with sacks of flour for breastworks. Precautions were taken against surprise.

This prompt action overawed the Indians. Though many in number, they hesitated to provoke a crisis. Bull Elk was arrested without resistance next day and sent to Fort Macleod, tried by Judge Macleod and sentenced to a term in the guard-room.

This clash brought the police as near an actual conflict with the Indians, perhaps, as any that had occurred, and the courage of officers and men averted what might easily have developed into such another war as those which, on the American side of the Line, have stained the soil with the blood of both red men and white.

In January 1883 the track-laying gangs on the Canadian Pacific Railway were only a few miles east of Maple Creek and by September trains were unloading passengers and freight in Calgary, where a town had sprung up east of the Elbow River and homesteaders and merchants were no longer dependent on the bull trains to deliver goods via Montana, as had been the case since 1874. Edmonton, although with much difficulty the Saskatchewan was navigated, had still to be reached mainly by horse- or cattle-drawn vehicle over the old prairie trails, as had also for a time the territory to the south, but now all the freight was distributed from points on the Canadian Pacific Railway nearest the various outlying towns. The steel line, too, had opened to western ranchers markets in the east and the cattle industry was on the high road to success.

Over a period of years survey parties had been at work exploring the various passes to determine the most feasible route through the mountains to the Pacific Coast. As in all great projects many unrecorded deaths occurred in this pioneer force. Men perished in forest fires, in flooded rivers, in snow storms on the plains, and avalanches in the mountains. Some were murdered both by Indians and by white renegades. The building of this great transcontinental highway is a story by itself, a story of heartbreaking toil and hardship, of hunger and cold heroically endured, a story of a gigantic enterprise carried through in the face of tremendous obstacles to a triumphant finish, and a story moreover inseparably linked with the opening of Canada's great West.

While the actual laying of the track was in progress, thousands of men of almost all nationalities were employed and the work of the Mounted Police was greatly augmented. Among the navvies were many 'tough' characters, a constant source of trouble, and the greatest vigilance was necessary to prevent the sale to them of quantities of fiery liquor. Gamblers, thieves, bootleggers and 'bad' men generally were to be found in close proximity to the construction camps. The Indians, too, became uneasy over this army of invasion and its peaceable purposes had to be explained to them. All these duties fell upon the shoulders of the Mounted Police, but throughout these difficult times they kept the upper hand and maintained peace. The following letter from the general manager of the company, dated 1st January 1883, to the Commissioner of the Force, speaks for itself:

DEAR SIR,

> *Our work of construction for the year 1882 has just closed, and I cannot permit the occasion to pass without acknowledging the obligations of the company to the North-West Mounted Police, whose zeal and industry in preventing traffic in liquor and preserving order along the line under construction have contributed so much to the successful prosecution of the work. Indeed, without the assistance of the officers and men of the splendid force under your command, it would have been impossible to have accomplished so much as we did. On no great work within my knowledge, where so many men have*

been employed, has such perfect order prevailed. On behalf of the company and of all the officers, I wish to return thanks and to acknowledge particularly our obligations to yourself and Major Walsh.

(Signed) W. C. VAN HORNE,
General Manager.

The Crees and Assiniboines at the Cypress Hills and in the vicinity of construction at Maple Creek were most troublesome. Horses stolen by them from contractors were recovered by the police and the thieves were taken into custody and punished. But in many instances horse stealing attributed to Indians was really the work of white desperadoes following in the wake of construction. Fires, too, were the cause of much anxiety and did much damage, both on the prairie and in the mountains, destroying quantities of valuable timber.

One instance of the manner in which the police handled troublesome Indians during Canadian Pacific Railway construction days is worth relating. A large Cree camp, of which Chiefs Piapot and Long Man were the heads, sat down squarely on the line of construction and halted the advance. They announced that they were there to stay and that they would not allow the work to continue. The railway authorities appealed to the Lieutenant-Governor, who communicated with the nearest police post and asked them to move the Indians.

A sergeant and two men went to the camp and gave the Indians half an hour to move, promising should they fail to do so to pull down the tents. The Indians threatened and wasted some powder but showed no intention of moving, so the three men proceeded calmly to flatten the tents, being apparently quite uninterested in any demonstrations by the Indians.

This was enough. The camp came down in a hurry and not a hand was lifted against the dauntless trio by the swarm of angry Crees surrounding them.

Strikes among the men on the work were frequent and these were also usually settled by the police. Undoubtedly the force was an important factor in making possible the rapid advance and completion of the Canadian Pacific Railway.

Sir Cecil Edward Denny, circa 1910.

XX

Old Man's River swallows a town

The Old Man's River had by 1883 about completed the destruction of Macleod village and was undermining the fort itself. A new fort was therefore built on the bench land and its present site in 1884 and the original abandoned. The need for a stockade was ended and the new fort was an open square, comfortable both for men and horses, in great contrast to the old cottonwood stockade built in 1874 with its mud floors and roof. It utterly disappeared this year and the Old Man's River today rolls over the site of the first fort built by the North-West Mounted Police in the present province of Alberta in those wild days more than half a century ago. The old nine-pound guns brought across the plains in 1874 at much cost in toil and horseflesh were also moved for the first time since placed in the old fort in 1874. While the fort was being built, construction was begun also on a number of buildings a little to the east and the new town of Macleod came into being. There was also a great contrast between the old mud-roofed log buildings of the first town and the neat lumber structures of the new.

Macleod had boasted a newspaper, the *Macleod Gazette*, founded and edited by a former police constable, C. E. D. Wood, in 1882. This was the second newspaper published in Alberta, the *Edmonton Bulletin*, owned and edited by Frank Oliver, being the first. It was established in the previous year. The *Calgary Herald* commenced publication in 1883.

It might be said that the official history of Alberta commenced in 1882, when Rupert's Land was organized into four provisional districts: Alberta, Saskatchewan, Assiniboia and Athabasca. In 1875 a separate legislative body under a lieutenant-governor was given the Territories. Provision was made for elected representatives in the North-West Council. When any district of one thousand square miles contained a white population of one thousand souls, an election might be held and a parliamentary representative sent to the Council. In 1876 the Hon. David Laird was appointed Lieutenant-Governor of the Territories and the first session of the North-West Council was held at Swan River on 8th March 1877.

In 1883 on the building of the Canadian Pacific Railway, Regina was founded and became the capital of the North-West Territory, with the Hon. Edgar Dewdney succeeding the Hon. David Laird as Lieutenant-Governor. Six elected members met in the Council that year, viz: Frank Oliver, Edmonton; D. H. MacDowall, Lorne; John C. Hamilton, Broadview; T. W. Jackson, Qu'Appelle; William White, Regina; and James Ross, Moose Jaw. In the year 1884 sixty justices of the peace were appointed. There were seventeen Protestant and eleven Roman Catholic schools in operation. The towns of Regina and Calgary were incorporated and permits were issued for nine thousand nine hundred and eight gallons of liquor by the Lieutenant-Governor.

The year 1884 also marks the beginning of the long fight for representative government between the elected and appointed members of the Government, for control of school lands, increased subsidies from the Dominion, opposition to railroad land grants, and responsible government. *Bona fide* residents and householders resident in a district for at least twelve months were entitled to vote.

When a district reached two thousand population it became entitled to two members. Any person qualified to vote was eligible for election. When the elected members numbered twenty-one, the Council then existing should cease and the elected members form the Legislative Assembly of the North-West Territories with all the powers vested in the Council. Assembly members were elected for two years. There was no provision in the Act for representation to the Dominion Parliament.

The clause relating to schools provided that as soon as any system of taxation should be adopted in a district, the Lieutenant-Governor, with the consent of the Council of Assembly, should pass all necessary ordinances in respect to education, but it also provided that a majority of the ratepayers might establish such schools as they thought fit and make the necessary assessment and collection of rates therefor, whether Protestant or Roman Catholic.

In 1882 regulations for homestead grants came into force. These were very liberal and calculated to promote settlement. Any British subject, the head of a family or of the age of twenty-one years, was entitled to take up a free homestead of one hundred and sixty acres upon payment of a fee of ten dollars, and another quarter section as a pre-emption. Cultivation and five years' residence entitled him to a patent. Residence requirements were afterwards reduced to three years, with six months' absence allowed in each year. The homesteader might purchase his pre-emption at one dollar per acre upon completion of his homestead duties.

'In 1880,' to quote from an early history of the future Alberta capital:

> the town of Edmonton consisted of only five white families and a number of half-breeds, but people were beginning to be attracted there and soon what was known as claim-jumping began to worry the few original inhabitants. As the country was unsurveyed, the settlers had no actual rights in the land and the newcomers attempted to squat and build themselves shacks

wherever they fancied. This led to the election of a vigilance committee, with Mr. Matthew McCauley, a sturdy pioneer, as its captain. Whenever a newcomer attempted to squat on land already claimed, he was promptly warned, and if he still persisted, the committee proceeded to throw his shack over the river bank into what was called the Vigilantes' Depository. This action was highly exciting at times but proved effective.

In 1883 the Canadian Pacific reached Calgary and all freight was teamed from there to Edmonton. There was also a weekly stage coach. The passenger rate for a quick journey – 'express' – was one hundred dollars.

By 1883, according to Dr. George Roy, an old-timer in Edmonton, there were between thirty-five and forty houses. In all the region between Calgary and Edmonton, except about the crossing of the Red Deer, there was no white settlement. The village grew into a town, and in 1891 the Canadian Pacific put on a regular service over their Calgary and Edmonton branch between the two points and, while the trip took two days, it was a vast improvement over the ox-trail. Shipments of grain and cattle went over the new road, the first real outlet for the agricultural resources of the north country. Lots on Jasper Avenue, now worth thousands, were sold for as little as seven dollars.

The days of the Hudson's Bay Company's trading monopoly were over, although besides the cash payment of three hundred thousand pounds, they were given one-twentieth of the land south of the North and main Saskatchewan rivers in settlement of their claims.

A striking illustration of the changes wrought by time is furnished by the values of furs in the eighties as contrasted with those of forty years later. Here are some illuminating figures of prevailing prices paid by traders for skins in 1884–5:

Beaver, $2.50 to $5.50; lynx, $1.50 to $2.50; mink, 75c. to $1.25; fisher, $4.50 to $6.00, though an occasional prime pelt of the highest quality might bring as much as $7.50; ermine – the best, 12 ½c.; muskrat, 4c. to 20c., the latter the highest price for the largest, heavily furred, prime spring pelts; badger, 75c. to $1.50; skunk, 75c.; coyote, 75c. to $1.00; wolf, $2.00 to $3.00; wolverine, $2.50 to $3.50; red fox (top), $1.50; cross fox, $3.00 to $15.00.

Of the commoner furs, otter was most valuable, being priced at $8.00 to $10.00, or possibly $12.00 for the best. A prime, dark, well-furred otter was a princely skin and one most prized by the Indians, and a beautiful otter skin double (that is, unslit) looped like a cuff, open at the top, adorning the head of an Indian, singled out the wearer as a person of wealth and distinction.

The silver fox (then extremely rare and found only in a wild state) topped the list, having a value, according to quality, of $50.00 to $75.00. A prime buffalo robe was worth $3.00.

Fur values since that date have catapulted in most cases to ten times these figures, and frequently much more. A beautiful fisher skin was sold some years ago for $500.00 and a single silver fox pelt has brought as much as $2,000.00. Mink have reached $30.00 or more and various other skins have scaled similar heights. It is doubtful if any other article of commerce has seen such phenomenal rises in value in recent years as have furs.

During the years 1882 and '83 the liquor business flourished, more particularly in Calgary, and the police found it most difficult to secure sufficient evidence for conviction, owing principally to the number of permits granted. Liquor was now seldom traded to the Indians; it was more profitable to dispose of it to white men in the towns now springing up along the line of the Canadian Pacific Railway.

The site of the present city of Lethbridge had until 1884 gone under the name of Coal Banks. It was owned by the North-West Coal and Navigation Company, of which E. T. Galt was manager. The stockholders were principally English capitalists. This company, during the building of the Canadian Pacific, had done a large coal business with that railway, shipping coal in barges down the river to Medicine Hat, but the present mines were not then developed and only a few miners had been employed. In 1885 the branch from Lethbridge to Dunmore on the main line of the Canadian Pacific Railway near Medicine Hat was finished, and with the railroad came the settlers. In the following year Lethbridge had a population of one thousand and buildings went up in all directions. When the town site was surveyed and laid out in 1884, the question of naming it arose. 'Coal Banks' was discarded and Government was petitioned to change the name to Coleridge. This was thought inexpedient as there was already a town of that name in Ontario. Then the coal company, really the founder of the town, offered to name it after its president, William Lethbridge, of London, England. There was no objection to this, so Lethbridge it became.

Lethbridge has grown into an important city, noted not only for the output and quality of the coal mined there but for the wealth of the surrounding country, now one of the most thickly-settled and best farming sections in southern Alberta.

I have been at pains to record how the leading cities of Alberta were named. It seems well that this should be done, that the beginnings as well as the naming of these places should be recorded, for as the years go by less and less will be remembered of their origin. I have often thought it a pity that more of the Indian names for prominent towns were not retained. Many of these were most appropriate and in most cases far more musical than the translations into English, such as Moose Jaw, Medicine Hat and others.

The duties of the police during 1883 and 1884 were extremely heavy. The field of their operations had been greatly extended and, as all over the country settlers were entering in large numbers, crime was much more prevalent. During 1884 five murders were recorded, two by Indians, two by white men and one by a Negro. The hanging of the last was the first execution to take place at Calgary.

XXI

A brutal murder and Calgary's first hanging

This murder was a particularly cold-blooded one. Late one night it was reported to Superintendent Steele, commanding at Calgary, that a man named Adams had committed suicide in the town. Inspector Dowling and Dr. Kennedy, dispatched to the store where he was employed to examine the body, decided that it was a case of murder and not suicide. A Negro named Williams had been seen in conversation with Adams earlier in the evening. He was trailed by Sergeant-Major Lake through the freshly fallen snow to the yard behind the Cochrane Ranch Company's butcher shop where, hidden under the corner of a hayrack, a leather glove stuffed with bills was picked up. A few minutes later he was arrested and the mate to the glove and a blood-stained razor were found in his shack. Stains on his clothing he explained as made by some beef he had been carrying, but the evidence against him was too direct and he ultimately confessed.

Calgary, first located east of the Elbow River, had by 1883 become a quite thriving town. Land originally taken by myself as a homestead but which had passed to the ownership of Major John

Stewart, was first selected by the Canadian Pacific Railway as their town site. However, the figure placed upon it was too high to suit the railway authorities and they went across the Elbow to the west side and built a permanent station and freight shed, with the result that the whole town followed. For some years the old site was abandoned and meanwhile the town grew into a city on the location where it has since remained.

Many cattle ranches were also launched during these years in the Calgary district. W. R. Hull and his brother brought in a herd of twelve hundred horses from a ranch they had in the Crow's Nest Pass and sold them to the Mounted Police and the North-West Cattle Company. Hull also located at Calgary, and Sproule and Walsh and A. P. Patrick near Ghost River. J. D. Geddes came in with a large herd of cattle. The Military Colonisation Company, under the management of General T. B. Strange, had leased and stocked with horses a large ranch adjoining the Blackfoot Reserve on the Bow River. There were other outfits and Calgary, being the supply point, became a busy and thriving place and was to know its first real-estate boom.

As mentioned in a previous chapter, the Cochrane Ranch Company was first located near Ghost River, west of Calgary, but owing to heavy losses moved to a new lease on the Belly River south of Macleod. This company purchased a second herd of some six thousand head in Montana and added them to the herd already on their range. These cattle were also in poor condition. At the beginning of the unusually severe winter of 1882–3, there were at least twelve thousand cattle on the Cochrane range west of Calgary. In the spring a scant four thousand remained. Dead bodies were heaped in every coulee; some of the long ravines were so filled with carcasses that a man could go from top to bottom throughout the entire length and never step off a dead body. Indians made very good wages for some time skinning the animals at twenty-five cents each.

Shortly after the arrival of the first herd, Colonel Walker resigned as manager of the Cochrane ranch and was succeeded by Frank White, a railroad man with little experience of stock.

Other large ranchers brought in thousands of cattle in '82 and '83. Fred Stimson, manager of the Bar U, sent Tom Lynch to Lost River, Idaho, for cattle to stock his range. He also imported twenty-one head of thoroughbred bulls. Lynch purchased a herd of three thousand, leaving Lost River in May and arriving at High River in September. He brought with him a coloured man named John Ware who became a noted character among the High River cowboys. 'Nigger John' was a first-rate rough rider, champion roper, and all-round cattleman. His quick temper often got him into trouble. He remained with the Bar U outfit for many years, finally going into ranching for himself. He was killed on the range in 1904.

One of the greatest menaces to stockmen, as the ranges became covered with cattle, was timber wolves. In the buffalo days the large timber wolf followed the buffalo herds in packs and on the disappearance of the buffalo took to the hills. When cattle came in, they preyed on them, causing great loss. A full-grown wolf was calculated to do a thousand dollars' worth of damage yearly. Young stock suffered most, though older stock was also killed. Colts were easy victims as the mares would run and the youngsters became separated from their mothers, when they were soon pulled down. Calves were not so readily got at, as cattle would bunch up and present a formidable front of sharp horns to the enemy. Stock of all ages was to be found all over the range badly mutilated and usually hamstrung so that they would eventually die or have to be killed. Bounties were offered,' both by the Stock Association and the Government, of five and ten dollars for a wolf scalp. Hounds of all breeds – wolfhounds, boarhounds, greyhounds and other dogs – were used to hunt the pests. They were dug out of dens and the pups killed, but as long as cattle in great numbers ranged southern Alberta, the large grey wolf continued to take toll of the herds.

With the advent of the farmer and the gradual disappearance of range cattle, the wolf vanished and is seen no more on the plains.

In the mountains, however, and in the wooded country towards the Peace River, the dark timber wolves are still numerous and in years when rabbits are scarce, most destructive of game, particularly moose, and instances are reported in which a solitary trapper or Indian has become their victim. Few are destroyed, however, and rarely by Indians, who consider it hazardous to kill a wolf, which they look upon as an evil spirit that, if injured, will haunt and do them injury.

In the year 1884, or ten years after the arrival of the police, forty-one companies and individuals held leases under the Government in the territory from the American boundary line to Calgary, totalling one million, seven hundred and eighty-two thousand, six hundred and ninety acres, on which cattle had been placed. There was, besides, eight hundred and seventy-five thousand acres under lease but as yet unstocked. The holders of leases had three years in which to stock them; after that they became forfeitable.

The North-West Cattle Association, with headquarters at Macleod, was formed in 1884. Through representations of this Association, specific districts were set apart by the Dominion Government for sheep ranching, and new regulations restricting leases to one hundred thousand acres and for terms not exceeding twenty-one years were passed. Also, the holder of a lease paid for the survey. A yearly rental of ten dollars for each thousand acres and horses or cattle to the number of one-tenth of the ranch acreage upon the lease within three years, were the conditions. The lessee might purchase a home ranch of one hundred and sixty acres within the lease at two dollars per acre.

Among the numerous leaseholders in 1884 were only six with leases of one hundred thousand acres or more: Jones, Inderwick, McCaul, Halifax Ranch, Cochrane Ranch Company and Sir John Waldron. By the close of 1884 there were at least forty thousand range animals between Bow River and the boundary line and the stock industry of Alberta was in a flourishing condition.

Colonel Walker, after quitting the Cochrane Ranch Company,

purchased their sawmill and timber limits and was in the lumber business in Calgary for many years. His successor, Frank White, resigned after the first two disastrous years of that company at Calgary and W. D. Kerfoot, an experienced stockman from Montana, took over the management. James Patterson became foreman of the Waldron Ranch. George Lane came over in '82 from Montana to become foreman of the Bar U for Fred Stimson. In later years Patterson was Stock Inspector for the Dominion Government at Winnipeg.

A reputed find of silver in the mountains west of Banff at this time started a mining rush which put Silver City, with a temporary population of two hundred or three hundred, on the map. But the excitement died when it was discovered that the specimens of rich silver ore which Joe Healy, a brother of the Benton sheriff before mentioned and one of the original owners of Whoop-up, and a man named Clinker Scott had, they made the public believe, come from claims they owned near Castle Mountain, had really been imported from Montana. The boom, however, lasted for more than a year but today all that remains of Silver City is a Canadian Pacific Railway siding and one shack in which old Joe Smith, ex-mayor and early pioneer, still lives in hopeful anticipation of another boom.

Previous to 1882 all money for the Indian annuity payments came from Fort Benton through the firm of I. G. Baker & Company at Fort Macleod and was in bills of American currency. Thereafter, until banks were established at Calgary and other growing towns, the money came direct to the Indian Agent from Ottawa, though in most inconvenient form. Uncut sheets of Canadian one-dollar bills were delivered in a box the size of a small tea-chest. In Treaty Number Seven, of which as Agent I was in charge, the payments were around forty thousand dollars. The task of reducing these sheets of eighteen units to bundles containing one hundred bills may thus be realised. It was thought that making all payments in one-dollar bills would lessen the likelihood of the Indians being cheated, as they would thus become more quickly acquainted with their value than if paid in bills of different denominations. This was probably true, but it entailed much extra work and anxiety on the part of the Indian Agent making the payments, which over all the years have been made in cash.

Before the coming of the railroads, the Agents travelled in light wagons from reserve to reserve, in some cases long distances over country without trails where guides were necessary and with large amounts of money, camping at night in all weathers and usually accompanied only by a single mounted policeman or the driver. That not one case of robbery or loss of this annuity money ever occurred shows, perhaps better than anything else, the respect for the law which had been established through the North-West Mounted Police. Across the boundary line conditions were vastly different. Hardly a month passed that did not bring its tale of stage robbery, mine hold-up, or murder. Even army paymasters were stopped and the money taken, and although many responsible for these crimes were hanged or shot, crime was still prevalent and maintenance of law and order suffered greatly in comparison with what obtained in the Canadian North-West.

XXII

Border raids create an international problem

E dmonton was becoming the centre of increasing settlement and Commissioner Irvine recommended that police head-quarters for the district be removed there from Fort Saskatchewan. For some reason his recommendation was not acted upon, which was a mistake, since by the removal much inconvenience as well as expense would have been avoided.

In 1883 a policy of establishing industrial schools in the Territories for the instruction of Indian children in mechanical arts, agriculture, and the ordinary branches of education was adopted. Three of these institutions were built, one at Battleford, the others at Qu'Appelle and High River. The following recommendation was made to Ottawa by the Indian Commissioner:

> *The Indians show a reluctance to have their children separated from them, but by beginning with orphans and children who have no natural protectors a beginning can be made and we must count on the judicious treatment of these children by the principals and teachers of the institutions to do away with the objection of the Indian parents to their children being placed under their charge.*

183

For several years the High River School, intended for the southern Indians, was occupied principally by the children of Cree half-breeds and orphans gathered from the different settlements. The Blackfeet and kindred Indians could not be prevailed upon to part with their children. The Indians on the Edmonton district reservations were doing fairly well, growing considerable grain and potatoes, but among them were numerous mischief-making half-breeds whose counsels created much unrest and dissatisfaction. These people, unwilling to settle down themselves, tried to prevent their relatives, the Crees, from doing so as well.

Colonel Irvine, the Commissioner of the Police, had in the previous year drawn the attention of the Canadian Government to the advisability of some arrangement being arrived at between the Dominion and American authorities by which an end might be put to such offences as horse stealing along the frontier. He states:

> *You are aware the press of Montana has again and again published articles denouncing in the strongest possible terms depredations said to have been committed by Indians south of the International Boundary Line. Such articles were no doubt fair expressions of the natural sentiment entertained by the settlers of Montana. The other side of the question, however, as viewed from a Canadian aspect. presents a very different story. I have already forwarded to you a very large number of affidavits duly sworn before magistrates at Forts Walsh and Macleod, also at Wood Mountain and Qu'Appelle. These affidavits furnish substantial and undeniable evidence to prove conclusively the many depredations committed on British soil by United States Indians. Of the two cases, American and Canadian, ours is much the harder.*
>
> *In the first place, the depredations on our side of the Line have been quite as numerous as those said to have been committed in the United States. These depredations in almost all cases take the shape of horse stealing. A large proportion of the horses stolen by our Indians in United States territory have been eventually recov-*

ered by the police and returned to their legitimate owners, while horses stolen by American Indians, are, almost without exception, never returned. Again, several of our Indians have been prosecuted and punished, under the Act 32–33 Vic., Cap. 21, Sec. 13, for having feloniously brought stolen property into Canada. This has certainly tended to prevent such depredations being carried on, while no such guarantee is given by United States laws. In all cases we have invariably afforded the United States authorities every possible aid in the recovery of property stolen in their country, whether by their own or our Indians. If the legislature of Montana could be induced to pass a law similar to the one referred to, not only would the bringing to justice of horse thieves on both sides of the Line be greatly facilitated, but the existence of such a law in both countries would doubtless have the effect of putting an end to horse stealing to a very great extent.

With the disappearance of the buffalo and their replacement by large herds of stock, cattle killing, and more particularly horse stealing, became prevalent. Indians, either Canadian or American, were not the only culprits; lawless white men from the American side crossed the Line to steal in Canada as being safer, for if caught at this practice in Montana they received short shrift from the Vigilance Committee and were likely to end their careers hanging from the handiest tree. In Canada, on the other hand, in the event of capture they were always assured of a fair trial and, at the worst, imprisonment. They were seldom caught, as it was easy for them to cross into Montana, where they found a ready market for the stolen stock

No assistance to punish these thieves or recover the stolen stock could be secured from the American authorities, since no extradition treaty between Canada and the United States to cover these cases was in effect for several years after the settlement of the North-West Territories, with the result that matters remained as I have outlined for a long period.

The report continues:

'This matter of raids by Indians and others, from both sides of the boundary line, was brought to the attention of the British Minister at Washington, Mr. Sackville West, who forwarded a communication from Mr. John Hay, Secretary of State for the United States, to the Canadian Government, asking that a statement of the Canadian side of the question be submitted. The Right Honourable Sir John Macdonald, the first minister, to whom the memorandum was referred, reported that previous to the transfer to Canada of the North-West Territories by the Hudson's Bay Company, the Indians of that country, on both sides of the Line, were allowed to roam at will in pursuit of buffalo; in fact the International Boundary might be considered unknown to the aborigines. Indians of the same race and lineage lived on both sides of the Line and were as one people. That since the acquisition of the country by Canada, every exertion has been made by the Canadian Government to induce British Indians to abandon their nomadic habits and settle down on reservations provided for them. That considerable success had attended these efforts in the more northerly portion of the Canadian territories, but it had been impossible to attain any marked progress with the Indians near the boundary line, owing to the presence in Canadian territory until recently of several thousand United States Indians [Sitting Bull's Sioux].

That these Indians having now returned to the United States, Your Excellency is aware that the policy of urgently pressing our Indians to leave the frontier and settle on reserves provided for them well in the interior is being pursued with increased vigour and with good hopes of success.

That in the case of the Blackfeet and Assiniboines, allied by blood to each other, who are settled by treaty both by the United States and Canadian Governments near to each other, it is not reasonable to demand that these people should not visit each other, but regulations may be introduced to allow this, while any proved depredation committed by individuals may be punished.

That it is believed that no military force, however strong, will prevent occasional raids from either side, as is shown by the repeated horse and cattle stealing expeditions from the United States to Canadian territory.

That the suggestion of Your Excellency that individual permits be granted by the authorities of both nations to their respective Indians who may wish to cross the border for the purpose of hunting and visiting relatives would, if adopted, place in the hands of the officials of the two countries the means of satisfying all reasonable demands of Indians of the various tribes who may be inter-married or may desire to hunt together. A short description on the permit of the Indian bearing it would prevent a transfer of it to any Indian having no right to carry the permit.

That in submitting the above for Your Excellency's approval, he, the First Minister, states that it is the earnest wish of the Canadian Government to prevent depredations by Canadian Indians on United States territory and at the same time to express their appreciation of the friendly desire of the United States Government to act in regard to the Indians for the same end, and it is confidently hoped that a thorough understanding between the officers on either side will facilitate the adoption of an arrangement which will regulate what cannot be prevented, namely, the movement of Indians across the Line.

Sir John Macdonald further suggests that the Government of the United States, be informed of the Statute of Canada 32–33 Vic., Cap. 21, Sec. 112, under which any Indian stealing cattle or other property in the United States can be tried for the offence as if the crime had taken place in the Dominion of Canada. If a similar law obtains in the United States territories the enforcement of the provisions would seem to afford an official check to the system of raids prevailing along the border.

Calgary, east side of Elbow River, Fall of '83.

XXIII

Handling Treaty Seven's seven thousand Indians

Since 1882 I had been in charge as Indian Agent of the Indians, numbering close to seven thousand, in Treaty Number Seven and of the two Indian supply farms. Monthly visits to the various reserves, in most cases long distances apart, with my duties in the office at Macleod, kept myself and clerk fully occupied. A farm instructor and ration issuer for each reserve, with my driver and three men employed on the industrial farm, completed my staff. The Indians on all reservations in the treaty did well with their crops in 1883. The Blackfeet, Bloods and Piegans turned in one thousand one hundred sacks of potatoes to be stored for their use in the agency root houses. The Piegans did particularly well, using their own horses and having as many as ten ploughs going at one time. At least six hundred acres of land were turned over in the agency during the year, none of it by contract; the Indians, besides the ploughing, did all fencing, building, etc.

The Bloods were more settled and contented than ever before and few left their homes to cross the Line on horse stealing expeditions, although on one occasion when I happened to be in camp a large band of stolen horses was brought in. I took possession of the animals, which were returned to the owners a few days later. These details are taken from my report to the Superintendent-General of Indian Affairs appearing in the Indian Department Reports for the year 1883. Further particulars follow:

The Stony Indians' cattle are doing as well as can be expected. A few have mixed with the Cochrane Ranch Company herds, but as this company are moving their cattle south, no further trouble from this source will occur. I have made a contract to have all the lumber cut by the Stonies rafted down the Bow River to the Blackfoot Crossing, to be used by those Indians as roofing and flooring for the buildings they are putting up. The timber on their reserve will last the Stonies for years if carefully used and they might be allowed to sell small quantities of the lumber which they make by whip-sawing. They are good hunters and trappers and I think before long they will be able to support and look after themselves. The Sarcees have about one hundred and seventy-five acres under cultivation, but have not been as quiet as I should have wished. A few of the worst characters have caused trouble during the summer, but have been arrested and punished.

Now that the railroad is in such close proximity to the northern reserves and the country is beginning to be settled, the interests of the Indians must be closely watched. They must be encouraged and kindly dealt with, as this change has come upon them so suddenly that they scarcely understand it, seeing that when given their choice of territory as reservations it was never contemplated that a great transcontinental railroad would soon be built and settlers be flocking into the country. I must say that, so far, the settlers who have come in contact with the Indians have treated them well and kindly, but as they get better acquainted this will likely change and, unless they are well looked after, petty depredations will take place and much trouble result.

By the fall of 1883 instances of our Indians crossing over to United States territory on horse stealing expeditions had largely ceased but there were still many instances of Indians and white men from Montana making raids on this side. The system of granting permits to Indians to leave their reserve was found unworkable, as an Indian wishing to go south on an unlawful expedition would be the last to ask for a permit and he could slip away unnoticed whenever so inclined. Also in making this provision the Government lost sight of the fact that one clause of the Treaty of 1877 distinctly stated that Indians had the right to travel in any part of the country, subject to the laws thereof. This clause the Indians never forgot, and when they were required to obtain permits it was always brought up and was impossible to overlook.

In the spring of 1883 I received instructions to have a trail cut through the Crow's Nest Pass to meet that being opened from the Kootenai on the British Columbia side. We were expected to cut a good cattle trail, as many ranchers were waiting for its completion to drive stock into the North-West Territories. Five men in charge of Mr. McCord, farm instructor on the Blood reserve, were engaged on this work, which was completed, twelve feet wide and with many small bridges, in two months at a cost of one thousand five hundred dollars. It was a good road, though used more by pack trains than by stockmen, and it was the principal, and in fact the only, trail into the Kootenai country until the building of the Crow's Nest railroad many years later. Liquor was also smuggled over this trail and a police detachment was stationed near the mountains to watch for the lawbreakers.

The liquor traffic, which in the first five years after the arrival of the Mounted Police had been nearly stamped out, again began to grow into serious proportions and its elimination was almost as disagreeable a duty as any the police had to perform. By the prohibitionists of the community they were condemned as being too lax, while the non-temperance partisans found them too severe. Information against these lawbreakers was almost impossible to obtain, as no settler, however much he was against the sale of liquor, would turn informer, and none of the traders themselves would do so for the half of the fine to be derived by giving such information. The profit was immense, as much as a hundred dollars being realised at times from the sale of a five-gallon keg. It was necessary that police detachments be stationed near the boundary line, as most of the liquor came from Montana. The trains on the Canadian Pacific had also to be watched, as liquor was also smuggled over the rails. The mails on that road from Moose Jaw westward were also under charge of members of the force. These men were sworn in as special constables of the postal authorities and carried out their duties greatly to the satisfaction of that department. It will therefore be seen how varied had become the duties of the force.

In 1883 and '84 many new police posts were established at points along the railroad and in the vicinity of the Indian reservations, and patrols were constantly on the move. A new town blossomed at Macleod, and Lethbridge was also on the map. Calgary showed symptoms of becoming a large town and Edmonton was slowly forging ahead. Ranches were now to be found here and there between that place and Calgary, and in greater number from there to Macleod and on to the Boundary. Regina, Battleford and Prince Albert were growing rapidly and innumerable villages were springing up along the line of railroad.

The Indians were beginning to reconcile themselves to the disappearance of the buffalo and to realise that their only salvation lay in trying to raise crops and stock for a living. It was not to be expected, however, that they should be immediately successful or that they would not for many years be more or less dependent upon the Government for help and support. They had been a free and happy race, knowing no law or restraint but their own will or the tribal rule, and were now like people suddenly shut off from light, having blindly to grope their way towards a new and unknown condition of which they had no conception. Their faults, many of them as we saw them, had been virtues to themselves. They were wards of the Government in every sense, not only of duty but by right, and only sympathetic and intelligent handling would prevent their sharing the fate of other primitive peoples.

The white settler coming into the country to raise cattle or farm cared little what became of the poor Indian. If a cow was killed or a horse stolen, the Indians were to blame. Their land was looked upon with covetous eyes and they were regarded as a nuisance and expense. The right of the native red man was not for a moment considered or acknowledged, though more from ignorance than actual hard-heartedness. He was an inferior being to the lordly white man and doomed to pass before advancing civilisation. The Canadian Government, therefore, was in duty bound to prevent this. Canada had always treated her Indians well and fulfilled her pledges to them, in marked contrast to the manner in which they were treated at times on the American side. The Superintendent-General of Indian Affairs, Sir John Macdonald, in his report for the year 1883 states:

> *It is now over a hundred years since the first treaty was made with the Canadian Indians, for the quieting of Indian titles and the surrender of the lands, and yet in all this time no drop of white blood has been shed by an Indian because of a broken treaty, and the reason is plain. The Indian saw himself regarded as an equal in all the treaties made and the rights and privileges guaranteed to him have been observed to the very letter. Confidence is a plant of slow growth, but it has taken deep root among the Canadian Indians, who have learned that the pledged word of the Great Mother, or her lawful representatives, is a bond which will not be broken. If reserves are set aside, they are secured for all time to their Indian owners. In Manitoba, Keewatin, Assiniboia, Alberta and Saskatchewan there are included in the surrendered*

*territories nearly thirty-five thousand Indians permanently set-
tled on reservations, among whom, now peaceful and happy,
are bands of Sioux, the survivors of those who in Minnesota in
1859 carried slaughter and desolation to the homes of so many
peaceful settlers.*

*Royal Canadian Mounted Police veterans, Calgary, 1925. Sir Cecil
Denny front row, fourth from left.*

XXIV

The North-West rebellion of 1885

The Deputy Superintendent-General of Indian Affairs, visiting the West in 1884, made a hurried trip to Fort Macleod. Although pressed by me to visit some of the Indian reservations, he declined to do so and after a few days he returned to Ottawa. He was backward even in meeting the Indian chiefs who came to Macleod to see him. This was unfortunate, as he might by personal observation during his stay have gained some knowledge of the conditions prevailing in Treaty Number Seven. In the following year I received from him an official letter, from which I take the following quotation:

> *I have to inform you that the Superintendent-General is of the opinion that there exists no necessity for employing a clerk in your office; consequently you will, after giving him a month's warning, discharge him, as it is considered that you ought to be capable of performing all the office work in your agency, as well as supervising the issue of rations supplied from the store. The storekeeper should therefore be dismissed and you are consequently required to act as storekeeper and to restrict yourself to*

one visit each month to each of the reserves within your district and on making your visits you are to lock your office and storehouse and take the interpreter with you to act as servant and interpreter. The Superintendent-General is of the opinion that no assistant instructors are necessary and that the employment of officials has a bad effect. The instructors ought to be able to supervise all the Indians in their district.

Upon my quitting my position on receipt of the above orders, Treaty Number Seven was divided into three separate agencies, each with an Agent at the same salary as that I received while in charge of the whole and aided by a clerk, farm instructor, assistant and other subordinates. The short-sightedness and absurdity of the above order is therefore apparent and evidence of a lamentable ignorance of western Indian reservations and conditions. This, with the orders sent to the different agencies after my resignation to cut down the rations, was, at least in some measure, no doubt a contributing cause of the outbreak among the Indians along the Saskatchewan in the following year. My answer to this epistle was to promptly forward my resignation to Ottawa for the reasons stated therein. My letter reads as follows:

I have the honour to inform you, in reply to letter Number 5989, that I have notified my clerk and also the storekeeper of the instructions contained therein. This is most hard on the clerk, who has only just arrived after a long journey. I beg to inform you that I cannot undertake to do this work and I therefore think it best to notify you of the same, as I have always, and shall always, do my work thoroughly and I do not see my way to do so in this instance. The work of a clerk in my office takes all his time from one month's end to the other and I cannot do this and look after the Treaty. I also cannot see my way to cut down the Indian rations as ordered, as to do so would without doubt bring on trouble. My work has been difficult since I came here but am glad to say that everything in the Treaty is in perfect order and I do not wish while I am here to see it upset. I therefore beg that I be allowed to resign my position as agent of this Treaty as soon as convenient to the Department. I have applied for leave from the First of March, and if my place is filled before that time I shall be glad while I am here to assist the new agent all in my power.

The Commissioner of the Mounted Police and the different Indian agents received this spring the order cancelling issuance of permits to Indians to leave their reservations mentioned in the previous chapter, a step recommended by the Deputy Superintendent-General of Indian Affairs. The Commissioner's comment on this order, when reporting to the Premier, was:

This shows a total want of knowledge on his [the Deputy Superintendent-General's] part of the treaties made with the western Indians, in which it was distinctly stipulated that they might travel anywhere through the country, subject to the law of the land, and I wish to point out that the introduction of such a system would be tantamount to a breach of confidence with the Indians generally, inasmuch as from the outset the Indians have been led to believe that compulsory residence on reservations would not be required of them and that they would be permitted to travel about for legitimate hunting and trading purposes. This concession largely contributed to the satisfactory conclusion of the treaty with the Blackfeet.

Towards the close of 1884 the Indians throughout the North-West were showing unmistakable symptoms of restlessness and causing much anxiety to both police and Indian Department officials in close touch with them and with the half-breeds, and aware of their real and fancied grievances. Representations made to Ottawa as to the danger of an outbreak were ignored or regarded as visionary, but the clash when it came in the spring of 1885 was no surprise to those familiar with the situation in the North-West. Among other incidents which portended trouble may be mentioned the following: Sergeant Fury of the police, with a constable and the interpreter, arrested at the Blackfoot Crossing a Blackfoot named Whitecap for horse stealing. They were surrounded by a mob of Indians indignant over a reduction of their rations, who threatened to release the prisoner by force. Fury was obliged to leave without the Indian, but upon his reporting, Superintendent Steele left at once with thirty men for the Crossing to arrest the leaders in the obstruction of the previous day. In the meantime, however, the latter, having become worried over the outcome, had gone by a different route into Calgary, where they were arrested and, after a reprimand from the judge, released.

At Crooked Lakes, near Broadview, a large camp of Crees had gathered to hold a medicine dance. They danced for a week when, their militant ardour having been sufficiently aroused, a large party broke into the agency storehouse and helped themselves to a quantity of provisions. A Mounted Police detail under Superintendent Deane was dispatched to the reserve but was unable to effect any arrests. Headquarters was wired for reinforcements, which arrived next day under Superintendent W. M. Herchmer. The augmented force moved towards the Indian camp but were halted by a large party of armed and excited warriors. A parley ensued and surrender of the ring-leaders of the raid was demanded. This was refused and a determined show of resistance was offered by the Indians, a house nearby bristling with the muzzles of levelled rifles.

Since most of the police were covered at short distance, it would have been foolhardy under the circumstances to advance. Following a second long parley, the police drew off and took up their quarters in another adjacent house. Two days' more of palaver resulted in the surrender of four of the Indians, one the chief, Yellow Calf. The latter, however, having aided the police in attaining their purpose, was later released. The other three were tried and discharged by Judge

Richardson at Regina, probably the most satisfactory conclusion, as the Commissioner stated in his report, to a troublesome affair.

Others among the southern Crees were becoming very troublesome, many leaving their reserves and going north. A man named Pollock was shot at Maple Creek, presumably by Indians. Sergeant Patterson followed the trail one hundred miles to the boundary-line without overhauling them. A band of horses stolen at the same time in the same vicinity was not recovered.

There was trouble, also, of a serious character among the Crees near Battleford. On Poundmaker's reserve, Farm Instructor Craig was assaulted by an Indian and his band refused to give the offender up. Superintendent Crozier went with twenty-five men to the camp to arrest him. The Indians were holding a sun dance and Major Crozier decided to defer action until its conclusion, meanwhile sending for reinforcements to Battleford and moving the provisions from the Government storehouse some three miles to an old building which his men converted into a temporary fort. As the police passed the camp on the way to this building the Indians staged a sham attack, their bullets whistling unpleasantly close to the heads of the police.

The building having been put into as good a state for defence as possible and the reinforcements having arrived, upon the conclusion of the sun dance negotiations were opened, but the Indians persisted in their refusal to surrender the culprit. In the end he was taken from them by force, but amid scenes of confusion and excitement that escaped almost by a miracle culminating in a bloody debacle. Prominent in this affair were Poundmaker, Big Bear, Lucky Man and other old chiefs who took a leading part in the second Riel Rebellion of the following year. Superintendent Crozier gave the greatest praise to the coolness and steadiness of the detachment under his command.

Twenty-five horses disappeared this fall from the vicinity of Maple Creek, a half-breed who was herding them being found dead. All but three were recovered later from the Bloods and

Piegans near Macleod, but the murderer was never identified. Two of the thieves were subsequently arrested and sent to the penitentiary for two years.

The Police Commissioner found it necessary this year to again recommend an increase to the force of three hundred men, to be stationed mainly at Macleod. Every assistance was given by the police to the Indian Department and it would have been impossible for that department to function without them. Frequently the annuity payments were made by the police, as at Fort à la Corne by Sergeant Brooks and at Green Lake by Sergeant Keenan.

The Commissioner reported in 1884:

> *The prevalence of horse stealing by white men, half-breeds and Indians indiscriminately throughout the Territories is a marked feature of this year's annals of crime and the settlers seem to think they have only to report the loss to have it immediately recovered. An instance of this occurred in June, when a telegram was received as follows: 'Piapot's Indians stole team of horses from me last night. Will you please find them?'*

These conditions continued throughout the winter and into the spring of 1885, gradually growing worse. The half-breeds and Crees along the Saskatchewan became constantly bolder and more defiant. In March matters culminated in open rebellion, an outcome foreseen as early as June of the previous year. The half-breeds in that summer had invited Louis Riel from Montana to champion their cause, as he had done in the previous rebellion of 1869. He was now acting as their leader. Following his escape and remission of the sentence of outlawry in '69, he had resided and taught school in Montana and had married there. He had led a wandering life in that territory, moving at times from place to place and living in the small camps of half-breeds along the Missouri River. Among the whites no more attention was paid to him than to any other of the half-breeds scattered through the country.

Throughout the fall and winter of 1884, reports reached the police of frequent meetings of the half-breeds, at which they listened to inflammatory speeches made by Riel.

The half-breed population of the North-West was settled mainly along the North and South Saskatchewan rivers in the vicinity of Fort Carlton, Prince Albert, Duck Lake and Battleford. Farming was little to their taste, for they were by upbringing and instinct essentially hunters, trappers and nomads. Many had followed the buffalo into Montana, and on the disappearance of the shaggy herds in that country they returned, with few exceptions, to the Saskatchewan, to find their means of livelihood seriously curtailed. In the old days, the half-breed trapper and voyageur had thrived under the fur companies, but with the arrival of the railroads and settlers had come an end to those modes of existence. Among their grievances was the system of land survey in square blocks of townships and sections. Previously the land had been laid out in narrow lots, two miles in length and fronting on the rivers, permitting close communal association. Under the new plan they were afraid of losing a portion of their holdings and turned to Riel as the man to head the popular agitation and secure redress of their real or fancied wrongs.

Riel was a man of weak personality. Indian, French, Irish and Scandinavian blood ran in his veins. He was vain, inordinately susceptible to flattery, and he welcomed any opportunity for theatrical display. His first meetings were held at Prince Albert and Duck Lake. The Mounted Police kept close watch on events in the north during the winter of 1884.

Superintendent Gagnon reported in December that the half-breeds of St. Laurent and Batoche had held a public meeting to adopt a petition to be forwarded to Ottawa. This petition was called the Bill of Rights. Its demands were: (1) subdivision of the North-West Territories into provinces; (2) the extension to all half-breeds of land grants of two hundred and forty acres and advantages enjoyed by the Manitoba half-breeds; (3) the issue of patents to all colonists then in possession; (4) the sale of half a million acres of Dominion lands, the proceeds of which were to be expended on building schools, hospitals and similar institutions in the half-breed settlements and in equipping the poorer classes with seed grain and agricultural implements; (5) the reservation of a hundred townships of swamp lands to be distributed among the children of half-breeds during the next hundred and twenty years; (6) money grants for certain religious institutions and better provision for the Indians.

Riel made the Indians believe that their title to the lands in the North-West had never been properly extinguished and he held out many promises of future rewards to the chiefs should they join him.

No attention was paid to the petition. Indeed it was ignored and the Government attached no importance to the rumours that discontent was widespread throughout the North-West. If these claims had been examined, it would have been found that there certainly was some ground for the half-breeds' grievances, more particularly in the matter of security in the holding of their farms, and had timely consideration been given to their claims and steps been taken to deal with them, it is possible that no outbreak would have occurred.

The half-breeds, despite their many human weaknesses, were found by the police over years of intercourse with them to be as a whole a law-abiding and loyal people so long as they were fairly dealt with. That when considerately treated they could be firm friends was shown at the time that Sitting Bull invited them to join in a war of extermination against the white man, their reply being that they would fight for the whites and not against them.

In 1885 many of them were openly hostile to Riel, and such men as Peter Hourie, Peter Erasmus and members of the McKay family rendered invaluable service as guides, scouts and interpreters to the Government forces engaged in military operations during that year.

On 10th March Superintendent Gagnon wired the Commissioner that the half-breeds were becoming increasingly active and that they proposed to prevent supplies going in after the sixteenth. A few days later Superintendent Crozier asked that a nine-pound gun and twenty-five men be sent to Battleford. He also telegraphed:

> *Half-breed rebellion liable to break out any moment. If half-breeds rise, Indians will join them.*

Colonel Irvine moved promptly. On 18th March he left Regina with all his available force – four officers, eighty-six non-commissioned officers and men and sixty-six horses. At the Salt Plain he learned from Crozier that some Indians had already joined and that others were likely at any hour to join the rebels. Their numbers were estimated as between two hundred and four hundred. At Humboldt further word reached him that some four hundred half-breeds had assembled at Batoche to prevent him joining Crozier. On the twenty-third the rebels broke camp and soon afterwards the colonel was notified that the mail station at Hoodoo had been sacked. Arriving there, he found that in addition to removing all provisions and grain the raiders had captured the stage-driver with his horses.

The Commissioner arrived at Prince Albert on the twenty-fourth, avoiding the half-breeds waiting to intercept him at Batoche by turning off and taking a north-easterly direction towards Agnew's Crossing of the South Saskatchewan, to the intense chagrin of Riel's militant adherents. At Prince Albert, Colonel Irvine remained two days to rest the horses after their march of two hundred and ninety miles, meanwhile enrolling a body of volunteers to protect the town, and then proceeded to Carlton. When within a few miles from that place, word came from Superintendent Gagnon that Crozier had met the half-breeds near Duck Lake in a hot engagement and been obliged to retreat after severe losses in killed and wounded.

From details of the Duck Lake fight in Superintendent Crozier's report, it is learned that he had on the morning of the twenty-sixth dispatched Sergeant Stewart and seventeen men, with Joseph McKay of Prince Albert as guide, to bring in some police provisions and ammunition stored with a trader named Hilliard Mitchell at Duck Lake. They were met near that place by a large party of armed half-breeds who insolently demanded their surrender and threatened to fire upon them. The police ignored this demand and McKay informed the rebels that the firing, should it commence, would not all be on one side. Stewart and his men held the insurgents off and retired towards Carlton, sending a man ahead to notify the commanding officer. Superintendent Crozier left Carlton immediately with all the men he could muster, numbering, with the Prince Albert Volunteers, one hundred, and with a nine-pound gun. He met and was joined by Stewart and his detail and continued towards Duck Lake to secure the stores they had been prevented from obtaining.

At the point where Stewart had encountered them, he found his further progress blocked by the rebels, who in the meantime had been strongly reinforced and had selected their position with much strategic skill. Superintendent Crozier posted his men to the best advantage, but they were in a hopeless minority. The sleighs were their only cover and, the snow being deep, rapid movement was impossible. The commanding officer writes:

> *I consider that the line extended to our right prevented the rebels surrounding us. There we sustained the greatest loss, because concealed from view to the right of the road on which we approached were two houses, in which were posted a large number of the rebels and from thence they poured upon us a fierce fire. From this point they tried to gain, and were working on, our right rear. The deep, crusted snow, however, impeded their movements, thereby preventing them from accomplishing their purpose before the termination of the engagement.*
>
> *The engagement lasted thirty minutes and although the rebels were on their own ground, entrenched in ambush, with the advantage of a commanding position, ready and waiting for us, we drove back their right, and had we been opposed by them on*

our right on anything like an equality, we could have done the same on their left, but we had to contend against the enemy in houses and in ambush. The right of my line did prevent the enemy gaining our rear. They attempted it at the cost of their lives. Both the police and volunteers who composed my little escort behaved superbly; their bravery and coolness under a murderous fire was simply astonishing. The enemy were in ambush behind splendid cover, while we were exposed. Yet not a man shirked or even faltered until the order was given to retire, and then they moved off quietly.

The guns did good service and no men could have worked better than the gunners did that day, under conditions that would have tried soldiers however well disciplined. I did not think when the line extended there was a house on our right and that the enemy were ambushed about it in large numbers, so that I did not purposely expose one part of the line to fire more than another. The sleighs I threw out for no other purpose than for cover and they were taken advantage of as such by the volunteers and police indiscriminately and if unkind or unfeeling remarks have been made, it was not by any of those who fought so gallantly together and received without flinching as hot a fire as men were ever exposed to. The strongest feeling of friendship exists between the Prince Albert Volunteers and the Mounted Police, because all those who were present that day know that no man shirked his duty or shrank from danger, but that each unflinchingly and bravely took his chances and did his work. Though unsuccessful in getting possession of the stores, I considered that one consequence of my action was to force the rebels to give up for the time the attack on Fort Carlton which they had meditated and would otherwise have made on the night of the 27th of March, and prevented the bloodshed that must have occurred. In concluding, I may report that it was the rebels who attacked me and began the action. They had their disposition most skilfully made and nearly succeeded in cutting

off my command, which they would have done but for the
steady valour and good discipline of the men under me on
which I justly relied before setting out.

In this engagement nine of the Prince Albert Volunteers were
killed and five badly wounded, while three police were killed and
six wounded. The Prince Albert Volunteers lost more heavily than
the police owing to several of them having been extended on the
right of the line and exposed to the fire from the houses.

Superintendent Crozier himself behaved on this occasion with
the greatest gallantry, coolly pacing back and forth in front of his
men, who were either lying down or under shelter behind the
sleighs, and encouraging them by his voice and example. I learned
from Peter Hourie that Gabriel Dumont, commander of the half-
breeds, had given an order that Major Crozier was not to be fired
upon while continually in plain view in front of the line. This order
the half-breed leader explained as having been prompted by the
admiration which the cool courage displayed by the officer had
excited in him. Nevertheless, the commandant of the loyal force did
not escape unscathed, for he received a slight wound in the face.
Some strictures were made on the preponderance of those killed
and wounded on the side of the Volunteers, but, as has already been
shown, these were entirely unwarranted.

With the Duck Lake fight, the half-breeds and Indians threw
down the gauntlet to the Government and went into open hostility.
On Superintendent Crozier's return to Carlton, Commissioner
Colonel Irvine, who meanwhile had arrived with eighty men from
Prince Albert, after a council with the assembled officers, decided
to abandon Carlton and fall back to Prince Albert to protect that
town, in which all the loyal settlers in the district had taken refuge.
Carlton was consequently abandoned on 28th March. At the
moment of departure of the force, this landmark of historic associations in Hudson's Bay Company annals accidentally caught fire
and was burned to the ground.

Prince Albert, which was in daily expectation of an attack by the rebels, welcomed with great relief the return of Colonel Irvine and his command. The defences of the town were immediately strengthened. The days that followed were anxious ones, both for police and volunteers, with the safety of some two thousand people, among them many women and children, in their keeping. The defenders numbered two hundred and twenty-five Mounted Police and three hundred volunteers. The scouts patrolling the district made some daring rides.

The Government at Ottawa was now fully awake to the gravity of the situation and troops under Major-General Sir Fred Middleton, Commander-in-Chief of the Canadian Militia, were rushed from the east to the scene of the outbreak. Commissioner Irvine received instructions by wire from Ottawa to place himself and his force at the disposal of the commanding chief officer. These instructions were in effect until the close of the campaign.

In the month of April troops began to arrive and Qu'Appelle became the base of operations. Three columns were dispatched, one under General T. B. Strange to operate against Big Bear in the territory east of Edmonton, another under Colonel W. D. Otter to relieve beleaguered Battleford, and the third commanded by General Middleton to strike at the heart of the rebellion at Batoche and relieve Prince Albert. The total of these forces, with the artillery, guides and scouts, numbered over two thousand men.

The history of the campaign of 1885 has been written many times. General Strange, an old artillery officer, marched north from Calgary with the Alberta Field Force, raised at that point and Macleod, to Edmonton and thence east along the north bank of the Saskatchewan to attack Big Bear whose cut-throat band of plains Crees had slaughtered nine defenceless whites at Frog Lake and taken a number of prisoners. At Edmonton, where Superintendent A. H. Griesbach was in command of the Mounted Police, no serious outrages had occurred, although the Indians of Bob Tail's and Ermine Skin's bands had plundered the Hudson's Bay stores at

Battle River and the settlers round Beaver Lake, who fled to Fort Saskatchewan for protection. Depredations were also committed at Lac la Biche. On the approach of General Strange's force the chiefs of these bands surrendered and there was no further trouble in that district, the settlers returning to their homes. General Strange defeated the Indians under Big Bear at Frenchman's Butte and released the prisoners held by him. Big Bear escaped after that engagement, but on learning that Riel had been routed and the rebel chief himself captured by General Middleton on the 11th May at Batoche, the old Cree leader gave himself up to the Mounted Police at Carlton, two hundred miles away from the scene of the Frenchmen's Butte engagement.

Poundmaker and other chiefs surrendered to General Middleton at Battleford. With the defeat and capture of all the leaders, the rebellion of 1885 came to an end. Louis Riel was hanged at Regina. Eight Indians, convicted of murders at Frog Lake and Battleford, were hanged in November at the latter place, a fitting punishment for their crimes.

Chief Big Bear was sentenced to three years in Stony Mountain Penitentiary but was released at the end of fourteen months. It was proven at his trial that while he was no doubt in sympathy – as was natural – with his relatives, the half-breeds, he had personally had no part in the massacre at Frog Lake, but, on the contrary, had tried to prevent it. He died shortly after his release on Little Pine's reserve near Battleford.

Poundmaker received a prison sentence of two years, but, like Big Bear, he did not long survive his liberation, dying while on a visit to Chief Crowfoot of the Blackfeet, his adopted father, in 1888 at Blackfoot Crossing.

Old Fort Saskatchewan

XXV

Keeping the peace among the southern Indians

In Southern Alberta the Indians had remained quiet during the winter. In the spring, however, when their rations were much reduced and unsettling rumours reached them regarding prospective trouble in the north, they became dissatisfied and restless.

Then came the news of the Duck Lake fight. I was called up at my ranch about three miles from Macleod late one night in March 1885, and told that Superintendent John Cotton, commanding the Mounted Police in the district, wished to see me at the fort. I went over at once – to find the barracks in a considerable state of excitement. Word had just been received of the outbreak of the rebellion in the north. The Superintendent was most anxious for me to again take charge of the Indians in Treaty Number Seven, which, since my quitting the previous year had been divided into three agencies under three separate agents. He informed me that matters were not going well with the different bands; that the agents were unable to control them. He feared also that these Indians might take advantage of the trouble in the north to start killing cattle and to commit other depredations, more particularly since their rations having been reduced they were not given sufficient food.

I declined to consider the proposal unless with the understanding that I should have full control and that there would be no interference from officials in Ottawa such as had previously occurred. I added, however, that I should be glad to do anything I could for himself or the Mounted Police. He said he would at once wire the Lieutenant-Governor my conditions and asked me to accompany him to the Blood reservation next day. He wished me to talk to the chiefs, who he thought would listen to me. We left in the morning accordingly and on our arrival were told by the Agent, Mr. Pocklington, that the Indians would not listen to him and were bent on mischief.

I sent word to all chiefs in the camp to come to the agency for a council, and in a short time they assembled to the number of about thirty. At Superintendent Cotton's request, I spoke, telling them of the outbreak of the Crees and advising them to remain quietly on their reserves. Complaints were many, the chief that they had not enough to eat.

The Crees, they said, were their long-time enemies and they would not join them as they had been asked to do; they would, however, if allowed, go on the war-path against them. The Agent was blamed for the decrease in rations and they had grievances against other white men on the reserve. Superintendent Cotton at the end asked me to tell them that anything I promised would be carried out.

Before the council closed a messenger arrived from Macleod with an answer from the Lieutenant-Governor to the Superintendent's wire the previous day and also a telegram for myself, the latter – still in my possession – reading as follows:

> *Regina, 6th April. You are authorised to act for the Government in Indian matters in Treaty Number Seven in any way which you may deem advisable. E. Dewdney. Lieutenant-Governor, North-West Territory.*

I determined then to again take charge of the Treaty for the period of the rebellion and so informed Superintendent Cotton.

On the Indians being told, they expressed their pleasure by shaking hands all round. Their rations, I said, would be increased and I instructed Mr. Pocklington to raise the issue to one pound each of flour and beef per head daily. The previous rations had been half of this. I promised them seed grain and potatoes for their farming operations. I told them it was no fault of the Agent that their rations had been reduced and so placed him on a better footing with them, for which he afterwards thanked me. They promised to do as I advised and during the whole time of the rebellion no trouble whatever was caused by the Bloods. I visited them frequently during the summer, they continued quietly at work and that year raised good crops. I also visited the Piegans, increased their rations and settled a few minor grievances, and like the Bloods they gave us no trouble in that troubled period.

In May I drove to the Blackfoot Crossing and found the Blackfeet more disturbed than any of the other tribes. They were nearer to the seat of the rebellion than were the Bloods and Piegans and in consequence many rumours reached them. They were in the habit, too, of visiting Calgary, where they heard plenty of mischievous tales circulated by parties trying to foment trouble. I increased the Indians' rations at this place and advised them to remain quiet. I made my headquarters at the Crossing with the Blackfeet during the summer, journeying to the other reserves at frequent intervals.

Although it has been stated in accounts of the behaviour of the Blackfeet during the rebellion that detachments of troops were quartered on their reserve, that they were visited by detachments of police, by Catholic priests and by various officials, who collectively were supposed to have kept these Indians in subjection, there is no truth whatever in these statements. I was particularly careful to advise that none of the militia or police stationed at Calgary visit the reserve and none did so in consequence. I had given permission on several occasions to Indians to visit Calgary, generally with a written permit, but the Blackfeet, many without permits, travelled back and forth as was their custom. These visits occasioned much unnecessary alarm, adding to the apprehension of Calgary's population caused by rumours of impending outbreaks among the southern Indians.

On 6th July I received a letter from Father Lacombe at Calgary, who had not visited the Blackfeet during the summer, of which I give a portion:

> *DEAR, CAPTAIN DENNY,*
> *The people of Calgary are very uneasy at the presence of a large number of Blackfeet in the town. Would you be good enough to come up and take them away. They say you gave them permission to come and they will not leave without you tell them, so please come up as soon as you can.*

I drove up the following day and sent the small party of Indians there, who were perfectly peaceable and much surprised at the excitement they created, back to the reserve. After this they followed my advice to remain quietly at home, since it was easily seen that these visits might lead to complications.

I was anxious for the Lieutenant-Governor to visit the Blackfeet and I wrote him stating that the Indians wished to see him and asking him to come. After being assured that they were perfectly peaceable and that he was in no danger, he decided to do so. He arrived in August. I met him with the chiefs and a large party of Indians at Gleichen station. He was rather taken aback at the sight of the crowd gathered to welcome him but drove with me out to the Blackfoot camp, where a very satisfactory interview took place. Endless promises were made by him for the future; some were kept, others not.

On the Governor's return to Regina he forwarded the result of the interview to Sir John Macdonald at Ottawa, who sent me the following telegram to be read to Crowfoot and the Blackfoot nation:

The good words of Crowfoot are appreciated by the Big Chief at Ottawa. The loyalty of the Blackfeet will never be forgotten. Crowfoot's words shall be sent to the Queen. All Mr. Dewdney's promises shall be faithfully carried out.
(15-4-85.) Forwarded to Mr. C. E. Denny, Fort Macleod.

Care was necessary in handling the southern Indians at this time and outside interference increased the difficulties, especially when such instructions as the following, wired in cipher, were received. Decoded they read:

REGINA, 1ST MAY.
A few Crees some thirty in number around Cypress skulking. Would like Blackfeet to clean them out. Could this be done quietly? Advise me before taking action.
E. DEWDNEY.

To this communication I replied:

BLACKFOOT CROSSING, 1ST MAY.
Will not send Blackfeet. Would all wish to start out. Could not keep track of them.
C. E. DENNY.

It can be seen from the foregoing that I had much to contend with this summer and I was kept busy while the rebellion lasted in combating ill-advised suggestions and keeping the Indians quiet on their reserves. The result of such action as advised would have taken all the able-bodied Indians out of Treaty Number Seven and started a nice little war to get them back again. I might relate several of these wise recommendations but the one will suffice.

Superintendent Cotton patrolled east from Fort Macleod towards the Cypress Hills during the summer and kept that section free from hostilities. Settlers in the south were not molested in any way.

My report to the Indian Commissioner, following, gives a general idea of how matters stood in Treaty Number Seven:

FORT MACLEOD, 17TH MAY 1885.

SIR,

I have the honour to report that Mr. Pocklington and myself visited the Blood reserve yesterday and held a council with the Indians. I gave them the message you sent Crowfoot, and also his reply, also a message Crowfoot sent by me to the Bloods and Piegans to the effect that they were to remain quietly on their reserves at work. The Bloods had a few complaints to make but most of them were easily settled. It was necessary that the beef rations of the Bloods should be increased, as they had already heard that the Blackfeet had extra beef. This extra ration throughout the treaty was most necessary, as the rations they were getting were barely enough to keep them alive. I am glad to say that I had an opportunity to place Mr. Pocklington on a sound footing with the Bloods, who had held him responsible for many refusals of applications made to him for articles, etc., which he had no authority to grant.

The Bloods if quietly handled will not leave their reserves, but will work on their farms. It is most important in dealing with the Bloods, Blackfeet and Piegans this summer that their attention should be withdrawn from anything going on outside this Treaty. There will be no doubt a change in garrison of the different police posts at Calgary and Macleod, and strict instructions should be given that when it is necessary for these men to visit an Indian camp for the purpose of making an arrest, they should be accompanied by an officer of the Indian Department, known to the Indians, and that in no case should a party of militia go to an Indian camp without this step being taken.

My reason for this is that the Indians are used to the police going to their camps for prisoners, but do not understand men dressed in another uniform doing this duty. Just before I left the Crossing quite a stir was made in the upper Blackfoot camp by Major Hatton, from Calgary, entering that camp in the middle of the night with a party of militia on patrol and great excitement prevailed for several days. It was only very rarely that any of the militia in the West visited the reserves, those in command being most careful on that point, leaving such matters entirely in the hands of the police and Indian Department, who have so far brought the Indians of Treaty Number Seven through the year without a hitch, while had inexperienced hands held the reins, an outbreak of the Blackfoot tribe would most certainly have taken place, causing great loss of life, and property, to say nothing of the cost.

Your obedient servant,
C. E. DENNY,
Indian Agent.

All the militia stationed in the West were withdrawn upon the capture of Riel and Big Bear and the end of the rebellion in the north. The men engaged in the militia received land grants of one hundred and sixty acres on the conclusion of their terms of service. The Mounted Police received none. Thanks and promises were profuse after the rebellion. I received many such, being thanked with others by Sir John Macdonald in Parliament. I remained in charge of the treaty during the following winter, with the understanding that I should be appointed inspector of the treaty the following year. This promise was, however, never fulfilled.

In the spring of 1886 the Mounted Police were increased from five hundred to one thousand men, and Lieutenant-Colonel Irvine retired from the commissionership of the force, being succeeded by Mr. Lawrence Herchmer. The increase of the force was justified by the rush of population in the North-West after the rebellion.

Settlers flocked into the southern Alberta ranching country and into the farming country to the north and east, so that the duties of the force were much extended. Many towns and villages sprang up and the newcomers had to be helped and protected.

In the year 1886 the Territories were visited by Lord Lansdowne, who succeeded the Marquess of Lorne as Governor-General of Canada. His tour, beginning at Indian Head, took in Fort Qu'Appelle, Regina, Dunmore, Lethbridge, Fort Kipp, Fort Macleod and Calgary. He was accompanied throughout the journey by escorts of Mounted Police.

XXVI

Rapid development of the North-West

Telegraph lines were constructed this year to many points, such as Macleod, Lethbridge, Wood Mountain and Edmonton, not directly on the line of railroad. The whisky traffic increased considerably in the south during the rebellion as many points were unwatched and the people flocking into the country created a demand which could not easily be combated. Horse stealing had also become prevalent, many American Indians and white men making a business of it during the summer.

Horse stealing was not confined to the North-West Territories, however, a police detachment stationed in southern Manitoba under Inspector Saunders finding the crime rife. He stamped it out and on returning to headquarters in the fall of 1885 reported that for some time previous to his leaving no case had been reported. Inspector Steele, previous to the rebellion, had been stationed with a strong detachment in the mountains along the line of the Canadian Pacific Railway, and his work, although difficult, was competently performed. He remained there until the outbreak of the rebellion, when he took command of a corps of scouts and did good service under General Strange.

The coal resources of Alberta played a large part in the development of the prairies. Mr. J. B. Tyrrell, in 1885 and 1886, explored northern Alberta, including the Edmonton district. His work was important in showing settlers where coal for fuel could be obtained. When the Canadian Pacific Railway reached the mountains the coal used was brought from the States. About 1881 the first coal seam was opened at Lethbridge and coal for the use of the Canadian Pacific Railway was afterwards taken by barge to Medicine Hat. In 1883 mines were opened at Anthracite and Canmore in the Cascade and Bow valleys, the coal produced being used for heavy construction work on the railway in the mountains. It was a great factor in the rapid completion of the road.

In 1881 one thousand five hundred tons were produced. The output has since increased until the annual tonnage now runs into the millions.

With the spread of population, the work of the Mounted Police underwent a change. Since the railroad now spanned the country and branch lines were in process of construction, good comfortable quarters were erected at different points for the use of police detachments. The long journeys of the past gave place to short patrols on which farms and ranches were visited and complaints promptly attended to. During the summer of 1884 some two thousand settlers took up homesteads in Alberta. This was the beginning of the small farmer influx and from then on the lease-holder had gradually to give place to the settler class. It was many years, however, before the big cattle ranchers and the free range were displaced and the years from 1884 to 1890 were the banner period of the cattle industry in southern Alberta.

The winter of 1884 and 1885 was as favourable a one as was ever experienced by the stock owners. Cattle, horses and sheep grazed the season through, the snow being never more than six inches deep, and came out fat in the spring. The loss of calves was unusually low, averaging only two per cent. Spring arrived in February and the rivers opened. Two hundred head of cattle were driven from the Halifax Ranch at Pincher Creek to Calgary in ten days. They arrived in good condition and were sold for beef to Angus Sparrow. Another lot of one hundred and fifty head was driven from O. S. Main's ranch on Little Bow River into the Calgary market in February. This shows what a remarkable open winter and early spring southern Alberta sometimes enjoys.

Difficulty arose between settlers and ranchers. Many squatted on leased land along the river-fronts and shut off the watering places used by the range cattle. Some only took up land with the hope of being bought out by the ranch company on whose lease they planted themselves, and although *bona-fide* settlers were in the majority, much bad feeling was caused. It was natural, of course, too, that the arriving farmer would look for the best location, one embracing a spring or a river flat, and the friction spread until the Government appointed William Pearce to deal with the situation. He recommended that the small farmers should leave their gates open in the fall so that the range cattle could gain access to the water-holes and shelter along the river-bottoms. The farmers objected to this, claiming that their cattle would drift away with the range stock.

In 1885 the Government, through the Minister of the Interior, the Hon. Thomas White, issued new regulations regarding leases and more encouragement was given to the settler. Homesteaders thereafter could take up land on any lease. Previously, it had been necessary to secure the permission of the lease-holder. No further leases of twenty-one years were to be granted, and where possible existing leases of that length were to be cancelled.

The greatest and last general round-up in southern Alberta took place in May 1885. It was held at Fort Macleod and was attended by more than a hundred men, with fifteen mess wagons and five hundred horses, the captain being Jim Dunlap, foreman of the Cochrane Ranch. The country was covered from Pincher Creek nearly to the Cypress Hills and from Calgary south, about sixty thousand head of cattle being gathered. It was found that round-ups of such extent could not be worked economically and it was decided that for the future they should be replaced by district round-ups.

> *The stockmen [says Kelly] north of Mosquito and Willow Creeks met at Shrine's ranch in September 1885, and formed the North-West Stock Association, electing Staveley Hill president, F. S. Stimson vice-president and G. Lavigne, of the Mount Head ranch, secretary. This association was composed of the Oxley, Bar U, Sheep Creek, Mount Head, Little Bow Cattle Company, the Military Colonisation Company, Winder, Shrine, Emerson, Inken and Quirk ranches.*

During the fall of this year great prairie fires swept the country both north and south. The Blackfoot reservation was burnt over from end to end and most of the grass on the Military Colonisation Ranch was destroyed. The Blackfeet, who had now begun to gather small herds of cattle, were much dissatisfied, blaming the railroad, no doubt with justice, for causing these fires. From the earliest days prairie fires had been a scourge, giving much trouble to the police, but with the influx of settlers they became more numerous and entailed much extra work.

Carelessness was often responsible. It was astonishing how fires once well started would travel and the distances they could jump with the wind behind them. Commissioner Herchmer reported an instance of a fire crossing the Saskatchewan at Lime Lake, where it is nine hundred feet in width, as a result of lighted bark from a burning tree being carried over by the strong southerly wind. That the prairie at one time was covered with timber, remnants of old logs and roots frequently dug up at considerable depth testify. We still see the process of denudation going on. Timber line in 1874 was only some forty miles north of Calgary. Today through constant burning there is little timber south of the Red Deer River. The same is true of the country about Edmonton. When I first visited the district in

1875 the land was heavily timbered. Now it is mostly open as far as Clyde, some fifty miles north of Edmonton, and beyond that still are large open stretches that once were thickly forested. In the north not only is the timber destroyed by fire but the top soil burns down to the clay, making large areas unfit for agriculture.

The death of Captain Winder, founder and manager of the Winder Ranch, occurred in the fall of 1885. He had left the Mounted Police some years previously. He was one of the first to receive commissions in 1873 and saw much of the early hardship undergone by the force. He had an enviable record as a police officer and as a ranch manager was most successful. He did particularly well in horse breeding, much of the stock raised on the Winder Ranch being purchased for use of the police.

Troubles between ranch owners and settlers continued during 1886–7. Homesteaders settled on leases, many on the Cochrane land, and refused to move. New regulations were passed by the Government enabling those who homesteaded on leases to preempt adjoining quarter sections at two dollars and fifty cents per acre, which rendered void the portions of the lease so occupied.

In the spring of 1887 William Pearce took a census of the cattle, horses and sheep on the ranches south of Bow River and reported the number to the Government as being one hundred and four thousand head of cattle, eleven thousand horses and twenty-four thousand sheep. G. A. Dennis reported twenty-five thousand sheep in the Calgary district. During 1886 thirty-four thousand cattle, two thousand five hundred horses and six thousand five hundred sheep came in, twenty-six thousand cattle, two thousand horses and six thousand five hundred sheep from the United States and the remainder from British Columbia. In this year for the first time a duty of twenty per cent was placed on all livestock brought in from the United States. A quarantine was also established at the boundary line, as mange had appeared during the year in herds from the south. Wolves continued to take heavy toll of the range stock. A. E. Cross started ranching on Mosquito Creek this year and out of a band of two hundred head of horses lost on an average ten to twenty-five colts yearly. This was considered about the average loss throughout the district from this cause.

The winter of 1886–7 was an unusually severe one and the loss in cattle was enormous. Stock drifted long distances and died by hundreds in the deep drifts in the coulees. Even the antelope perished in hundreds, often wandering into the settlements and being killed in the streets. I. G. Baker & Company brought in the previous fall the first herd of beef steers, only to lose most of it. At least twenty-five thousand head of cattle were estimated to have died and in Montana losses were even greater. The previous winter had been the mildest ever known and the ranchers had failed to put up sufficient hay. This was a severe blow to the stock industry in Alberta. The price of beef took a considerable drop this year and for the first time cattle were exported to England as an experiment. The market proved a good and profitable one, forty-five dollars per head being realised after payment of all expenses.

This severe winter was a costly lesson to the stockmen. Thousands of horses and cattle were brought in to replace the losses, but from then on stock owners were careful to put up all the hay possible in such locations that it could be easily fed to cattle on the range during a hard winter.

Tweed and Ewart founded the Medicine Hat Ranch, with Ezra Pearson, an old-time stage-driver between Lethbridge and Medicine Hat, as manager, in 1883. It was stocked with cattle from Drayton, Ontario. Besides being the largest, it was the first of many that located in the Medicine Hat country in later years.

The first agricultural fair in southern Alberta was held in October at Macleod and a private bank was opened at the same place. This institution charged three per cent per month for money loaned and was the cause of many a small rancher going bankrupt. A fortune was made by the owner, but I understand it did not long remain with him. He held mortgages on the property of many new settlers, who being unable to pay the ruinous rate of interest lost not only their farms but their stock. I remember the case of one man who had borrowed six hundred dollars from this bank, giving a mortgage not only on his homestead but on several lots in the town of Macleod and one hundred and ten head of horses. Failing to pay the interest at the exorbitant rate, it was compounded and, the mortgage being foreclosed, he lost everything. The banker afterwards sold the farm alone for two thousand dollars and no wonder he quickly became rich. During the winter of 1885–6 Jim Dunlap, foreman of the Cochrane Ranch, had the misfortune to freeze his feet while riding between Fort Macleod and the Cochrane Ranch and, although every effort was made to save him, he eventually died from the effects. Dunlap came from Montana in charge of a drive of the first Cochrane cattle and was one of the best cattlemen in southern Alberta.

Major L. N. F. Crozier, Inspector and Asst. Commissioner of N.W.M.P.

Superintendent Crozier, who had been appointed Assistant Commissioner of the Mounted Police under Commissioner Irvine, left the force on the appointment of Mr. Lawrence Herchmer as the latter's successor. Superintendent Crozier was a most efficient officer. His dealings with the Sioux under Sitting Bull, his work during the rebellion and in fact his success in all he undertook stamped him as one of the most capable men of the force. The commissionership was most certainly due him, not only for the services he had rendered but because he was next in seniority. His resignation on the position being given to an outsider was regretted by all his companions in the force.

In January 1885 the Canadian Pacific Railway Company threw open lands for sale within twenty-four miles of the railroad at two dollars and fifty cents per acre, and in the same month that company completed its telegraph line from the Atlantic to the Pacific. In the autumn of the same year the North-West Territories were visited by the Hon. Thomas White, Minister of the Interior, who received many petitions, among them one for the abolition of the North-West Council and others for the formation of a Legislative Assembly, the extension of the Habeas Corpus Act to the Territories, improved mail service and the opening of odd-numbered sections for homesteading. At an election for the Territorial Council held at Macleod, Calgary, and Edmonton in the fall of this year, those elected were: Calgary, Lauder and Cayley; Edmonton, F. Oliver and H. C. Wilson, M.D.; and Macleod, H. Boyle and J. C. Ines. The seventh session of the Council which followed these elections was opened in November by Lieutenant-Governor Dewdney.

XXVII

The Mormons come to Canada

The advent of the Mormon settler in Alberta is of considerable interest. It was in the year 1885, following the Riel Rebellion and the completion of the railroad from Lethbridge to Dunmore, that the late President Card arrived with a small party of eight or ten Mormon families from Utah and took up land in the section south of Lethbridge now known as Cardston. Other families soon followed. These people were well adapted to develop a new country, being thrifty, experienced in farming and stock-raising, and themselves the children of pioneers of western United States Territories. They were the first to demonstrate the advantage of irrigation, as they were also the first to introduce red winter wheat to Alberta.

For a time they were looked upon with suspicion by other settlers on account of their peculiar religious and social views. The country was as yet sparsely settled and the communal settlement by these people upon large tracts of land was not relished. On their arrival pledges were given to the Government that they would refrain from the practice of polygamy and although at times complaints were made that they were violating that compact, investigation showed

227

the charges to be unfounded. They have proved themselves excellent farmers and stock-raisers, as well as law-abiding citizens, and have been most successful. A crop failure is unknown in the Cardston district.

The Cochrane Ranch, containing sixty-seven thousand acres, was purchased by them at six dollars per acre, nearly five times the price paid by Senator Cochrane. Some years afterwards part of it was sold for thirty-five dollars per acre.

As a general thing the Mormons live in village communities because of the religious and educational advantages, the church and schools playing an important part in their lives. Their farms, of one hundred acres or more, surround the settlement and it is extremely enlightening to drive through the Mormon farming district through waving fields of grain and see what these industrious and intelligent farmers have accomplished.

The town of Raymond, named after Raymond Knight, whose father was one of the largest ranchers and land owners among the Mormons, was founded about 1890. He owned at one time sheep numbering thousands herded on leased lands for miles along the Milk River. Bad winter storms and wolves caused heavy losses and the sheep were gradually replaced by cattle. As the land along the Milk River was excellent farm land, it was not long before it was occupied by settlers and many small towns and villages sprang up.

At Raymond was established the first beet-root sugar factory in western Canada at a cost of over one hundred thousand dollars. Although a success as to operation, it was found eventually that the cost of labour in gathering the beets was so high as to make it unprofitable and it was shut down. More recently it has been found possible to operate it more economically.

The climate of Alberta, with its dry sunny atmosphere, cannot be surpassed for healthfulness. The temperature sometimes rises in summer to ninety degrees in the shade during the day, but the nights are always cool. As far north as Fort Vermilion (latitude 58° 90') the mean summer heat is 61°, the same as Edmonton (latitude 55° 56'), and at Macleod (latitude 49° 12') the average is 60°, at Cardston (latitude 49° 12') and at Calgary (latitude 51° 2') it is 59° at midsummer. There are eighteen hours of sunshine daily, a circumstance which greatly favours the growth of vegetation.

At the boundary line the altitude is four thousand feet while seven hundred miles north it is less than a thousand, a reduction in altitude which is equal to several degrees of latitude and has a marked effect on the climate. Another factor of great importance is the phenomenon known as the chinook winds that blow from the west through the passes of the Rocky Mountains along the whole range as far as Peace River and are caused by the compression of the air and the condensation of the moisture as the currents descend from the mountain tops, liberating heat, and in the winter they melt the snow with great rapidity. It is not unusual for a chinook wind to raise the temperature as much as sixty degrees in a few hours.

Alberta is one of the richest districts mineralogically in the North American continent. Geological surveys have shown that the province south of Lesser Slave Lake is practically one vast coalfield in seams of varying thickness, and it is believed by scientists that the formation continues north. On the eastern slope of the Rocky Mountains anthracite of good quality is being mined, and as far north as the Yellowhead Pass, a little south of latitude 53°, outcrops of anthracite have been discovered. Lignite, also, of good grade occurs on the banks of many of the southern rivers and of the Smoky and Peace rivers in the north. In the early seventies I visited a burning coal seam some distance up the Red Deer River from the point where it was generally forded. The ground was baked and cracked open, with smoke issuing in many places. The Indians had no recollection or records of a time when this seam was not burning.

South and central Alberta has in late years been proven rich in petroleum, and along the Athabasca River and as far north as the lower Mackenzie other important reservoirs have been located. The so-called tar sands of the Athabasca, saturated with petroleum, indicate the presence of oil in immense volume.

The extent of these sands near Fort McMurray make them poten-
tially enormously valuable. In a native state or with very little
refining, they may be used for paving, roofing and other purposes.

In the far north, where the same deposits have been found, they
have been used for a century, not only for roofing purposes but
often for fuel. Of themselves they provide two of the essentials for
a glass-making industry, the fuel and the silica, for the tar sand
burns freely if supplied with sufficient air and consists of grains of
pure vitreous quartz suitable for the manufacture of fine white
glass. A process of extracting the bitumen is being developed, for
which strong claims of success are being made.

In the north near Fort Smith there is on the surface an extensive
bed of salt, and farther south an oil-prospecting concern during
boring operations penetrated a layer of rock salt fifty feet in thickness. Gypsum is found in large cliffs in several localities in the
extreme north-east and extensive beds of limestone occur near
Calgary and Bankhead, as well as many other places in the south,
west of Macleod. Placer gold in paying quantities has for years been
taken from the North Saskatchewan and Peace rivers, and in the
farther north, at Great Bear Lake, extensive deposits of pitchblende,
source of radium, are now being worked, while on lakes Athabasca
and Great Slave what are expected to prove some of the richest gold
mines in the world are in process of development.

In the early years of the Mounted Police in the West, there were
many tales of gold having been discovered by prospectors from the
south. As mentioned in a previous chapter, gold was said to have
been taken from a party murdered by Indians up the Old Man's
River. Gold was found in the paunch of a cow killed for beef by the
contractor at Macleod and a more circumstantial story came to me
personally in 1878.

XXVIII

A weird story of gold and guilt

Among the prisoners made in the first few years following the arrival of the police were some strange characters and the tales they told were often of great interest and worthy of preservation. The following is one of them.

It was my duty to arrest, with two others, the narrator of it, capturing them not far from the mountains with fifty gallons of alcohol and six hundred buffalo robes, the proceeds of whisky traded to the Blood Indians. An Indian had reported that a party of traders were camped some forty miles up the Old Man's River and I had been detailed to take three men with our saddle horses and a pack animal and bring them in. I dropped on their camp that night and, taking them by surprise, made an easy capture. Placing a guard over the camp and horses and building a bright fire, I concluded to remain on watch myself, letting the men, with the exception of the guard, turn in for a well-earned sleep. One of the prisoners, a half-breed Mexican, requested to be allowed to remain up also and sit with me by the fire. I was glad of his company, as I expected his stories would help to pass the long night, and I was not disappointed.

He began by telling me that he was born in Mexico but had been obliged to leave that country on account of a horse stealing scrape he had got into. He then for many years knocked about in most of the western territories, turning his hand to anything that offered. He frankly stated that he had been a horse thief, stage robber and gambler; also a gold miner. During some years spent in Montana he had heard reports that to the north and across the boundary line, and on some of the streams near the mountains, rich gold washings were to be found, but that the plains Indians, and particularly the Blackfeet, were so hostile that it was impossible for a small party to venture in there and remain for any length of time without being discovered and attacked.

However, he found a partner who shared with him the cost of several horses, mining tools and sufficient provisions to last a year. They took with them another man who professed to know the north country and the three started, skirting the mountains and prospecting as they went, until well towards midsummer, when they came to a creek which seemed worthy of closer investigation. They followed up the stream and well into the mountains, and found a pocket where they washed out considerable coarse gold.

Here they remained until late in the fall. They had accumulated about a thousand dollars in gold dust, which was kept in two separate buckskin bags.

Then bad luck overtook them. His partner, whom he called Fellows, went one morning to look for the horses, being followed shortly afterwards by the third man, Fred Bailey. Some hours later he thought he heard shots and started out to investigate. About a mile from the camp he came suddenly upon Bailey in the act of rifling the body of his partner, who lay on the ground. Bailey, on seeing him, fired, and although the range was short, missed. Whereupon he in turn fired and shot the man dead.

He examined his partner, who although shot through the body was still living. Being unable to move him, he made him as comfortable as possible and returned to camp, and after catching and packing the horses he went back, it being then dark, with the loads. Fellows he found had died during his absence. He covered the body with stones, but left Bailey lying where he fell and moved down the creek. He camped that night at a spot not far, he said, from where we now were. He remained at this place for several days and was visited by some Blood Indians, who although to all appearance friendly while in camp, that night stole all his horses, leaving him afoot. He was in a bad predicament, knowing that he was in danger of being killed at any moment.

Although he saw nothing more of the Indians, he knew they were not far away. He determined to hide the bag of gold-dust he had kept by him. That belonging to his partner he never discovered, he said, although he looked everywhere. He placed his buckskin sack in a cleft of rock, covering it with earth and stones and marking the place by some notches on a tree nearby. Then taking his gun, a blanket and what provisions he could carry, he made his way south as best he could, travelling only by night. He was weeks before meeting with a human being, but eventually he reached the camp of some cattle men well into Montana. But he had never, up to this time, had an opportunity of revisiting the spot where he had hidden his gold.

He stated that he had been induced to join the whisky-trading party solely in the hope of recovering this treasure and made me the offer of pointing out the place where it was hidden on the condition of being allowed to escape. The story as to the discovery of gold if true, which I doubted, gave rise to the suspicion of foul play on his part. We proceeded the following day to Fort Macleod, where the prisoners were tried by Colonel Macleod and fined two hundred dollars each, while the robes, horses and wagons were confiscated and the liquor destroyed. None of the men was able to pay the fine so they were sentenced to six months' imprisonment with hard labour in the barracks.

The half-breed Mexican, whose name I have forgotten, insisted before Colonel Macleod on the truth of the story he had told me, and stated that he would point out the cache if allowed to go there with an escort and with this gold pay his fine. The Colonel like myself was sceptical but he finally agreed and two men were sent with the Mexican to try to locate the spot. However, the prisoner led them to the place he had indicated and, on clearing away the earth and stones, a crevice was found in the rock. The buckskin sack had disappeared, a few remaining fragments only showing that it had been destroyed by some animal. The gold it had contained was scattered and mixed with earth so that it was impossible to recover much of it or to calculate the original amount. At any rate, as was afterwards ascertained, about one hundred dollars' worth was gathered up and taken with the prisoner back to Fort Macleod. On again being brought before Colonel Macleod, the rest of the fine was remitted and the prisoner released. He returned to Montana and we never heard of him again. The remains of a human skeleton were found near the spot and the few bones recovered, buried; but as to the truth of his story regarding the killing of the two men no inquiries were ever made for them and so the matter ended. Life was cheap in those days.

The unveiling of the memorial cairn commemorating the arrival of the NWMP at Calgary in 1875. This ceremony took place exactly 50 years later.

XXIX

The North-West Council requests widened authority

Returns made at the opening of the seventh session of the North-West Council in November 1885 showed the rapid advancement of the country. Revenue had more than doubled; sixty-eight new school districts had been organised. A memorial sent to Ottawa embodied the following requests: representation in the Senate and House of Commons; power to incorporate companies having only territorial rights; a survey of the old established trails; the adjustment of old settlers' claims; reduced freight rates on the Canadian Pacific Railway; the right of Habeas Corpus for the Territories; the establishment of a territorial Court of Appeal; application of the Torrens registration system to the Territories; the purchase of police and Indian supplies in the Territories; disposal by the Government of their interests in town-sites; encouragement of branch railway construction by subsidising or guarantee of bonds instead of by land grants; reduction or abolition of duties on agricultural implements and lumber; the vesting of money voted for expenses of government, including roads, bridges, schools, public printing, ferries, etc., in the Council as representative of the people; abolition of the

North-West Council and the formation of a Legislative Assembly.

Messrs Perley, Ross and Wilson were appointed a delegation to go to Ottawa and present the memorial to the Government at the following session of the Dominion Parliament. Sums of three hundred thousand dollars for destitute Indians and sixty-seven thousand five hundred and ninety-five dollars for rebellion losses were voted and a grant was made for the Banff National Park, which was established in 1886.

At elections for the council held this year in the south, Hugh Cayley and T. Lauder won in Calgary and Lord Boyle in Macleod. In both districts the ranching industry had steadily grown in cattle, horses and sheep. The North-West Coal and Navigation Company at Lethbridge was turning out large quantities of coal. The territorial school population in 1886 was two thousand seven hundred and eighty-six with seventy-six Protestant and fourteen Roman Catholic school districts. These figures show how rapidly was progressing the conquest of Canada's prairie West and, as a further development, when the North-West Council met again in the fall of 1886 the members were informed that seventeen out of twenty-seven requests in their memorial had been granted. The Habeas Corpus Act was extended to the Territories, a court of appeal was established, a commissioner was appointed to settle half-breed claims, Assiniboia was given two representatives in the House of Commons and Alberta and Saskatchewan one each, and these combined districts were given two senators. On 1st January 1887 the Torrens regulation system in respect to real estate and lands came into effect. In 1885–6 the total revenue of the Territories was about twenty-two thousand dollars, receipts thirteen thousand dollars, expenditures eight thousand nine hundred and two dollars. The population of Alberta was five thousand and the Territories twenty-eight thousand, Indians not included. With Indians, Alberta's quota was made up as follows: Edmonton district, males two thousand eight hundred and ninety, females two thousand seven hundred and twenty-six; Calgary and Red Deer, males three thousand

and thirty, females two thousand four hundred and thirty-seven; Macleod, males two thousand two hundred and forty-four, females two thousand and eighty-one; Medicine Hat, males four hundred and ninety-five, females two hundred and thirty-seven. Total: eight thousand eight hundred and twenty-seven males and seven thousand four hundred and eighty-one females. The census of livestock for the same year showed seventy-six thousand three hundred and twenty-five cattle, ten thousand and twenty-five horses and twenty-one thousand three hundred sheep.

Calgary, now a flourishing town, suffered a bad setback in the fall of 1886 through a fire which swept away a great portion of the town. The loss was put at one hundred thousand dollars, one-third only covered by insurance. However, the progressive spirit of the people soon repaired the damage and the town rebuilt was three years later considered the most substantial west of Winnipeg. Three solid stone buildings, the Alberta Hotel, the Bank of Montreal and the Alexander Block, were erected and building permits totalling half a million dollars were issued.

Many prairie fires occurred during the year, resulting in serious losses to farmers and ranchers. One of these, started by a hunting party in the Porcupine Hills near Pincher Creek in the fall of this year, threatened with destruction the town of Macleod. It burned over a tract of country ninety miles long by twenty wide. The combined efforts of the settlers, Mounted Police, and citizens were required to save the town. Fire breaks were ploughed and slaughtered steers attached by ropes to the horns of their saddles were dragged by riders on each side down a line of flame, effectually smothering it. The individual responsible for starting the fire was arrested and fined fifty dollars by the magistrate at Pincher Creek. Considerable hay and grain was also destroyed this year by prairie fires.

During the winter of 1886–7 the first steamboat to navigate the Athabasca was built by the Hudson's Bay Company at Athabasca Landing for use on that and the Little Slave River. From then onwards until well into 1900 steamers in increasing number were

engaged in freight and passenger service on the Athabasca, but
the railroads which reached the river both above and below the
Landing at this time supplanted them and have since handled the
traffic to the Peace and Mackenzie river basins.

In 1886 grants of three hundred and twenty-acre homesteads on
even-numbered sections were made to members of the militia who
had served through the rebellion of the previous year. In 1887 similar grants were given to men of the irregular forces engaged. In
later years all Canadians who served during the South African War
of 1899–1902 were granted two adjoining quarter-sections of land
available for homestead entry and many receiving these grants settled either in Saskatchewan or Alberta. They were settlers of the
best class and a valuable element in the development of the country. In 1887 leases of ranch lands comprising six hundred thousand
acres were cancelled in the Macleod district alone and thrown open
for settlement. These included lands along Willow Creek from the
Winder Ranch to Mosquito Creek, and all east of the stream to the
Little Bow; also all land east of a line drawn from Macleod to Belly
River with the exception of the small leases of Bell and Patterson
and Dug Allison; and the stretch between Pincher Creek and the
south fork of the Old Man's River as far as Lee's Creek, a small lease
belonging to Jones and Sharp excepted. There were several other
leases cancelled.

Stock losses occasioned by the severe winter of 1887 were in part
offset by the mild season of the following year, when cattle wintered
well on the range, though in some districts blackleg or anthrax took
toll of the young stock. Blackleg vaccine was found ineffective.
Relief came when stockmen moved their herds to new pasture. As
a whole, this was a prosperous year for the cattlemen. Large tracts
of leased lands held by speculators in the east were still unoccupied
and many new settlers, unable to procure the requisite written permission of the leaseholders to homestead, became 'squatters'. In this
year a government regulation changed the old law requiring a lease-
holder to have a head of stock to each ten acres to one on every

twenty acres of his lease. Forty-four leases were also cancelled in this year. The stockmen were now improving their herds by importing pure-bred animals, chiefly shorthorns and Herefords, although for a time the Polled Angus were in favour and some of the most successful ranchers used these bulls. It was found, however, that while the quality of the meat was finer and that owing to their thick coats they could stand a severe climate better, steers of that breed took longer to mature than either the shorthorns or the Herefords.

The ranchmen, after the lesson taught by two severe winters, began to put up hay and feed their calves during the cold season. The Bar U fed seven hundred calves and two hundred cows during the winter of 1888–9 and had but few losses. It had been the habit at the round-ups to segregate all mavericks, or unbranded animals. Some were killed for use at the time, the others sold and the proceeds placed to the credit of the Stock Association. This practice was strenuously objected to by the small cattle-owner, with his stock under fence, whose unbranded calves sometimes escaped and were captured and sold as mavericks. Their objections, however, went unheeded, as the homesteaders who were now coming into the country in increasing numbers were far from popular with the leaseholder, who used every means short of actual force to keep them out.

Kelly, in his *Range Men*, gives the following list of ranches occupying the country from High River to the boundary line in 1888: A. M. Morden, Stewart Ranch; George Lavasseur, E. Wilmot, Alberta Ranch; Morgan and Cummings, W. Berry and Sons, Breaneau and May, C. G. Geddes, Martin Holway, I. H. Bray, N. F. Scobie, along Pincher Creek; W. S. Lee, F. W. Godsal, D. A. Blain, Jones and Sharp, Garnett Brothers, between the south and middle fork of the Old Man's River; I. G. Baker & Company's cattle scattered everywhere; Cypress Hills Company on the Belly River between the Little and Big Bow rivers; Ricardo and Williams, north of Bow River; A. G. Whitney, H. W. Savery, at Kipp; J. S. Norris, Pioneer Ranch at Macleod; A. E. Browning, the Cornish

Cattle Company, Trefoil Ranch, Winder Ranch, Willow Creek Ranch, C. A. Lyndon, F. W. Craig, New Oxley Ranch Company, Victor Ranch on Willow Creek; F. C. Inderwick, Waldron Ranch Company, Macleod Cattle Company, Whitney and Daly, L. Brook, Mansell Brothers, Dug Allison, Peter MacLaren on the Old Man's River and its north and middle forks; Sheep Creek Ranch Company, Lucas Eastman and Wallace on Sheep Creek; Glengarry Ranch Company, R. W. Whitney, on Trout Creek; Alexander Ranch, Cross Brothers, Powder River Cattle Company, on Mosquito Creek; Jerry Potts on the Piegan Reserve; Tom Lynch, John Quirk, Little Bow River Company, J. T. Sullivan, W. Skrine, North-West Cattle Company, on High River; Primrose Ranch, W. G. Conrad, W. Podger, Hubert Samson, on the Little Bow; R. W. Patterson, James Bell, George Emerson, J. D. Murray, Belly River; Walter Huckvale, Main and Denis, R. H. Wilson, Frank Strong, Sam Brouard, on the Belly River; A. C. Sparrow between Elbow and Fish Creek; Brown Ranch Company, St. Marty's River below the mouth of Lee's Creek, Porcupine Hills.

The above were the most noted leaseholders and stockmen of southern Alberta in that year. Many afterwards became prominent in the territory, either as farmers or in business in the cities which grew up in Alberta. Among those who have passed away is Frank Strong, who died in Victoria. Strong was one of the oldest stockmen in Alberta, arriving in 1880 from Montana as manager for I. G. Baker & Company's stock interests. He owned a horse ranch and bred splendid animals, of which he sold many to the Mounted Police. In the fall of 1888 as many as five thousand head of prime Alberta beef cattle were sold in England, the average price to the ranchers on the range being between forty and fifty dollars.

In July Jim Patterson and Charlie Sharples, representing the Oxley and Winder ranches, left Macleod in search of a good trail to Medicine Hat over which they could drive their beef herds for shipment. They picked a route and the Oxley and Cochrane outfits shipped a number of fat, wild steers from that point early in the fall for the English market. Both these shipments were too early for the beef markets, arriving about the time the heavy cargoes of Argentine steers landed; in addition to this, the wildness of the Cochrane cattle was such that they had to be slaughtered at Deptford immediately on arrival, which tended to prejudice the sale. The Bar U, which ranch seemed always to land 'in clover' when there was any clover to be found, delayed their export beef until late in October, when they shipped the second trainload ever sent east out of Calgary, for England, the first shipment being one of fifteen cars which Sir Lister Kaye had sent earlier in the month from his Mosquito Creek Ranch. Both these trainloads reached the British market at the right time and netted good prices and profits, the Bar U shipment bringing possibly a little more than seventy-six steers from farther south.

The Canadian Pacific Railway though it had not a very complete equipment for shipping stock, did its best and rushed the stock through as fast as possible. The Cochrane cattle averaged one thousand three hundred pounds when they left the train at Montreal. These were the animals that met the poor market. One remarkably successful shipment was made very early in September, arriving at Aberdeen, Scotland, on 20th September and being sold for prices ranging as high as a hundred dollars each, the average price for the whole three hundred and eighty-six head being seventy-five dollars.

XXX

Scope of police duties steadily extended

The prices for beef cattle in Alberta at this time, although the local demand was not great, were fairly good, seven cents a pound live weight being the average. Horses were generally of an inferior class and there was little demand for them. R. G. Robinson, of the Elbow Park Ranch, bought a band of mares from John Lineham for forty dollars a head. He brought in good stallions and raised a superior class of animal, making a success of the venture. Many other ranchers followed Robinson's lead. The Waldron Ranch went in exclusively for Clydesdales; the Quorn, English thoroughbred stallions and three hundred Irish mares.

A man named Bush, from Oregon, sold four hundred saddle horses in the Macleod district and an effort was made on the different ranches to improve the class of horses generally. Thousands of horses ran wild on the range from the mountains to the junction of the Red Deer with the Bow. A great number of ranches had been established in Alberta for the breeding of horses exclusively. The cattle ranches, too, usually owned several hundred animals of inferior quality for use by the cowboys in riding the ranges, rounding up cattle, etc. These horses were allowed to run freely on the prairies and wandered great distances from the home ranch. Many were never recovered and in the course of a few years joined bands of wild horses and themselves became wild. Young stallions grew up among them and wild mares with colts became numerous.

These bands of wild horses ranged to the east of the established ranches near the foothills, the principal range being the extensive country lying towards the junction of the Belly River with the Bow and forming the South Saskatchewan. Much of this country is composed of sand-hills, with feed and plenty of water. It was ideal grazing ground and in time several hundred animals, divided into separate bands each headed by a stallion, ranged through it. It was almost impossible to capture or herd these horses back to their home pastures. Parties of the best horsemen rode for days in the endeavour to rope some of them but without success. As an instance, while at my ranch at Willow Creek, near Macleod, I had nearly a hundred head of mares and geldings running on the prairies towards the Little Bow River. Not one of these horses did I ever recover, and on leaving the district in 1890 they were still running wild towards the mouth of the Big Bow River and as far as I know none were ever captured by anyone.

Of course during hard winters many horses died, and as the country became settled many were caught and many shot, for the reason that any work horses belonging to settlers that happened to join these bands were hard to recover. Thus they became a nuisance and were killed whenever an opportunity arose.

While in the western part of Montana in the year 1890 I met an Umatilla Indian from Oregon who informed me that the Indians on the reservation of that tribe were overstocked with horses. They had become so numerous and cheap that the Indians were killing them and feeding the meat to their hogs. He asked me to try to sell horses for him on my return to Alberta. He would sell bands of over five hundred head for two dollars a head; for a less number he wanted five dollars each. On returning north the following year I mentioned this offer to several dealers at Calgary, with the result that they went south and purchased a considerable number of these animals, which were shipped to Ontario and I understand sold at a good profit.

The first recorded damage by hail in Alberta appears in 1888, incidentally revealing also how settlement had increased and how the great cattle ranches were gradually being divided into homesteads occupied by men engaged in mixed farming and stock raising. Hailstorms in July destroyed forty acres of crop on the Canadian Pacific Railway farm at Gleichen, forty acres for W. N. Williams, ten acres for Magnus Begg, twenty-five acres for Dan Martin and fields for many others. John Clark, the Crowfoot horseman and rancher, lost thirty acres of splendid oats. The following night Gleichen was visited and hundreds of panes of glass were broken. Sheep, horses, and cattle in Johnson Brothers' corrals broke out and stampeded across the prairies. Hailstorms at Kipp destroyed Long and Wilkes's promising crops and a number of farmers in the Calgary district lost their grain.

J. C. Nelson, Dominion Land Surveyor, was caught in a severe hailstorm on Willow Creek, near Macleod, and had his instruments broken. He was beaten black and blue before he could reach his buckboard, underneath which he took shelter, and he told me the hailstones were as large as hen's eggs.

During the year the work of the police was greatly increased. There were constant patrols. Settlers were visited and their complaints attended to. More than a hundred stolen horses were recovered and the thieves apprehended and punished. The Montana Stock Growers' Association in the spring of 1888 offered three thousand dollars reward for the capture of horse thieves operating in the Teton range in Montana, a portion of the money to go for the recovery of the horses.

The police also had their hands full in trying to stamp out the increasing liquor traffic. Liquor arrived in a great variety of ways: alcohol as red ink; Jamaica ginger in sacks of oats; whisky in loads of hay; a hundred devices were used to evade the law. Horrible concoctions were invented by the smugglers to make quantity take the place of quality. Raw alcohol was usually imported and the trader, once it was safely cached in Alberta, proceeded to lengthen his stock by mixing it with water, bluestone and tobacco. Instances of men being killed by the last draught from such kegs were not at all rare. The police received no assistance from the settlers in their endeavours to suppress the traffic, but on the contrary much opposition, as the following notice, which appears in a Moosomin paper in 1883, testifies:

> *Indignation meeting. – A meeting will be held in the Orange Hall to-morrow night to protest against the late mean and despicable action taken by the police in subpoenaing respectable and worthy citizens to give evidence as whisky sneaks, thus interfering with the liberty of freeborn subjects and as likely to intimidate good citizens from entering hotels. Everyone should attend and protest against such a resurrected tombstone, iron-heeled law, to bear which is to suffer worse than the slaves in Siberia. Arouse ye all.*

The claims of the half-breeds, following the rebellion, received consideration at the hands of the Government. Patents for their farms were granted and other steps were taken to re-assure them as to their security of tenure. But the very nature of their mixed descent was bound to manifest itself in a spirit of unrest and a reluctance to adapt themselves to the new life forced upon them. In the old days, before the country had been invaded from the east, existence had been easy and pleasant. Buffalo hunting, trapping and trading with the Indians enabled them to live well and luxuriously. When the buffalo disappeared, they did very well at freighting, but this work ceased with the advent of the railroad and the old cart and pack trains were gradually abandoned. The half-breeds thus found their means of livelihood cut off. It was hoped they would settle down to farming, but in this the authorities were disappointed. To cultivate small fields and raise just sufficient for their own use seemed the limit of their aspirations and they made little effort to compete with the white settlers who were now fast taking up the land around them. They preferred the wandering gypsy-like life many of them still pursue, moving from place to place, mostly back in the woods north of the Saskatchewan, trapping and hunting what game is still to be found.

The Indians, being forced by circumstances to remain on their reserves, were gradually taking to farming and stock-raising, but there was considerable unrest among them for many years after the rebellion and in fact until the older generation, which had been used to the wild, free life of the early days, died out. Murders were committed and horse stealing and drunkenness were prevalent, giving an immense amount of work to the Mounted Police. But the enforcement of the Liquor Act was the greatest difficulty. Under cover of the permit system, by which citizens were allowed to have up to five gallons of liquor in their possession, much illicit liquor was run into the country. Few Indians were proof against the wiles of the whisky trader. One of these worthies had only to take a keg of spirits into camp to be sure of making a profitable sale. Many horses changed hands for it and the Indian had to thank the trader's liquid goods for the trouble he brought on his neighbours and himself. The police had no blessings for a law which by its elasticity allowed contraband liquor to pass in under their very noses.

One cause of discontent among the Indians I have before mentioned. This was the ban against stolen property – horses – being brought into the Dominion. They did not so much object to being punished for stealing horses on the Canadian side of the border but they felt it unjust to suffer for similar thefts from Americans, the more so since there was no reciprocal provision south of the Line. But taking it as a whole, the Indians were slowly making progress in the right direction. Many of the old men were dying off, but there was promise, supported in after years, that the oncoming generation would become civilised and self-supporting. It would have been unreasonable to expect, so short a time having elapsed since the plains Indians were wholly wild, that they should within a few years become as civilised as the white men who had supplanted them.

In 1887 the Federal Parliament had been dissolved and a general election held. Alberta, with only one seat, elected D. W. Davis. He has been mentioned in previous chapters as the American in charge of Fort Whoop-up in 1874 on the arrival of the Mounted Police. He afterwards was I. G. Baker & Company's agent, taking charge of their store first at Calgary and then at Macleod. He had later gone into ranching extensively on the Belly River and prospered. At this election he ran as a Conservative, being opposed by Dr. J. D. Lafferty, Liberal, and R. Hardisty, Independent. Mr. Hardisty, later appointed senator, was the well-known old-time Chief Factor of the Hudson's Bay Company at Fort Edmonton.

In 1888 the Dominion Government made considerable provision for the North-West Territories. Appropriations were made for the bridges over the Bow and Old Man's rivers and for the maintenance of five supreme court judges and five sheriffs. The following gentlemen were appointed to the judgeships: the Hon. Hugh Richardson, of Regina; the Hon. James F. Macleod, C. M. G., of Fort Macleod; the Hon. Charles B. Roleau of Calgary; the Hon. Edward W. Wetmore, of Fredericton, New Brunswick, and the Hon. J. Maguire of Kingston, Ontario. The five judicial districts were Eastern Assiniboia, Western Assiniboia, Southern Alberta, Northern Alberta and Saskatchewan. In consequence of these appointments the original system of administering justice by stipendiary magistrates was abolished and with it the right of appeal to the Court of Queen's Bench of Manitoba. At this same session the Alberta and Athabasca railway, projected from Calgary to Edmonton and the Athabasca River – three hundred miles – received a land grant of six thousand four hundred acres a mile. A similar grant was made for the eight miles of the Medicine Hat Railway and Coal Company.

XXXI

The Territories secure Parliamentary representation

B y the North-West Territories Act, passed in 1888 by the
Federal Parliament, a measure of responsible government
was granted the Territories. The Legislative Assembly supplanted the North-West Council. Nineteen electoral districts were
formed and twenty-two representatives provided for. Assiniboia was
assigned ten, Alberta seven, and Saskatchewan five. In addition
three legal experts were appointed but these had no vote. The new
assembly was empowered to elect its own speaker, control electoral
proceedings but not the qualifications of voters, institute direct taxation for municipal and territorial purposes and enact ordinances
relating to the following subjects: establishment and tenure of territorial offices and payment of costs thereof out of territorial rev-
enues; establishment, maintenance and management of prisons,
municipal institutions and licenses; incorporation of companies
except as provided in the other provinces; solemnisation of mar-
riages; property and civil rights; administration of justice except the
power of appointing judicial officers; expenditure of territorial
funds and such portion of any money voted by the Dominion
Parliament as the Lieutenant-Governor should, with the advice of

the Assembly, be authorised to spend, and generally all matters of a local or private nature in the Territories.

The Assembly was to be elected for three years, subject to earlier dissolution by the Lieutenant-Governor. Any person not an alien or an Indian, a *bona fide* male resident and householder of adult age, resident in the Territories for twelve months and within the electoral district for three months previous to the election, was qualified to vote. Voting was to be open. An Advisory Council of four members chosen by the Lieutenant-Governor from the Assembly and acting with him, formed an Executive dealing with finance. The sessional indemnity of members was five hundred dollars and travelling expenses; of the legal experts, two hundred and fifty dollars; of the Speaker, five hundred dollars; of the Clerk of the Assembly and Lieutenant-Governor's Secretary, two thousand dollars per year. These payments were to be made from the Dominion Consolidated Fund.

In July Lieutenant-Governor Dewdney resigned to become Minister of the Interior in the Dominion Government, and was succeeded by the Hon. Joseph Royal. In the same year, under an amendment to the liquor law, beer was allowed to be sold under certain restrictions.

The first elections were held in June, the successful candidates in Alberta being Thomas Tweed, Medicine Hat; F. W. G. Haultain, Macleod; John Lineham and Hugh S. Cayley, Calgary; Robert G. Brett, H. C. Wilson and Frank Oliver, Edmonton. The Hon. Messrs. Justices Macleod, Richardson and Rouleau were declared to be legal experts. F. W. G. Haultain, D. F. Jelly, William Sutherland and Hilliard Mitchell were named advisers to the Governor and Herbert C. Wilson was chosen speaker, the aforementioned being appointed on the meeting of the first Assembly in June.

One of the first matters to be brought up was the liquor question. According to the *Macleod Gazette* the prohibition law was broken daily over the whole country. Public opinion was overwhelmingly against a law that was as unsatisfactory as it was ineffective. The permit system then in force gave the greatest trouble to the Mounted Police. The Indians, although now on their reserves, were still unsettled as a result of the rebellion and the increasing white population, and the great herds of cattle, in close proximity to and in many cases grazing on their lands, were a source of constant irritation and temptation to the red men. However, they gave less trouble than the liquor traffic, since the police because they had for years conscientiously endeavoured to understand them and to put themselves in the Indians' shoes, had their confidence, and this was reciprocated. Furthermore, because they believed the Indian had rights as well as the white man and acted in that belief, the Mounted Police played a large part in the peaceful development of Canada's West.

Among other duties of the police was the prevention of prairie fires. These were becoming more frequent each summer and causing considerable damage. Settlement, instead of reducing the work of the force. added to it greatly. A traveller passing through the Territories at this time would have seen police engaged in fighting prairie fires, enforcing quarantine regulations, collecting customs dues, watching for smugglers, chasing horse thieves, conveying lunatics or prisoners, taking charge of mails on the Canadian Pacific Railway and performing various other duties required by the several departments of the public service. While, as has been said, the Indians did not give much trouble, there were times – as, for instance, when sixty thousand cattle were running in the vicinity of the Blood Reserve where two thousand Indians were living and receiving rations – that the temptation to kill cattle was great and necessitated a vigorous watch by the police to prevent it. Had they been withdrawn, cattle ranching by white men would have been impossible.

Three years later the force was reduced from a thousand to seven hundred. It seemed at the time an unwise step, but the police had acquired such a reputation that at points where considerable bodies were formerly stationed only a few men were now required. Danger from Indians and half-breeds now being a thing of the past, police duties differed in many respects from those of the early days. Detachments were posted throughout the country, with comfortable buildings and stables, and from these centres patrols of one or two men covered quite extensive areas, visiting ranchers and the Indian bands. It was all a striking realisation of Sir John Macdonald's dream of a mounted force for the West which should be a credit to Canada.

Speaking in the Senate in 1894, the Hon. W. B. Ives, then President of the Privy Council, said:

> *The State of Montana is immeasurably smaller in extent than the territories over which the North-West Mounted Police have jurisdiction. There are about the same number of Indians of similar character in Montana and Dakota as in the Canadian North-West, and whereas we use a force of seven hundred men, who have been successful to a degree in preserving order in that country, the smallest number of troops the United States have found sufficient for a much smaller territory is three thousand five hundred to four thousand men. Anyone familiar with the state of things in their country and ours must admit that our force, though only a small fraction of theirs, has succeeded admirably.*

At the first meeting of the Legislative Assembly a resolution was passed declaring that a vote should be taken of the people to decide between prohibition and high licence, and that if the Government at Ottawa did not approve of a plebiscite, they should give power to the Assembly to decide the question.

At the second session of the Legislature a deadlock occurred between the Council, led by F. W. G. Haultain, and the Lieutenant-Governor in relation to the finances, and because the former did not approve of the Governor's interpretation of his powers and those of the Council, the members of that body resigned. The Governor endeavoured to go on with public business with other advisory councils, but the Assembly refused to co-operate and a deadlock ensued.

The Assembly now requested the Dominion Government to grant it enlarged powers and better terms, including an increased subsidy, the right of trial by jury when desired by the party charged, and authority to deal with the franchise. Resolutions asking for the repeal of the clause in the North-West Territories Act which provided for the printing in French of the Ordinances, Votes and Proceedings and other public documents, for the right to legislate in matters of education, and to abolish, if deemed wise, the separate school system, and that a grant of land be made in each territorial district for university purposes, were also forwarded to Ottawa.

After prorogation the Governor carried on business through another Advisory Council, and on the House again meeting this council was ignored by the Assembly and the deadlock between that body and the Governor continued. While matters were in this state the Dominion election of 1891 took place and D. W. Davis was again elected as against J. Reilly to represent Calgary. In May of this year Messrs. Brett and Betts, members of the Advisory Council, went to Ottawa to urge on the Federal Parliament the granting of a full measure of responsible government. This was refused, being opposed by the territorial representatives on the ground that the people did not desire it until such time as the Territories were formed into provinces. Following this a Bill was introduced by the Hon. Mr. Dewdney empowering the Lieutenant-Governor to dissolve the Assembly and order a new election; this Bill also enlarged the powers of the Assembly.

The Legislature was dissolved and another election held in November 1891, the leading issue being prohibition versus licence, settled in favour of the latter. At the next meeting of the Legislature a regular cabinet was formed, with F. W. G. Haultain as premier and Messrs. Clinkskill, Neff and Tweed as his associates. An ordinance to regulate the liquor traffic was passed and local option was provided for where desired.

In consequence of the resolution asking for better terms, Mr. Haultain was invited to Ottawa and as a result of his representations to the Government, the territorial subsidy was raised to three hundred thousand dollars, which was sixty-eight thousand seven hundred and twenty-eight dollars less than was asked for.

The death of Sir John Macdonald in 1891 was keenly felt by the old members of the Mounted Police. As has been seen, in all his administration the Premier kept control of the force in his own hands and he always took the liveliest interest in the welfare of the men and the work they did. He defended and praised their record at all times, but the day came when neither in the East nor the West did they fear criticism. But it was due to the guidance and support of Sir John Macdonald in its early and stormy years that this was true, and his name will always be associated with and honoured by the North-West Mounted Police.

Two stock associations had been formed in southern Alberta, the South West Stock Association and the Alberta Stock Growers' Association, both in the Macleod district and afterwards merged under the title of the first-mentioned. In 1889, F. S. Stimson, George Lane, A. Barter, D. MacPherson, W. R. Hull, A. E. Cross and other stockmen met at High River, with the intention of forming an association which should be the leading one of the districts and the old Alberta Stock Growers' Association was re-formed under different rules and management.

In 1892 Great Britain placed an embargo on all cattle coming from Canada, the cause being alleged cases of pleuro-pneumonia among them, but a rigid examination of all herds in the East and West failed to disclose any animals suffering from the disease. In spite of repeated representations, however, the embargo was continued up to a very recent date. In 1891 J. Christy, who had for many years dealt extensively in horses and was the first to bring any number of Montana horses into Alberta, sold his ranch at Pincher Creek and went into the cattle business near Calgary. The horses supplied by him to the Mounted Police in the late seventies were

N.W.M.P. Veterans at Calgary Jubilee (1875–1925), July 1925.
Sir Cecil Denny is in the centre.

the first of the class of western animals used by the force, and were found better fitted for the service and hardier than those previously brought from Ontario.

George Lane, who, acting for the contractors, had furnished beef to the Government on the Blood reserve, this year went into ranching on his own account in the Porcupine Hills, purchasing the Flying E Ranch. This was the beginning of the great stock interests which he controlled until his death a few years ago.

Among later accessions to the cattle business about this time was P. Burns, who began as a contractor with the railroad then being built by the Canadian Pacific Railway from Calgary to Edmonton. From this modest start he in time built up the largest packing and livestock business, not only in the West but in Canada. The country was now fast being settled and although great cattle ranches still existed, mixed farming was beginning to take the place of cancelled leases. The end of the wide free range for all stock was in sight.

Many men who have attained prominence in business, politics or in other lines of endeavour came into Alberta from 1889 onward, in most instances taking up homesteads or working for some ranch owner as a beginning. The large ranch companies were generally operated by English capital, but I know of none of them repaying the outlay. They began usually with several thousand head of range cattle, inexperienced managers and large expenses that ate up all profits. Losses, too, were often great. On the other hand, ranchers who made a beginning with a few hundred head as a rule did well.

The best-known and most famous horseman who ever came to Alberta, which is saying a good deal, was Johnny Franklin, a young Texan who arrived in 1889 and worked on the Strong ranch. He rode the worst outlaws to he found on the range and it was said that no horse ever threw him. He was for years champion rider of the West and carried away the biggest prizes at all fairs and stampedes. In after years he retired to his ranch and did well at horse breeding.

Royal Canadian Mounted Police veterans Sir Cecil Denny and John Herron, Calgary, 1925.

XXXII

The 'short-cut' to the Klondyke: a tragic record

U ntil 1888, when such an Act was passed, there existed no brand ordinance in the Territories. Brand recorders were appointed in the different districts. A brand on an animal was *prima facie* evidence of ownership and a penalty of a hundred dollars' fine or thirty days' imprisonment was imposed for using another man's brand. It worked a hardship, however, on the farmer owning only a few cattle and having no brand. It was calculated that by the fall of 1889 there were at least a hundred thousand cattle and several thousand horses in the district from High River to the boundary. Sir John Lister Kaye brought out many Scotch and English families and placed them on his ten farms near the Blackfoot reserve, with J. R. McIllison as manager. Sir R. W. Cameron purchased fifty thousand acres on Bow River near its junction with the Belly for a horse and cattle ranch. Land was cheap at this time, the Coal and Navigation Company selling blocks at a dollar and a quarter an acre. Mackenzie and Mann bought the Glengarry Ranch in the Porcupine Hills, of which A. B. Macdonald was manager, but despite the immense tracts occupied by large companies and the thousands of cattle and horses on free range, settlers continued coming in in increasing numbers, wire fences, that bane of the cattleman, were going up and the homesteader was gradually infringing on the rancher. The big lease-holders also were now purchasing land and going in for mixed farming.

Modern Edmonton dates from the building of the Canadian Pacific Railway, the first surveys for which were run along the North Saskatchewan in close proximity to the old Hudson's Bay Company post. The hopes of the few settlers were lifted high. A boom in town lots started, but on the railroad being diverted two hundred miles to the south it suddenly collapsed. The men who came in the early boom days kept hope alive. To their faith and energy Edmonton owes its development from a little frontier town to capital of the province. The Calgary and Edmonton Railway reached the south bank of the Saskatchewan River opposite Edmonton in July 1891. The terminus, first called Strathcona, later became South Edmonton. For a number of years the new town site promised to outgrow the ancient centre of the fur trade and the rivalry between the two places on several occasions threatened to pass the bounds of law and order, the most notable instance occurring shortly after Strathcona began to assume the proportions of a town.

The Dominion Land Office had been established in Edmonton many years before Strathcona came into being. The new town's citizens looked with envious eyes on this Government institution and determined to attempt its forcible removal to the south side. Edmonton, fully aroused, was just as determined it should remain where it was. The Strathcona-ites at one time even had the books of the office loaded on a wagon to carry away, when the alarm was sounded and in a few minutes two hundred Edmontonians had assembled. The wheels were taken off, the horses unhitched and driven across the river. The Home Guards of 1885 were called out and possession was taken of the books until word was received from Ottawa that the Land Office was to remain in Edmonton.

Edmonton was incorporated a town in 1892, Matthew McCauley being first mayor. The future city grew very slowly until

1897, when the great rush to the newly-discovered gold-fields of the Klondyke started a boom which set Edmonton on its feet and the population in a few months increased from a few hundred to several thousand. Edmonton has forged ahead steadily, both in wealth and population, ever since.

Edmonton was the outfitting point for many parties of gold seekers who went by the overland route to the Klondyke. They came in droves of all sorts and conditions, men and even women, grizzled prospectors, city clerks, soldiers, sailors, lawyers, parsons, with every conceivable scheme of travel in mind – pack trains, houses on wheels, canoes and boats of all descriptions, afoot, ahorseback, even barrels fitted with axles – and Edmonton was the point of departure. Goods of every description were in demand and the merchant reaped a rich harvest. Others came to share this golden opportunity, went into business and remained, and so the Klondyke gold-rush was the making of modern Edmonton. Had this not occurred, Strathcona might have been the principal city; as it is, Strathcona is South Edmonton and a part of the city.

The rush to the Klondyke by the overland route through Edmonton spelled tragedy for many a poor fellow. Men unused to hardship, unprepared, with useless transport, excess of baggage, inadequately provisioned and with clothing utterly unsuited to a winter or even summer, in the northern wilds, joined the stampede. Many of them were childishly ignorant of what lay before them, how or by what route they would reach their destination. Some were even known to draw a line on the map from Edmonton to Dawson and say, 'Oh, that's easy.'

Those with pack horses found after going a certain distance north that all trails ceased. Miles on miles of swamps and muskegs stretched ahead; horses were abandoned and they plodded on afoot, packing what they could on their backs. Few ever reached the Klondyke. They went up the Peace River to the Liard and the Pelly and even down the great Mackenzie, and many left their bones in the forests and swamps of the north. They scattered to the four winds, some crossing the mountains by the Peace River Pass, to find themselves at last on the Pacific coast but far away from their objective. Many managed to return over the way they had gone but broken in health and with empty pockets. Some got no farther, if as far, as Athabasca Landing, only a hundred miles north of Edmonton, and they were the fortunate ones. Their effects – wagons, buggies, sacks of flour, guns and ammunition, blankets, clothing, patent stoves and tents – were strewn along the ways they travelled for hundreds of miles in the north. The Beaver Indians on the Upper Peace, the Dog Ribs on the Pelly and the Crees everywhere beyond the North Saskatchewan had fat pickings for years after they had passed.

Hundreds of horses were left. Some died during the winter, others were killed by wolves and still others taken and used by the Indians. Not a few, running wild in the woods, were in evidence for years afterwards.

Some of these wild animals became a nuisance. For instance, while I was in charge of the Mounted Police pack-train of fifty horses with the party cutting the Peace River – Yukon trail in 1904, I camped one night at a creek near the Finlay River. The horses, after being unloaded, were hobbled and turned out to graze. During the night we were awakened by a tremendous commotion among our pack animals. Tired though we were, all had to turn out, thinking the herd had been stampeded by bears, which were numerous. We found that a band of wild horses had rushed among our animals, squealing, kicking, and making a terrible uproar. One of these outlaws I shot. He was a great, ragged, rawboned beast. Several more shots were fired before they were driven off and a day was lost in rounding up our herd, which was scattered through the timber for miles. A number of the animals were badly injured.

On this expedition we frequently came across old tumbledown cabins, windowless, poorly constructed and often containing the bleaching bones of some poor creature who had tried to pass the winter there. Scurvy was the malady of which most died, I have been told by survivors. Men herded in these small cabins seldom took any exercise, brooded over their troubles, and being lost in the wilderness and without fresh vegetables, they fell an easy prey to the disease. Often we stumbled upon such a cabin buried deep in the woods far from any trail with the mute evidence of tragedy in the skeleton outside where it had no doubt been dragged by wild animals, and it was not difficult to reconstruct the gruesome details.

Unscrupulous concerns advertised this overland route as an easy road to the Klondyke all over the world, directing their dupes to Edmonton where supplies and full information could he obtained, and dozens died a miserable death in the pitiless north before learning how greatly they had been misled. True, many were cautioned by the police and others to avoid this route but few followed the advice. Profiting from the tragic record of the Klondyke rush by the overland trail, the authorities have since intercepted parties going into the far north and unless they are physically fit and have supplies sufficient for at least a year, they are not allowed to proceed. Against those who for gain advertised in glowing colours the advantages of this route, thereby sending many to their deaths, there will always stand an indictment of inhuman indifference toward their fellow men.

As illustrating the hardships undergone by those who followed the Edmonton route to the Klondyke, the experiences of a party who attempted it, told by one of their number, may here be set down.

Mr. Crawford, the narrator, was living in Chippewa Falls, Wisconsin, when news of the fabulous discoveries in the Klondyke reached him. He purchased a ticket in St. Paul over the Soo line for Seattle. The train was crowded with people bound for the new gold-fields. Most of those on the train by which Mr. Crawford travelled were going to rush into the Klondyke by an admirable route that they had drawn on their pocket maps. It began at Edmonton and reached the promised land via the Athabasca, Great Slave Lake, Mackenzie and Liard rivers to the Divide and down the other side to the Yukon. This route they called 'the short-cut.' It looked good to them on the map, the only one worth considering. Mr. Crawford threw in his lot with this party and they branched off for Edmonton. Here they tossed their tickets to Seattle to the winds and embarked enthusiastically on 'the short-cut'. It proved a short-cut to untold privation, suffering and death, a short-cut along which young men in the flower of manhood died like sheep and others lost their reason.

The start from Edmonton was made early in April 1898. The party followed the Athabasca and Slave rivers to Great Slave Lake and across the lake to the Mackenzie River, four hundred miles down the Mackenzie to the mouth of the Liard and thence up that river hundreds of miles to the Divide. Mr. Crawford's description of the country as far as the Mackenzie River pictures it as well watered territory with a fertile soil upon which almost anything would grow. At Fort Simpson, in latitude sixty-two degrees north, they saw fine beds of cucumbers, while crops of wheat and barley were ripening at the beginning of August.

North of the Liard they passed through a low, level country, in places heavily timbered. The lakes and rivers teemed with trout and other varieties of fish. Ducks and geese were everywhere, while in the forests bears, moose, cariboo and other big game abounded.

Their troubles commenced with the start of their ascent of the Liard. The Liard is a broad and swift stream. Until they reached its mouth they had been going with the current, but thereafter the water was against them. Portage succeeded portage and rapid rapid. 'Tracking' had frequently to be resorted to. It was labour to try men's souls. Winter overtook them on the Liard. They had two years' supply of food, clothing and prospecting equipment with them, but weakened by the strenuous day by day toil and hardship, they had to abandon a large part of these supplies.

Scurvy broke out among them and, of the five men in the party, three died within three weeks and one went insane and was left with the authorities at a post on the Liard.

Of what was known as the Hamilton party, numbering eight

powerfully-built men including A. D. Stewart, chief of the police force of that city, only one survived.

Finally these parties, which had so far journeyed separately, after struggling to the headwaters of the Liard, crossed the Divide at the Dease River and having insufficient supplies to continue to the Klondyke country, the remnants banded together and headed for the Stikene and the coast, whence they caught a steamer to Vancouver, the place from which they should have started. They reached Vancouver in September 1899, over twenty-one months from the time they had left Edmonton, or more than eighteen months after they should have reached the Klondyke had they gone via Seattle or Vancouver. From Vancouver the survivors of the two parties turned east, satisfied to be alive and with no further desire to seek their fortunes amid the glacial waters of the Yukon and its tributaries.

XXXIII

The Indian trades his scalping knife for a plough

After the second general election of the Territorial Legislature in 1891, the Lieutenant-Governor no longer had a seat in that Assembly and regular parliamentary government was established. Messrs. Haultain, Clinkskill, Neff and Tweed comprised the executive. The Dominion subsidy was increased to a hundred and ninety-three thousand two hundred dollars. In his closing message to the Legislature in 1892, the Hon. Joseph Royal, Lieutenant-Governor of the North-West Territories, said: 'The Legislature today enjoys all the rights and privileges of self-government.' This was the conclusion of Governor Royal's term of office and he was succeeded in the following year by the Hon. C. H. Mackintosh.

The number of schools in the Territories this year was seventy-two, with eight thousand pupils. In Alberta under the British North America Act, which provided that one-eighteenth of all land in the North-West Territories be allocated for the benefit of education in Canada, over seven million acres were so reserved. This land was sold from time to time, the proceeds being placed in a school land fund. These lands could not be leased for farming but permits might be granted for coal mining, grazing and to cut timber. All moneys realised from the sale or leasing of school lands were to be invested in Canadian securities and the interest, after deducting costs, paid into the school fund. It will thus be seen that the educational endowment of Alberta could hardly be more liberal. Instruction in Alberta is free in the primary schools and attendance is compulsory from seven to fifteen years of age. Also, if in an area five miles either in length or breadth there are four residents who would be assessable for school taxes and eight children between the ages of five and sixteen, inclusive, that area may be created a school district and as such may issue debentures for the erection of a school house. Liberal grants are made towards teachers' salaries. The district selects the teacher, who must be qualified and certificated by the Alberta Board of Education.

Excellent laws regarding neglected children are in force in Alberta. The Children's Protection Act is modelled after the statute of Ontario of the same name. In after years permanent homes were found for many hundreds of little ones, with complete success. Shelters were also established by the Department of Neglected Children in the larger cities and have been well conducted and most successful.

In the death of Lieutenant-Colonel Macleod, which occurred in September 1894, after a long illness, the Territories suffered the loss of one who took a leading part in the opening of the country to peaceful settlement. He joined the North-West Mounted Police on the organisation of the force in 1873 as Assistant Commissioner, did excellent service during the long and arduous march of 1874, commanded that portion of the force which penetrated into the stronghold of the outlaw whisky traders in that year, and founded the fort on the Old Man's River which bore his name. His tact and knowledge of human nature, coupled with great forbearance and patience, enabled the North-West Mounted Police to establish law and order in a hitherto wild and lawless territory. By his skilful handling of the savage and warlike Indian tribes, he gained their complete confidence. The main secret of his success was that when he made a promise it was scrupulously kept, as the Indians learned. While commanding the force later as Commissioner, he also carried out the duties of stipendiary magistrate. His dealing with the turbulent element was based on stern justice, and although he handed out many severe sentences, he retained the respect and confidence of all classes of the white population, including the criminals themselves.

Upon leaving the force, he was appointed judge of the Supreme Court of the Territories, a position he occupied until his death, and in that responsible office no higher praise can be given than that he was an upright and just judge. He died a poor man. Although he had many opportunities to acquire wealth, he took advantage of none.

Previous to 1895 commissioners had been appointed to deal with the claims of half-breeds and their families to script, to be taken either in land or money at their option. Land script, being transferable, was open to manipulation by speculators. The half-breeds being by birth and upbringing hunters and trappers, placed little value upon it and for the most part it was soon disposed of, as often as not for whisky. In later years they bitterly regretted having thrown away the chance of obtaining free farms. Those who fraudulently secured this land script in many cases located it on lands which became very valuable, or sold the script at a big profit. It was some years before all claims for script were satisfied, the Commissioners journeying even to the Peace River country, where many half-breeds, but few white men, had settled previous to 1890. Even into remote districts the speculator followed the Commissioners to exchange for the script issued liquor or small sums of money.

Throughout the ranching country from 1890 to 1897 the cattlemen generally were prosperous. The market was good and prices fair, forty dollars for steers being the average. Horse ranchers did not do so well. The class of animals being raised was poor. Some hundreds of horses were shipped to England but they were hard to sell. As a result, many large horse ranchers went out of business, losing considerable money.

The manager of the Oxley Ranch, Stanley Pinhorn, committed suicide in the year 1891, while in poor health, and was succeeded by A. R. Springett, formerly Indian Agent. Pinhorn was a most successful manager, and his untimely death was certainly much regretted.

In 1892 quarantine against United States cattle was inaugurated, and for a time strictly enforced. Posts were established along Milk River, where all cattle coming from the south were detained for ninety days. The regulation was enforced by the Mounted Police. Its enforcement was difficult, since Montana cattle were continually drifting north; besides, thousands of Canadian cattle had been driven south during the winter storms. Following many complaints, and failure to find any disease among stock driven in, the quarantine regulations, after being in force only a single summer, were discontinued.

Settlers were now taking homesteads all through the range territory near Fort Kipp, on Mosquito Creek, and in the Saint Mary's district, where many families had arrived from Utah to swell the Mormon settlement at Cardston. Still others went into the Pincher Creek district, where there was now a population of nearly five hundred, and along the High River; in fact, settlers were securing homesteads in almost all parts of Alberta south of the North Saskatchewan River, and from 1895 dates the rapid break-up of the great cattle ranches and the ousting of their owners, who for many years following the disappearance of the buffalo had held almost undisputed possession of that portion of Alberta south of the Red Deer River. Each year saw the open grazing areas reduced. Railways were built across them, wire fences cut off the watering places; the free range was fast vanishing. But instead of decreasing with the closing of the free range, there was more livestock than before and livestock of a better quality. Nearly every settler owned some cattle, and these were steadily improved by careful selection in breeding. They ran no more at large, but were well fed and housed during the winter.

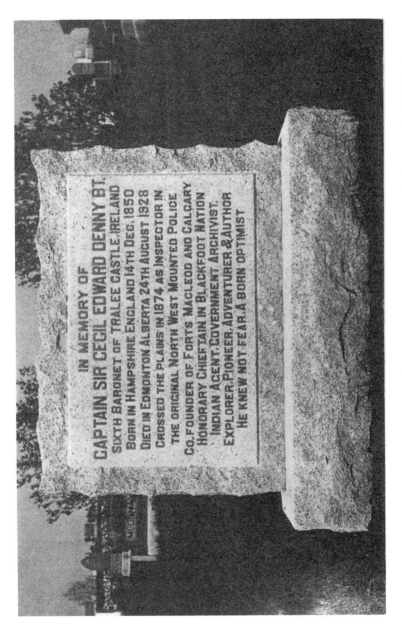

The stone erected to the memory of Sir Cecil E. Denny at Union Cemetery, Calgary, in R.C.M.P. plot.

A change no less radical, too, had taken place among the Indians. Only a few years had passed since they were placed on reserves and rationed. Most of the older men, the hunters and warriors, were dead, succumbing to the restrictions of the reservation life. They had passed away quietly, and the younger generation, to whom the old wild life was unknown, were to prove that the provisions made for their benefit by the Government – the shepherding of them on the reserves, the schools they were required to attend, the instructors sent among them to teach them farming and stock-raising – had been wise provisions. By 1895 most of the tribes had large bands of horses and cattle, and knew how to care for them. Cattle killing and horse stealing had practically stopped; the Indians had turned to more lawful pursuits, and on many of the reserves were earning money in making and selling hay during the summer.

They did freighting, too, the Bloods regularly hauling coal on contract with their own teams from Lethbridge to Macleod. Good houses were replacing the tepees on the various reserves, some even of brick, and they were well furnished. For a time the mortality among them was great, but this had ceased with education in sanitary matters, and there is good cause to anticipate that the Indian will not only survive but that the race will increase both in population and wealth, as it comes more and more under the influence of civilisation.

Schooling has done wonders for the red man, and to one who had known the Blackfeet in the days when they were among the wildest and most warlike tribes on the continent, and had some part in bringing about the change, it affords a certain feeling of satisfaction to contrast the present with the past. I received a letter some years ago from the head chief of the Blackfeet Indians. I knew his father, Running Rabbit, well. He was a great war-chief, and led many a party against the southern Indians in the early days. He did not long survive the day of the buffalo, but while he lived he was a good friend to the police and the whites. His son, a comparatively young man then, does not remember the old wild days, except as a child.

His letter was worded very much as he would speak, and was of interest as showing what only one generation had done for a Blackfoot.

The contrast between the son writing of his crops and the loss occasioned by their failure and the father only a short time previously leading war parties against the Sioux, and living altogether off the buffalo killed by him, is a most graphic illustration of the change in the Indian's mode of life. He signs himself 'Your son', going back in memory to the time when his father, with the other plains Indians, used the term in speaking of the officers of the Mounted Police in gratitude for the fatherly care and interest taken in their welfare from the early days of 1874.

One of the greatest guides ever known in the North-West Territories, Jerry Potts, died at Macleod in the summer of 1894. He was engaged at Fort Benton as guide and interpreter for the Mounted Police by Colonel French in 1874, and remained in the force until his death.

Jerry had a wonderful sense of location. No matter how fierce the storm or how difficult the trail, he led straight and true to the point aimed at, and was never known to be at fault. As a half-breed Piegan Indian he had great influence with the Blackfeet tribes, and many a time trouble was averted solely by his influence. As an interpreter also he ranked high. Indians are often rambling in their speech in council, saying much that has no bearing on the question at issue. Potts would get to the gist of the matter in a few short terse sentences.

Many of the chiefs having long names when literally interpreted had them shortened by Jerry. Crowfoot, whose full name was Crow-big-foot, through Jerry came to be known by the abbreviated title. Eagle Tail, the Piegan chief, was originally named Many Eagle Tail Feathers. Many places in Alberta also took their names from his interpretation of them from Blackfoot into English; as High River, the Blackfoot name for which was Spitze, meaning Tall or High Timber. Blackfoot Crossing, Sheep Creek, the Old Man's River, 'the river the Old Man played on' and many others owe their names to Jerry Potts's free translation of them from the original Blackfoot.

Jerry had been retired on a pension a few years previous to his death from tuberculosis. He left a family of several children.

XXXIV

The North-West Mounted Police in the South African War

The Calgary and Edmonton Railway was completed in 1892, and a regular train service established from Macleod to the future capital. Immigration about this time began to pour into the Red Deer River district, and the country along the North Saskatchewan. During 1893 the Dominion Government cancelled all outstanding leases, and cattlemen were given the privilege of purchasing ten per cent of their holdings at $1.25 per acre.

On the outbreak of the Boer War in 1899 Canada had committed herself to military assistance in defence of the Empire, and dispatched a battalion of infantry of one thousand officers and men from Quebec on the 31st of October. On the 18th of December following the Government determined to raise a second contingent for South Africa, and the following authentic information regarding the raising of that battalion has been furnished by Lieutenant-Colonel J. D. Willson, who was one of this contingent, and served with distinction throughout the war. I quote from his account:

On the 27th December the list of officers was complete and orders were issued for the raising of four squadrons of Mounted

Rifles, the whole forming a regiment of two battalions and a brigade of artillery. Of these squadrons, 'C' and 'D' were recruited in the North-West Territories, the officers, with very few exceptions, being drawn from the North-West Mounted Police. The order was received with satisfaction throughout the Dominions and hailed with enthusiasm by thousands of young men in the West. Recruiting proceeded rapidly, the only embarrassment being the numbers who offered their services in excess of the total authorised.

By the fifth of January, two complete squadrons had been assembled at Regina. From every hamlet and settlement of the North Saskatchewan between Edmonton and Prince Albert, from Wetaskiwin and Red Deer, men hurried on horseback and in sleighs and by rail to Regina to enrol in 'C' Squadron, while the plainsmen about Calgary, Macleod, Lethbridge and the foothills flocked to Macleod to fill the ranks of 'D' Squadron. Meanwhile, horses had been assembled at both Regina and Macleod.

Perhaps in no country in the world was there finer recruiting ground for light cavalry, for though the population was sparse and widely scattered, most men rode and a considerable portion of them were horse-owners and daily in the saddle; horses were plentiful and cheap, the southern portion of the Territories swarming with animals admirably fitted for military use, bred from a small but hardy class, but improved by well bred sires. Our horses would have compared favourably with those of any light cavalry in the world for speed, strength and beauty, and even superior to most in toughness, developed by their birth on the plains, and there most of them had lived during the heat of summer and through the long cold winters.

Our ranks were filled with every class of the West, generally drawn from the farmers and stockmen, of a physique rarely equalled by any regiment I have ever seen. The oldest and best-known families of Canada were well represented. There were probably some seventy-five men drawn from the North-West Mounted Police, on leave from their duties for a year, for service with the Battalion, with a very few men who had seen service with the Imperial Army, besides a number of ex-members of the Mounted Police.

The whole Battalion was under the command of the late Lieutenant-Colonel Lawrence Herchmer, then Commissioner of the North-West Mounted Police, who had been in the Imperial Army in India in his youth and had lived in the West in more recent years. 'C' Squadron was commanded by the late Major Joseph Howe, Superintendent of the North-West Mounted Police, with Captain Cuthbert second in command. 'D' Squadron was commanded by Major C. E. Saunders, also of the Mounted Police, with Captain A. C. Macdonell as second in command.

In Regina and Calgary much hard work was necessary before organisation was completed. Every man was subjected to a test in practical horsemanship on high-spirited and often only half-broken horses. No attempt was made to teach equitation, so that, though the men were generally good horsemen, they never attained or attempted to learn the approved cavalry seat. The stock saddles, as also the Whitman bit long used by the Mounted Police, was adopted.

By the 18th of January, all being in readiness, men and horses left Regina for Ottawa, where an inspection was held by the Governor-General, Lord Minto, and after a day or two for rest, they proceeded to Halifax and embarked on the S. S. Pomeranian on the 26th of January.

The voyage was long but uneventful. The horses were crowded below decks, each animal so boxed in that he could not lie down, and it can be imagined how difficult it was to clean the stables, as was done daily. No attempt was made to groom the animals. Though I had known horses all my life, until this voyage I never realised what these animals, to which civilisation owes so much, could endure. I cannot speak too highly for the manner in which our veterinary officer handled the situation. To his orders regarding diet and general treatment we owe it that during our long voyage we lost but nine animals, which was a record rarely, if ever, reached by Imperial cavalry regiments.

The service rendered by this regiment during the South African War is well known, many of the officers as well as men who served in the ranks, becoming prominent in after years, and more especially in the Great War. There was Captain A. C. Macdonell who was later to raise and command a regiment of Mounted Rifles that reached South Africa near the close of the war and also to command the Strathcona Horse for several years before he led it overseas and attained the distinction of brigadier-general commanding the Seventh Brigade, and still later as major-general to command the Twelfth Division of our Canadian Army Corps in the Great War.

One of the youngest of the regiment was Billy Griesbach, a trooper in 'C' Squadron, who had his share of hardship and battle during the year of service in South Africa, to return to Edmonton and to eventually raise and take overseas the 49th Battalion (Edmonton Regiment) and later become brigadier and command the First Brigade to the close of the war.

The 49th Battalion in the Great War had also many in its ranks who had served through the South African campaign in other regiments besides the Mounted Rifles. As an instance. I may mention R. H. Palmer. He served in the Strathcona Horse as a trooper during the South African campaign, was wounded and earned a commission and returned to Edmonton. On the outbreak of the war of 1914 he went overseas as lieutenant in the 49th Battalion, being steadily at the front until the end of the war, returning to Edmonton in command of the battalion as lieutenant-colonel, a most enviable record.

Edward Hillier was sergeant-major of 'D' Squadron and

remark- able for his efficiency and energy in that rank. He gained a commission later in the Canadian Scouts, and still later as captain in the S.A. Constabulary. He also returned to Canada and on the outbreak of the Great War went overseas with the 5th Battalion as adjutant, was promoted to lieutenant-colonel and afterwards to brigadier.

Fred Jamieson, too, then a boy, was also a trooper in 'C' Squadron, returned to Canada, later to become lieutenant-colonel in the Alberta Dragoons in the Great War.

Many other men from Alberta could be mentioned who taking part in the South African War, in after years became noted either in civil or military life. Mention of the part Alberta took in the Boer War in 1899 brings out in great relief what had been achieved in only twenty-five years, that is from 1874, in the North-West Territories.

We in the early seventies had little idea that a country then populated almost solely by Indians who lived by hunting the buffalo would in our day send volunteers in thousands of the finest type of manhood, fully equipped, by a great transcontinental railroad to join in a war of the Empire on the other side of the world. The transformation that had taken place in such a short space of time in the North-West was great – a transformation such as I doubt any other country on earth could show over as brief a period.

XXXV

Northern Indians admitted to Treaty

The summers from 1895 to 1897 in southern Alberta were very dry and the crops almost a complete failure. In the Cardston district irrigation, introduced by the Mormons, had been wonderfully successful. A charter had been applied for in 1890 by Messrs. Pearce and Bone for the irrigation of the Calgary district. A ditch was dug, but partially destroyed in the wet season following. In 1903 the Canadian Pacific Railway Company undertook the gigantic irrigation scheme at present in operation. Colonel J. S. Dennis was at the head of the enterprise. In the early nineties much damage was caused by prairie fires, and their origin was attributed to the railway locomotives. This led the Canadian Pacific Railway in 1895 to place eight foot fireguards on each side of their line. The smoke stacks of their locomotives were also screened. As a result the number of these fires was greatly reduced.

One of the first acts of Lieutenant-Governor Mackintosh was to sign the charter for the incorporation of Calgary as a city, dating from 1st January 1894. The Edmonton city charter was dated ten years later – 1904.

The year 1897 saw the construction of the Crow's Nest line,

subsidised by the Dominion Government to the extent of $11,000 a mile for three hundred and fifty miles from Lethbridge west. The Canadian Pacific Railway, which undertook the building of this road, turned over to the Government as an offset some valuable timber limits in British Columbia in addition and agreed to reduce their freight rates and to operate the road under the control of the Railway Committee of the Cabinet.

Nearly a quarter of a million dollars' damage was caused by floods in 1897. Many people were driven from their homes in the Macleod and Pincher Creek districts, and numerous railroad bridges were washed away. For several years previously extremely dry seasons had prevailed, and this exceptionally wet season was unlooked for.

In 1900 Hon. A. E. Forget succeeded to the lieutenant-governorship of the Territories and the political future of the country became a live issue. Hon. F. W. G. Haultain was particularly active in presenting the financial constitutional position at Ottawa, and more especially the question of provincial autonomy. The Dominion Government, however, came to the conclusion that the time was not yet ripe to form the North-West Territories into provinces.

Premier Roblin was anxious to have a portion of the Territories annexed to Manitoba, and travelled through the country advocating this idea, but the response was cold, the wish of the people being for the establishment of a separate province or provinces.

In the federal election of 1904, the Hon. Frank Oliver and Dr. McIntyre, Liberals and J. Herron and M. S. McCarthy, Conservatives, were the successful contestants in Alberta, North and South. In the following session the question of provincial autonomy was definitely settled by the passage of an Act dividing the Territories into two provinces, with a joint area of five hundred and fifty thousand three hundred and sixty-five square miles, or slightly less than half the total area of the country. The census of 1901 gave the combined population as one hundred and sixty thousand. Crown lands were to remain vested in the Dominion, the plea of the provinces that they be turned over to them being negatived on the ground that the Territories had been purchased by the Dominion Government from the Hudson's Bay Company and could, therefore, by no line of reasoning be regarded as anything but federal property.

North of Edmonton lay a vast country, which, while partially surveyed south of the Peace River, was to the north of it practically all unsurveyed and uninhabited, except by Indians. In 1899 Indian Treaty Number Eight with the tribes of the great Athabasca region was concluded. At this treaty an enormous tract of country was ceded. The boundaries were very irregular, that on the east being near Lake Athabasca, about 105° west longitude, and in a triangular form south as far as 52° north latitude; that on the west at 130° west longitude, and as far north as the Macleod Bay of Lake Chippewyan.

This territory was inhabited by several tribes, among them the Slaves, Dog Ribs, Yellow Knives, Chippewyans, Crees, Beavers and Iroquois. These Indians had for generations lived by hunting and trapping, and their contact with the white race had been extremely limited. They were a primitive people, with few wants that the country they inhabited did not supply, and in their own way they were honest. The lives they led were lives of hardship and privation. Dogs in winter and canoes in summer were their only modes of travel. Caribou, which roamed the country in immense herds, and fish which abounded in the numerous lakes, were their principal food, and the trapping of every kind of fur-bearing animal in northern Canada their regular occupation. From these tribes came most of the fine furs sold in the markets in the south. The traffic for two hundred years had been confined almost entirely to the Hudson's Bay Company. It was not so much to preserve order as to protect them from the whites who, now that the country south was fast settling, would surely encroach on their domain, that this treaty was made.

The Chief Commissioner was former Lieutenant-Governor Laird, a man with an extensive knowledge of Indian character, who had negotiated the treaty with the Blackfeet in 1877. The region covered by Treaty Number Eight is one of great rivers, lakes and forests, with here and there extensive tracts of rich soil. In the long days and brief nights of summer grain and vegetables of many kinds would grow prolifically and ripen in spite of a season shorter than that farther south. Down the Peace River, at Fort Vermilion, three hundred miles north of the Peace River Crossing, wheat has been grown successfully, and a grist mill been in operation for many years.

It is also worthy of note that in 1876 wheat grown at Lake Athabasca won the prize at the Centennial Exhibition in Philadelphia. At Vermilion, it must be remembered, the altitude is only nine hundred and fifty feet above sea-level, while Edmonton and Calgary are two thousand one hundred and fifty-eight and three thousand three hundred and eighty-nine feet respectively. The difference in altitude offsets to a great extent the difference in latitude in the matter of growing crops, although doubtless the long hours of sunshine during the summer months in the north is also a favourable factor in their ripening.

At the same time that Lieutenant-Governor Laird made this treaty with the northern Indians, Lieutenant-Colonel James Walker issued script to such half-breeds as were to be found in the north, and both these commissioners concluded their labours satisfactorily.

XXXVI

Peace River — and the end of the trail

It is only by making a trip through it that one can grasp the extent and fertility of the Peace River basin and the country beyond. Such a trip was made by a party of the Mounted Police in 1904, of which I was a member. This party, consisting of thirty-two constables and two non-commissioned officers, was commanded by Superintendent Constantine and Inspector J. Richards. I had charge of the pack train of fifty or more horses.

Starting from Peace River Crossing, the work assigned to the party was the cutting of a seven-foot pack trail from that point across country to Fort St. John; thence across the Rockies through Laurier Pass to Fort Graham on the Finlay River, and then over the Coast Range to the Pacific, connecting with the telegraph line running to Dawson City. The purpose of this trail was the establishment of an all-Canadian route to the Yukon, the only way previously into that country being by steamer up the coast and through United States territory to the Klondyke. Two years, it was estimated, would be required to complete the task, and this estimate proved correct.

We left Fort Saskatchewan on sleighs early in March, and

followed up the Athabasca River on the ice to Mirror Landing. Here we crossed to Lesser Slave Lake, thence to Peace River Crossing, where we were held up for some time waiting for the river to clear of ice. From the Crossing two hundred miles to Fort St. John we had some cutting, but the country was fairly open, with in many places beautiful park-like stretches. The soil was a rich loam with water plentiful in small creeks winding through it. There was a luxuriant growth of grass, peavine often being up to the horses' knees. Game was plentiful.

We encountered some small bands of Cree and Chippewyan Indians, but few white settlers. At Fort St. John we found only two or three log buildings occupied by the Hudson's Bay Company trader. The country throughout is timbered, but to the south of the Peace towards Big Pine River, and up the stream to the mountains, stretches of open country occur, and it has since become a first-class farming district.

Steamers were running without hindrance to St. John and sixty miles farther up the Peace to Hudson's Hope. There navigation is blocked by the Rocky Mountain Canyon, fourteen miles long and impossible for boats. The river here is a boiling cauldron, compressed between high, rocky walls. Logs and trees entering the upper end come out as matchwood at the exit. It is often called the Black Canyon, a name more appropriate than the one in common use, as it is in reality nearly a hundred miles from the Rocky Mountains.

Above the canyon the river widens again, and is navigable to the Parle Pas Rapids, where it enters the mountains. Peace River proper ends about fifty miles above Mount Selwyn, or nearly two hundred miles above Fort St. John. At this point the junction of Parsnip River from the south-west with the Finlay from the north-west forms the Peace.

There is no Peace River Pass, so often misquoted.

A little below the junction before mentioned, the Finlay Rapids, an ugly stretch of boulder-strewn water over which a swift current boils in foamy waves and whirlpools, block the way. The view down the river from above these rapids, tossing between giant mountains forest-flanked almost to their rocky summits, was a beautiful and awe-inspiring one. But to follow down that river in a canoe alone, as I undertook to do in the following year, is another matter.

For days I drifted, range succeeding range of mountains. There seemed no end to them. As I rounded bend after bend, I looked anxiously ahead, hoping each was the last, but there were more and yet more to come. I was kept continually on the watch for rapids, sunken rocks – or uprooted trees, which were worse. And when ill-fortune carried one, as it did me, into a whirlpool, the chance of getting through seemed remote. I was powerless in the grip of the current, running with full force against a precipitous wall of rock. I drifted helplessly in its clutches for at least an hour, and when at last I did escape was unable to tell up-stream from down. Thankful to be alive, I made for shore, and spent the remainder of the day recovering from my exhaustion.

It is a relief finally to reach the open level country and leave the mountains with all their grandeur behind. It is astonishing how the Peace River, including the Parsnip and the Finlay, winds for hundreds of miles through the heart of the Rocky Mountains. Fort Graham, lying a hundred miles up the Finlay River from its junction with the Parsnip, was the second wintering-place of the party cutting the Peace River-Yukon trail, the first winter having been passed at Fort St. John.

We had left St. John early in the spring, cut a seven-foot pack trail through two hundred miles of largely timbered country, and over the Laurier Pass through the Rockies to Fort Graham. This route had been seldom travelled, and an Indian guide was necessary. Some open territory was encountered before entering the mountains, with the rich soil and luxuriant grasses before described. Not a human being did we meet in all this long distance, not even an Indian; this opulent section lay waiting and inviting settlement. Once the mountains are entered they continue to the coast. Fort Graham lies in a generally open valley, surrounded by mountain ranges.

West of the Finlay River towers Mica Mountain. Seams several feet in width can be traced from the summit down. Numberless claims have been staked, but no work has been done, and they have lapsed. The problem is to get the mica to market. At present that is impossible, but the time must come when a way will be found, for these seams must be most valuable. The mineral in large blocks is to be seen lying on the mountain-side, having broken away from the ledge.

Gold is found on the bars of the Finlay River. The valley, a beautiful, partly-open one, with level country between the river and the mountain ranges to the east and west, extends almost due north from Fort Graham, the river being as wide as the Saskatchewan at Edmonton, and runs for several hundred miles, still north, to its source not far from the headwaters of the Nelson River.

Snow lies deep in the upper Finlay valley. We wondered as we journeyed through the woods before reaching Fort Graham to see snowshoes, both grown people's and children's, hanging thirty feet above the ground from the branches of trees and marvelled that Indians could climb that height to hang up their winter footgear. We learned later that the snow was at that level when the Indians hung them there. This gives an idea of the snowfall. Horses were almost unknown to the Beaver Indians, who hunt and trap in that region, snowshoes and dogs in the winter and cottonwood dug-outs or birch-bark canoes in the summer being their means of travel.

I was interested while at Fort Graham to meet a Beaver Indian, brother-in-law of the Hudson's Bay trader at that place, with three or four dogs carrying packs. He came from the headwaters of the Nelson River, far to the north-west. He had been taught how to use a gold pan by Mr. Fox, his brother-in-law, and advised us to use it on some streams in the Nelson River country. I happened to be in Mr. Fox's house at the time of his arrival. He had come all this distance for ammunition.

But what interested me most was a moose-skin bag he showed us containing several fair-sized nuggets of gold, and some gold dust mixed with black sand. He said that he had panned this gold in a small stream flowing into the Nelson many days' travel distant. Fox took the gold with him on his next journey for supplies to Fort Macleod at the headwaters of the Parsnip River. It went on to Vancouver, and I heard from him subsequently that it weighed more than two ounces, worth around $50.

The excitement this would have caused had it become known may be imagined, but having no wish to see a gold rush in this section of the country, Fox kept the information to himself. During the Klondyke rush he had been obliged to feed and clothe many victims of the short-cut from Edmonton to the gold fields who staggered starved and ill into his post.

There is no doubt that somewhere about the head-waters of the Nelson River placer gold exists in quantities, and will some day be discovered, but it is a difficult country to enter. Horses cannot get in. Forests, swamps, mountain ranges and deep winter snows at present bar the way. Had I at that time been younger and able to purchase supplies for several years, I think I should have set out with this Indian as guide for this place, but it was not to be located by me. I left Fort Graham in September, going alone down the Finlay and Peace Rivers, and reaching Athabasca Landing after many weeks of hard and dangerous travelling just as winter came on in earnest.

I have ventured in this description of a journey into the upper Peace River territory to give some idea of what a vast region lies to the north of the great province of Alberta, waiting with its wealth of minerals, timber and grazing lands for the coming of the thousands who will some day open and occupy it. It will not be my fortune to see this, the active portion of a long life having passed, but I have here tried to show the gradual transformation which has taken place in the territory covered by the present province of Alberta since the early seventies. No doubt in some future day, when the vast country to the north is also opened, and the wealth there stored is known to the whole world, and railways connect the towns and cities scattered over its enormous area, another historian will tell of its pioneer development, although with a different background from that here depicted, and perhaps recall pioneers mentioned in this volume who helped to bring law, order, and civilisation to the province of Alberta, at that time a portion of the great North-West Territories of Canada.

Index